P.O.W.

Richard Garrett

P.O.W.

DAVID & CHARLES
Newton Abbot   London

British Library Cataloguing in Publication Data

Garrett, Richard
P.O.W.
1. Prisoners of war – History
I. Title
365'.45   JX5141
ISBN 0-7153-7986-0

Typeset and printed in Great Britain
by Butler & Tanner Ltd, Frome and London
for David & Charles (Publishers) Limited
Brunel House   Newton Abbot   Devon

CONTENTS

For those who didn't get away

'To be a prisoner has always seemed to me about
the worst thing that could happen to a man.'

John Buchan, *Greenmantle*

AUTHOR'S NOTE

Many people have helped me to prepare this book. The works that I have consulted are all mentioned in the Bibliography, but their authors deserve more than to be mere names on a list. A large number of them were, themselves, prisoners of war, and I should be doing less than my duty, if I did not express my gratitude to them for so diligently – and, often, so entertainingly – setting down their experiences. Without them, a general history of life in wartime captivity would have been impossible.

But I should like to thank especially Mr Don Bruce, Mr L. G. B. Eastwood, Mr W. J. Hudson, Mr H. Jeffrey, Mr Norman Insoll, Mr Edward Lee, Mr Harold Payne OBE and Mr S. D. Stubbs, all of whom talked to me at great length about their experience; and Mrs Joy Fawcett, Archivist of the British Red Cross Society. My thanks, also, to Mrs Joan Laing for allowing me to quote from her late husband's writings; and to the librarians of the Ministry of Defence Library, the Imperial War Museum, the National Maritime Museum and the London Library, and to officials at the Public Records Office.

In Chapter 7, I quote from an unpublished manuscript by the late Mr J. Stuart Castle. This is reproduced by permission of Mr Castle's literary executor.

At the end of the Prologue, I mentioned that one of the reasons for writing this book was to exorcise a bad dream. Should anyone wonder whether I succeeded, I can now report failure. The dream, indeed, has become worse. Despite having been a POW, I had no idea of the depths to which man can sink in his treatment of captives. I can only marvel at the reasonable treatment received by some of us who spent part of World War II in German prison camps. When compared to many infinitely less fortunate captives in that war and in others, it was almost beyond reproach.

Richard Garrett

PROLOGUE

I have always preferred to keep my own experiences out of my books, to be an anonymous observer reporting the deeds of others. In the present case, however, I feel bound to make a personal appearance. The matter is one that, for the better part of thirty-eight years, has occupied my day-time thoughts and my night-time dreams. It is impossible to be detached, for *PO/W* owes its origin to an event that occurred in my life very early in 1943.

On 8 November of the previous year, British and American troops had landed in North Africa under General Dwight D. Eisenhower. They moved eastwards into Tunisia. With the 8th Army advancing from Libya, and these Anglo-American forces driving towards it, it seemed inevitable that Rommel's Afrika Korps would be squeezed to death in the middle.

My own appearance upon this historic scene did not take place until February 1943. I remember my arrival in the front line well, for the first thing to catch my eye was a rough wooden cross. It bore the name of an officer in, I think, the Royal West Kent Regiment.

Next morning, I saw a line of Bren gun carriers strung out along the road in front of our positions. There was nobody inside them: there had, I believe, been a truce to bury their crews. Apparently they had been caught in a trap, wiped out to a man by German machine-gunners, who occupied concealed positions on the hills on either side.

Somewhat to my surprise, I saw no other evidence of the enemy. Wherever they were – which was somewhere in the vicinity of the three hills (Sugarloaf, Greenhill and Baldie) to our front – they were well hidden. They only proclaimed their presence when, from time to time, they fired shells at our positions.

The war, on the whole was going well for the Allies. On this small sector of the front, however, it might have died from inertia. There had been heavy fighting before our arrival. Now, everything was strangely quiet.

One day, towards the end of February, we were hurried away to a town several miles to the south – to reinforce some other battalion that was having a rough time of it. Presumably our presence was unnecessary, for we spent all day doing nothing, and I was able to visit a dentist at divisional headquarters. That night, we returned to our old positions – or, rather, not *quite* our old positions. This time, we dug in on another range of hills a few miles to the rear.

The fighting began round about lunch-time, when the Germans attacked us. I cannot remember how long it lasted, but it must have been several hours, for the light was already beginning to fade when I had my first close-up view of an enemy soldier.

Something had gone badly wrong. The rest of the battalion was now in full retreat. At some point in this confusion of events, the man beside me had been hit in the stomach. The wound was serious: in the shelter of a slit trench, I was now trying, not very successfully, to contain the damage with a field dressing – at the same time, feeding him with what I suspect was an injudiciously generous number of morphine tablets. To judge by his cries, they were doing little to ease the pain.

There seemed to be a lull in the fighting and, then, I saw this character standing on the edge of the trench, regarding me with mild curiosity. He was pointing a light machine-gun in the general direction of my chest. By means of signals, he instructed me to stand up – ideally, with my hands above my head.

Although our encounter was a very brief one, I can still remember his face. He looked tired, but it was his teeth that, for some reason, have remained in my memory. They were brown and uneven, and suggested that he might have done well to visit a dentist (it's funny how teeth seem to keep on recurring, but there you are). His uniform would have disgraced a parade ground: his chest was decorated with a medal ribbon that, somebody told me afterwards, indicated that he had seen service on the Russian front. On this last day of February 1943, he was serving as a sergeant-major in the Hermann Goering parachute regiment.

Once he had removed my revolver, he did not seem to worry very much about whether my hands were up or down. For want of anything better to do, I offered him a cigarette. He accepted it with a smile. When he lit it, I noticed that his hand was shaking. There was, perhaps, a second or two of companionship, a recognition of the fact that, although we were on opposing sides, we were united in danger. He assured me that the man injured – fatally, it transpired – would be looked after. Then he detailed one of his NCOs to escort me away from the battlefield.

By this time, it was almost dark. I have a dim memory of meeting an officer. Speaking in English, he wished me a good evening (which seemed a funny thing to do under the circumstances), promised that the wounded man would be in a doctor's hands before long, and ushered me into a *Kübel* ('bucket' – a light car based on the Volkswagen, which was used by the German Army throughout the war). He, too, appeared to be tolerably friendly but such is the nature of war. Front-line soldiers have always seemed to me to be much more humane than the ferocious little men who occupy desks miles away from the sound of guns.

I cannot remember anything at all of that night. The shock of events may have acted as an anaesthetic and I do not believe that I gave very much thought to my long-term plight. It was more a question of living from one moment to the next – accompanied, perhaps, by curiosity and by concern for my immediate needs. I suppose I must have felt frightened during the battle, but I cannot recall any fear. Nor do I remember feeling tired, though I hadn't slept for the better part of forty-eight hours.

The next colour-slide in this series of disjointed memories shows me in a small and austere room in the town of Mateur, about ten miles from the front line. I was, I gathered, to be interrogated. My inquisitor was wearing an immaculate green uniform, his boots were well polished, and he seemed many more than ten miles removed from that dishevelled sergeant-major who had captured me. He was well built, with a fair complexion, and he actually had a scar on one of his cheeks that might have been caused by a sabre cut. During the years leading up to the war, he had been employed by a travel agency in London's Piccadilly. This doubtless accounted for his fluent English, and I can only assume that he had been manager of the establishment. He was much too imposing to have been anything else.

He invited me to sit down, and I reminded myself of the requirements of a prisoner of war under these circumstances. I should, as we had so often been told, confine myself to supplying such personal details as my name, my rank and my number. Nothing else needed to be divulged.

As it happened, he did not wish to know anything else. Once I had mumbled my name, he permitted himself a small smile – and proceeded to tell me the number of the platoon that I had recently commanded, the company to which it belonged, the battalion and the brigade. He also, as it happened, knew the name of my current girl friend. There was no question of any inquisition: he was more than adequately informed already.

It is possible that he acquired this knowledge from a batch of mail that had, or so I heard, been captured. I cannot think of any other way, for few prisoners had been taken, and none of my friends were among them.

Since he had so little to ask me, I decided to undertake a small investigation of my own. For the past few weeks, we had been regarding the bland slopes of those three hills in which the Germans were established. There had been rumours of elaborate fortifications to the rear – even a special bunker to accommodate the commanding officer's mistress. I had approached them on several occasions during nightly reconnaissance patrols, but I had not discovered a great deal. With such an amiable interrogator, it seemed an opportunity to satisfy my curiosity about the set-up.

This time, he actually laughed. But he was not prepared to tell me anything. As he not unreasonably pointed out, his job was to ask the questions; mine, in the present situation, to answer them. It would not be appropriate if we changed roles. He then suggested that I might like some breakfast. An orderly took me into another room, where I was given a bread roll and some coffee.

An artillery officer whom I vaguely knew, and who had also been captured, was in the room with a villainous-looking character in the uniform of the French Foreign Legion. The latter claimed to speak no English, and he certainly did not seem to be friendly. The gunner suggested that he might be a plant, that his English might be much better than his peevish shaking of the head suggested and that his task was to take a careful mental note of everything we said. We should, he suggested, speak with circumspection.

He may have been right. After a while, the Frenchman made it clear that he wanted to go to the lavatory. He was led away by the orderly and never returned.

There was an agreement between the German and Italian governments that, no matter who their captors might be, all prisoners of war taken in North Africa should be handed over to the Italians. Two days later, after uncomfortable lodgings in a pen at Biserte, where we slept on the floor and were given little to eat, we were put on board a cargo ship bound for Naples. The idea was that we should spend the time battened down in one of the holds. However, the vessel was manned by an Italian crew, with German artillery men responsible for a couple of guns that had been mounted fore and aft.

Hitler and Mussolini may have been good friends, but the spirit does not seem to have extended to the rank and file. The German gunners despised the Italian crewmen: the Italians detested the arrogance (or what they considered to be the arrogance – they seemed a rather decent collection of men) of the Germans. One result was that, as soon as we had left port, the hatches were removed, and we were invited on deck. The voyage passed quite pleasantly: for most of it, we seemed to be the only people who were on speaking terms with both sides.

Campo PG66, a collection of wooden huts surrounded by barbed wire, was intended as a transit camp. It was situated at Capua, a few miles from Naples, with a good view of Vesuvius. From here, we were assured, we would presently be dispatched to permanent camps where the conditions would be better. In fact, I spent three months there, during which time I re-read and then re-read again Alice's Adventures in Wonderland and her trip to the far side of the looking-glass (the collected works of Lewis Carroll was one of the few books in the camp). The nights were spoiled by a community of bed-bugs that, no matter how vigorously we applied ourselves to the task of extermination, seemed always able to summon up reserves.

Part of the day was occupied by groping through the dustbins in search of discarded cabbage stalks to supplement our diet. We received one hot meal a day, usually a thin soup with one or two fragments of meat floating about in it. On Sundays, as a treat, we were given macaroni.

In addition to this, there was half a Red Cross parcel per person per week. The contents of these packages which, in theory, should have been issued at the rate of one per person per week, depended upon the country of origin. The Canadian version, for example, contained a large tin of powdered milk named Klim, whilst the British provided a can of condensed milk. But, in most ways, they were similar: butter or margarine, jam, sugar, chocolate, tinned meat and cheese. They ensured, I imagine, a reasonably balanced diet. We had not, however, become accustomed to our new circumstances, and were fresh from the vigorous, open-air life of active service. The result was that we were perpetually hungry. The Italians always promised that, *domani*, we should receive a complete parcel each but it never happened.

The accommodation was in wooden huts. At the edge of the compound there was a concrete block containing about half-a-dozen lavatories. The walls were decorated with graffiti in several languages, which ranged from bawdy rhymes to algebraic equations. One of the cisterns had some strange malfunction that caused it continually to flush itself. Throughout the day and night, the sound of its maniac ablutions could be heard in the camp. During the dark hours, it was rather weird – as if some phantom prisoner had a nasty attack of dysentery.

Many people became ill when they first entered 'the bag'. Jaundice was a common ailment, though I escaped with nothing worse than a sore throat. But I think a more general complaint was introspection. There was, perhaps, a feeling of guilt at having fallen into the enemy's hands. Should one have fought it out to the last round and died gloriously? War has an insatiable appetite for heroics and there was nothing heroic about surrender.

Time and again, not only during my spell in captivity, but over the years that have followed it, I have court-martialled myself for doing less than my duty – or, at any rate, for doing the wrong thing. A great many mistakes were made on that occasion. In the opinion of the jury in my mind, which stubbornly refuses to retire, I made at least one and, possibly, two.

I was just twenty-three, and I doubt whether my concern for a single wounded man would qualify for inclusion under the title of 'Daring deeds of our gallant lads'. I should have left this to somebody else, and given my attention to matters on a rather larger scale – such as thinking, 'What the hell do we do now?' Extempore medicine is best left to doctors: a platoon commander's job is to fight and never mind the casualties.

There was also, of course, the question of the future. All of us wished to remain at Capua for as long as possible, for it was in the south of Italy. It could not be long (or so we hoped) before the Allies landed and we were released. Unfortunately, the Italians came to a similar conclusion, and one day (in June, I think) we were moved north to a camp on the outskirts of Modena. It cannot have been far from Maranello where, nowadays, they manufacture Ferrari motor-cars. Conditions here were very much better.

As in any other self-respecting POW camp, somebody had managed to construct an illicit wireless set. When, at the beginning of September, Mussolini was elbowed out of power, and Marshal Badoglio agreed to an armistice with Eisenhower, the SBO ('Senior British Officer' – he was, in fact, the commanding officer of a battalion of New Zealanders) urged us to remain calm. He told us that messages had been received over the radio from Whitehall. Paratroops would soon be landing at Leghorn and Genoa: they would be with us before long. If we broke out and littered ourselves across the countryside, we might get in their way. 'Be patient,' he said, 'and stay put.'

Some people refused to stay put. For much of one day, you could see a stream of ragged figures climbing over the wall and vanishing into an orchard beyond. They doubtless did the right thing, though I have never been able to discover the truth of the matter. According to some accounts, there was no communication from Whitehall: it was all a very clever deception by the German intelligence authorities. In *MI9* by M. R. D. Foot and J. M. Langley, however, we read that the order really did come from London, at the instigation of Montgomery, who 'always liked neatness and order, and abhorred the slovenly. He was not much attached to irregular operations of any kind. He therefore insisted that directions were sent to Allied prisoners on Italian soil that they were to stay in their camps until the advancing armies overran them'.

This, presumably, is the truth. It is also true that Montgomery's preference for 'neatness and order' cost one SBO his life. Unable to forgive himself for what he regarded as his misjudgement of the situation, he committed suicide after the war.

No paratroops arrived, and the Allied advance had ground to a standstill many miles away to the south. Instead, on Italian Armistice Day plus one, a company of Waffen SS marched into the camp and took over where the Italians had left off. Within twenty-four hours, we were on our way to Germany, squashed into cattle trucks for two days and two nights, given neither food nor water and half suffocated by the heat-wave that had lasted throughout the summer.

If Italy had been a place of blue skies and shining sun, Germany was grey. The days went by much more slowly and, as the Allied bombing intensified, food became scarcer and Red Cross parcels non-existent. For most of the time, we lived in a camp at Weinsberg, a rather pretty little town about sixty miles to the north of Stuttgart. In the late spring of 1945, we were moved eastwards to a huge multi-national camp at Moosburg, not far from Munich. It was there, on a May morning, that American tanks rumbled into the compound and we were set free.

Having become adapted to a life of captivity, we now had to become used to freedom. It was not easy. Prisoners of war, in my experience at any rate, were highly civilised communities. There was a tolerance, a loyalty, a sense of humour, an honesty and a friendliness such as I have certainly never experienced in civilian life. Dog did not eat dog: if needs be, dog helped dog – even to the point of considerable self-sacrifice.

Life as a POW continues to occupy my sleeping mind. At least once a month, sometimes more often, I dream that I am back in captivity again. In these dreams, it is another war, though the camp and the faces are the same. Sometimes, it is a not unpleasant experience, and one relives the companionship of those days. On other occasions, it is a nightmare. The hostilities are nearly over, and we are all about to be executed. In one such dream, I was chased by no less a person than Hitler. It sounds silly, though, in the opinion of my subconscious, it was a desperate situation.

In 1970, when I fell victim to a dread of flying, I managed to exorcise it by writing a children's book about flight across the North Atlantic. Perhaps, if I were to write a history of prisoners of war, it might help to remove my guilt and my nightmares. It should, you must understand, deal not only with the valiant exploits of those who escaped (who were, really, quite a small minority) but, also, with the lot of the more average captive. The man who, with varying degrees of patience, did his best to come to terms with the situation and hoped that, some day, somebody might rescue him.

Since the confrontation in which a man who has been disarmed finds himself at the mercy of an armed enemy is as old as warfare itself, the story begins a good many years ago ...

I

THE PRICE OF FREEDOM

When man came down from the trees, or crawled out of the primeval swamp, or began to infest the earth's surface by whatever means, he showed at least one unfortunate tendency. He was apt to fight. These early creatures may have been the long-lost ancestors of poets, musicians, doctors and holy men. They were also, alas, the forefathers of those who built the atom bomb, who waged war and who killed, sometimes, for the sheer pleasure of slaughter. In this respect, they were somewhat lower than the animals, who nearly always have a valid reason to taking life.

In the first instance, one assumes that combat (it could not really be called 'war') was a simple matter of acquisitiveness. A man wanted something that belonged to his neighbour. The neighbour, not unreasonably, tried to protect his possessions, and the upshot was that they fought – with the winner taking all (including his opponent's life).

But man was not by nature a solitary creature. He organised himself into tribes. Warfare in the modern sense of the word was born. There was still the tendency to grab, but the undertaking became invested with more exalted trappings. To fight was to demonstrate unity, to show that the ideas of Tribe A were superior to those of Tribe B. This, of course, was a thoroughly dishonest attitude, for it served to disguise an unpleasant adventure as something glorious. Unfortunately, it has persisted ever since.

In these conflicts, some people were killed, many were wounded and a number found themselves unharmed but, nonetheless, at the enemy's mercy. 'Mercy', in this instance, is not a very apt word, for they seldom received any. They were usually murdered, and so – in a crime that passed for revenge – were their women and children. Occasionally, the latter were taken away as slaves but this depended upon the whims of their captors. If they were in good health – which means to say, if they had the strength to work hard – and if there was sufficient food to keep them alive, they might be permitted to spend the rest of their lives in servitude. But politics of a kind also affected their fate. A chief might decide that a mass slaughter would impress his enemies, reducing them, or so he hoped, to a state of terror. In such a case, there would be no survivors. It was, sometimes, the better of two horrible alternatives.

As the Romans developed into the world's foremost military power, warfare became more sophisticated. The Roman army was a highly disciplined body of men, armed with relatively effective weapons. By the fourth century AD, it had occurred to Roman thinkers that this diabolical sport, which clearly had mankind in its thrall, needed some sort of rules. The Emperor Augustus, many years earlier, had already gone some way towards limitation of arms, by stipulating that a professional force should consist of no more than 300,000 men. Whether this was inspired by an ideal of limiting the scope of a conflict, or whether it was based on logistics – the knowledge that no more than this number was required to produce Roman victories – is, perhaps, doubtful.

But now, rules were established. Before war could be declared, a country had to send its prospective opponent an ultimatum. The document had to be lucid, making the demands clear and without ambiguity. If the recipient complied with the terms, that was the end of the matter. There should be no more harassment.

Heralds and ambassadors were to be exempt from any kind of ill-treatment, but the fate of the captured still depended very much on the attitude of the captors. Caesar, when the mood took him, would be generous. He sometimes allowed a captive to become a freed man within the Roman Empire. There was, also, the possibility that freedom (or survival in many instances) could be bought by payment of a ransom. During the Middle Ages in Europe, the going rate depended on the status of the prisoner. The higher it was, the more his friends and relations could afford to pay.

These rules did not apply to barbaric opponents, who were probably unable to understand them in any case. Nor did they apply to enemies who held the wrong religious beliefs and were, therefore, infidels. But religious tolerance was never a strong force in such matters. After a battle, European soldiers were apt to strip the dead of their clothes and possessions for the very sensible reason that such items added to the loot. The more militant sons of Islam went a stage further. They decapitated the dead – thereby denying them any chance of an after-life and making sure that they did not contaminate paradise.

A prisoner is a member of the losing side who does not run away fast enough. In assessing the amount of quarter given, it is often difficult to disentangle the truth. After the Battle of Hastings in 1066, for instance, the only living beings upon the field of conflict were Normans. The men of Harold's army did not linger to see what happened. Most prudently, they seeped away into great forest and later, presumably, returned to their homes.

Those who did not move sufficiently quickly were no doubt cut to pieces – most certainly, the wounded who could not move at all were killed. But if a Norman soldier were brought before a latter-day war-crimes tribunal, he would have protested that it had been done in the heat of the battle and that his victim was still a source of danger.

Unfortunately, in those early days, there was small distinction between combatants and non-combatants. The Norsemen, when they raided Britain, did not take prisoners, not least because it would have been impossible to accommodate them in their ships. Consequently, they killed everybody. Afterwards, and with less excuse, the wholesale slaughter of civilians as well as soldiers continued. It is impossible to find any reason for it, other than the sheer enjoyment of mass murder, which is a regrettably human characteristic. Just as the runner must unwind after a race, so must a professional killer (which was, after all, a soldier's calling) take time to extract himself from the ecstasy of violence.

By the time Edward III embarked upon the Hundred Years War, a somewhat vague code of practice, based upon the concept of chivalry, had been worked out. To break the rules was not illegal, for there was no authority to enforce them. It was, however, considered to be dishonourable, which was just as bad and, possibly, worse.

Since the conflict was between England and France, two Christian nations, the members of which were neither barbarians nor infidels, tolerably humane standards were recommended for prisoners. On the face of it, these laws of war may seem to have been an improvement on those of previous generations. But any admiration for them should be tempered by the realisation that they made shrewd economic sense.

War was an expensive business, not only for the sovereign. All freemen in England were bound by oath to put in forty days a year military service, at their own expense. For example, in 1415, a knight named Thomas Tunstall contracted to serve the King in France for one year. The agreement, which was written in French, stipulated that he must provide and maintain six men-at-arms and eighteen horse archers. The latter had to be 'well mounted and equipped suitably to their condition'. In addition to this, he had his own servants to pay. His reward for such services was the far from princely sum of two shillings (10p) a day.

The rate depended on a man's place in society. Dukes received 13s 4d (67p) a day; earls, 6s 8d (33½p); barons, 4s 0d (20p); knights 2s 0d (10p); other men-at-arms, 1s 0d (5p); and archers, the worst paid of all, 6d (2½p). Admittedly, the king pledged himself to repay the money – in Henry V's case to the extent of pawning his crown. Nevertheless, the income was a long way short of generous especially since, the higher a man's place on the scale, the greater were his responsibilities. Henry V's brother, the Duke of Clarence, was expected to provide 240 men-at-arms and 720 horse archers, adding up to a weekly wages bill of £250.

If, then, a warrior serving in France was to make any profit from the undertaking, he must find other sources of income. Looting the enemy's property was an accepted practice. What, after all, would be the point of a war, if there were no spoils? If the local inhabitants objected, it was just too bad. Their sovereign should have kept them out of the mess by acceding to the aggressor's demands.

But objects were not the only negotiable assets to be taken from the field of battle. People, too, were a marketable commodity. The better-off prisoners might reasonably be expected to have families who would pay dearly to have them back at home. The lower orders, whose relatives could not afford to redeem them from this pawn shop of humanity, could be sold off as slaves. Either way, there was money in it.

As it happened, the practice had a merciful fringe benefit. Since there was no market for corpses, a man was of more value alive than dead. Consequently, it made sense to spare his life and, during his period of captivity, to keep him in reasonably good health. The lot of the slaves, of course, depended upon their eventual employers. As in the distant past, there were some households compared to which death on the battlefield would have been an acceptable alternative.

The price of a ransom depended on the standing of the prisoner. The more important he was, the more money he might be expected to fetch. When Henry V announced before Agincourt that he had no intention of being taken alive, he was not indulging in a highfalutin, do-or-die speech. He was simply, and very decently, reassuring his subjects that they would not be required to pay exorbitant taxes to bail him out.

In theory, a prisoner belonged to whoever captured him. When a common soldier helped himself to a captive, however, he was required to pay one-third of the ransom to his knight and another one-third had to be delivered to the king. Although the amounts were often negotiated in cash, money was not the only commodity. Horses, jewellery, anything of reasonable value would do.

Sometimes, a prisoner produced a disappointing return. When the Archdeacon of Paris was captured by a gentleman named John Ballard during the siege of Calais, Mr Ballard must have congratulated himself upon his good fortune. But when the worthy cleric came on to the market, nobody was prepared to offer more than £50. By contrast, when the Earl of Warwick took possession of the Archbishop of Sens at Poitiers, he was afterwards made the richer by £8,000. Since he also had a three-quarter share in the Bishop of Le Mans (another victim), the earl did very well from the campaign.

Certain prisoners, the highest-ranking losers, were the property of the king, no matter who captured them. Indeed, the monarch was involved in the business right up to his illustrious neck. Sometimes, he bought captives at cut prices from his subjects, and then resold them at the going rate. Again, after Poitiers, Edward bought three of his son's (the Black Prince's) better POWs for £20,000. This was not surprising, for the Black Prince acted as his father's procurer. By judiciously shopping around, he purchased another fourteen for £66,000. The King, no doubt, disposed of them at a handsome profit.

It was this battle that broke some sort of record for the ransom stakes. Among those captured was no less a person than the monarch of France, King John. He was treated with fitting respect. On the evening after the battle, the Black Prince entertained him and a number of leading noblemen to dinner. The prince himself served the unhappy sovereign, performing the duty (as became a king) upon his knees. There is no record of the menu, though all the food was looted from French provision wagons. The English had received no supplies for three days.

The prince was courteous and reassuring. He praised King John's conduct in battle, his personal courage and his stoicism in the face of defeat. He would, he assured him, be well treated. It was, perhaps, easy to be polite. The captive sovereign's personal possessions, his gold and silver and jewels, had already been discreetly removed. As for the ransom, that would be enormous.

During his stay in Britain, King John was quartered in the Savoy Palace. Later, he was moved to a house in Lincolnshire and, later still, to Berkhamstead in Hertfordshire. King Edward III (who happened to be his cousin) seems to have enjoyed his company, and sometimes invited him to Windsor. Doubtless, whenever he looked at his guest, Edward could see his features dissolve into bags of money. The asking price for his freedom was 3 million gold crowns (about £500,000). As for the French king, he may have been less than happy to recall that the King of Scotland, David II, was still a prisoner in England – and had been for the past eleven years.

It took some time to raise the money, which was levied from the long-suffering French public in the form of taxes on salt, wine and other goods. John's eleven-year-old daughter Isabel also contributed. She was sold off in marriage to the son of a particularly unpleasant Duke of Milan.

Between 1360 and 1370, Edward is said to have received £268,000, though John was allowed to go home after four years in England – in October 1360, when two-thirds of the first instalment had been paid. Three of his sons, however, were required to remain behind as hostages. When one of them, the Duke of Anjou, broke his parole four years later, John's freedom came to an end once more and he was summoned back to London.

He returned to a magnificent welcome, and none was more delighted to see him than the English king who, it seemed, had missed his cousin. Indeed, the hospitality appears to have been too much for King John's constitution. Shortly afterwards, he died, at the age of forty-four. Before his body was sent back to France, he was honoured by a requiem in St Paul's Cathedral, which was more than could be said for any other prisoner of war.

The Duke of Anjou may have broken his parole but his conduct might have been excused by the fact that he had a beautiful young wife waiting impatiently for his return. Most prisoners seem to have been more punctilious under these circumstances. There was, admittedly, the French-man who offered information to Henry V after he had escaped from captivity in a manner 'unbecoming to a knight'. Henry ignored his offer, and suggested that he go back to his own side and get himself killed. The king might have done better to have taken the suggestion more seriously. It would have saved him and his army a lot of unnecessary marching.

During the days before Agincourt, the English army was tired and under strength, and many of the men were ill with dysentery. After the fall of Harfleur, the more well-to-do citizens had been released on parole after they had paid sufficient sums of money. The poorer inhabitants, who couldn't afford the price of freedom, were shipped to England. But now King Henry was anxious. The French forces, he learned, had been substantially reinforced. The time had come, he suspected, to retreat from Harfleur to Calais.

After a march of 260 miles, much of it in bad weather, and with the army's supplies of food only just sufficient to ward off malnutrition, he found the way blocked at Agincourt. Henry was in a sombre mood. He was prepared to renounce his conquest of Harfleur if he were allowed to march to Calais unmolested. The French replied that this was not sufficient: he must give up all pretensions to the throne of France. Eventually the negotiations broke down. The date was 14 October 1415. The battle named Agincourt would be fought on the following morning.

Before he retired that night, Henry gave orders that all the prisoners that had been taken during the march from Harfleur should be released. But there was a condition. If, on the following day, he should win a victory, they must return to captivity. Sure enough, after the great clash of armies was over and the French had been soundly thrashed, the forlorn captives trotted obediently back into the English camp.

Prisoners of war were chattels. As any other commodity, there were brokers prepared to do business in them. After the fall of Calais in 1347, Edward III had done his best to turn it into an English town. Merchants and tradesmen were enticed across the Channel with offers of free houses and privileges for themselves – and, indeed, for their heirs. Those Frenchmen who could not afford the price of a ransom were allowed to remain there, provided they took an oath of allegiance to the English king. Their more affluent neighbours were required to pay up.

During the early days of the occupation, however, sixty knights and two hundred gentlemen were released on parole, and given the opportunity to raise money personally in an effort to make their freedom more permanent. This may seem to have been a generous gesture: in fact, it was an early example of public relations. The idea was that the men would speak well of their treatment and demolish some of the antagonism towards the English.

As time went on, Calais became a kind of Wall Street for the prisoner business. The brokers bought and sold these unhappy characters, and a captive might change hands several times before, at last, he was ransomed. With each transaction, of course, the price increased and many English fortunes were amassed by the trade.

The rate for a French knight was about £1,500 but when, in 1347, Sir Thomas Dagworth sold the French count, Charles de Blois, to Edward III, he was rewarded with £5,000. The king, quite clearly, did not require de Blois for the pleasure of his company. He retailed him for a much larger sum.

Several of the big country houses in England owed their origins to this traffic. Sir John Cornwall was particularly successful. He sold the Count of Vendôme to Henry V. Later, after Agincourt, he spotted a knight named Gilbert de Lannoy trying to crawl out of a blazing building. Lannoy had been wounded in the knee. If Cornwall would spare his life, he promised to pay him 1,200 gold crowns and throw in one of his best horses. Cornwall was, presumably, busy at the time. The deal sounded reasonable and he accepted.

In combat, Sir John was as gallant as the next man but, when not fighting, he built up a sizable business as a speculator in captives. The money eventually bought him a mansion at Ampthill in Bedfordshire and the title of Lord Fanhope.

Lesser people also benefited from the trade of prisoners: even lowly men-at-arms found campaigning could be a profitable occupation.

'Hundred Years War' is something of a misnomer. Quite apart from the fact that it is not statistically correct, the fighting was punctuated by longish periods of peace. For much of the time, the English forces performed garrison duties, acting much like any other army of occupation. In Calais, however, the brokers were still eager to do business and, throughout the occupied territory, the soldiers were only too pleased to assist them.

The result was that a species of Mafia developed. Harmless citizens were snatched from their beds, taken to Calais, and sold on the market. If anyone questioned the justice of what really amounted to kidnapping, he would be brusquely informed that the captive was a declared enemy of the King of England. But few people tried to raise any objections and everybody, from the king downwards, needed the money.

Likewise, and again after the style of the modern Mafia, a protection racket flourished. Villages were forced to pay dues – either in cash, or with livestock, food, wine or some other commodity. If they failed to stump up, their homes were burned and some of them were executed on trumped-up charges. Similarly, toll booths were set up on highways. French travellers making long journeys were compelled to present themselves at each and to pay for safe conduct to the next point along the route.

Extortions such as these flourished during the reign of Edward III. Henry V was more reasonable, though it is hard to excuse his conduct to the prisoners taken at Agincourt.

Contrary to all expectations, the battle had gone well for the English. By early afternoon, there were no Frenchmen still fighting. However, Henry was uneasily aware of the fact that, although the first and second lines of French cavalry had crashed to destruction on the English defences, the third line had not yet committed itself. The enemy soldiers showed no signs of being about to advance but neither did they appear in any hurry to depart.

To add to his anxieties, there were parties of stragglers from the first and second lines wandering about and needing, it seemed, no more than the presence of an enterprising knight or two to refashion them into an effective fighting force. If this should happen, the enormous numbers of prisoners at the rear of the English position might decide to join in. They had, after all, only removed their helmets. Otherwise, and given some weapons, they were in full fighting trim.

At the same time, parties of French peasants were raiding the English baggage train. It had been only lightly guarded and those men who should have been standing sentinel were busy, like the rest of the army, helping themselves to the spoils of war. Indeed, the bulk of the English warriors were systematically sorting through piles of fallen Frenchmen. The wounded (or those who seemed likely to recover sufficiently to be worth a few gold crowns on the market at Calais) were separated from the dead. The dead were being hurriedly and rapaciously stripped of everything they had, until the scene of glory was littered with naked corpses, stacked in obscene piles upon the mud.

The plunder of the baggage train was proceeding to the peasants' advantage – they had now removed several horses, quantities of gold and silver, a casket or two of jewels, several swords and even a crown. Indeed, the pickings were so good that several French knights joined in, creating a rough-and-ready organisation from what had originally been a disorderly mob. It was surely time that some of the English troops were ordered to constrain their greed and return to the task of protecting their own side's possessions.

But King Henry was still preoccupied by what he regarded as a threat to his hard-won victory. When he saw three French knights ride out to the stragglers in no-man's land, he assumed that they intended to regroup them. His own men were now very tired and, even without counting heads, he could see that the throng of prisoners far outnumbered his own soldiers. The threat was not to be endured any longer. The more exalted of the captives would be spared – not for mercy, but for the value they represented. The remainder must be slaughtered.

The English soldiers were loath to see so much potentially hard cash destroyed in an orgy of blood-letting. Some of them protested: many refused to have any part in the affair. But the king was adamant. Any man who failed to do his duty would, he said, be hanged. To show that this was no idle threat, he appointed an esquire and two hundred archers as executioners. They could either apply their talents to rebellious English soldiers or else assist in the massacre of the French.

It is impossible to say how many died on that terrible afternoon. According to some estimates, more men were killed in the blood-bath than perished in the actual battle. As one contemporary observer wrote, 'all those noblemen of France were then killed in cold blood and cut in pieces, hands and faces, which was a fearful sight to see'. They were, according to an historian writing in Tudor times, 'sticked with daggers, brained with poleaxes, slain with mauls and paunched in fell and cruel wise'.

Despite Henry's insistence that the nobility should be spared, at least one was slain by mistake. This was the Duke of Brabant. In the belief that, by attending him, they might indicate that here was a man of substance who would be worth a handsome sum in ransom money, his servants had departed. The Duke had taken off his helmet, nobody recognised his face and there was nothing about his dishevelled garb to indicate his identity.

He was unmercifully chopped to death along with all the less-exalted victims.

As matters turned out, the massacre had been unnecessary. The third line was in no mood to attack; the prisoners did not pose a threat from the rear; and the knights would have been unable to do very much with the stragglers. Nor, as one rumour had suggested, were any French reinforcements on the way. But, afterwards, nobody appears to have been dismayed by the king's decision. After all, people seemed to say, anyone can make mistakes. In any case, as somebody suggested, the French themselves were not above such acts of inhumanity. In 1396, French troops had departed for Greece on a crusade intended to assist the Hungarians against the Turks. On the eve of the battle of Nicopolis, they had killed about a thousand prisoners – asserting that they could not afford the soldiers to guard them. They would, after all, be better employed fighting on the field than hanging about behind the lines, policing a dejected collection of captives. But these were Turks and, therefore, infidels. They did not count in the quaint code of honour that distinguished between Christians and the rest of the world.

When the slaughter at Agincourt was over, King Henry seems to have taken trouble to be pleasant to the few captives who survived. He allowed some of them to wait upon him at dinner that night, which was a privilege they would have cheerfully foregone. On the march to Calais – a slow business: overloaded with booty, the column could cover only about eleven miles a day – he sent them morsels of bread and wine from his own table. Often he rode beside them, seeming, it sometimes appeared, to prefer their company to that of his own men. His conversation must have been tedious. According to the Duke of Orleans, a fairly typical example was, 'Noble cousin, be of good heart. I know that God gave me the victory over the French, not that I deserved it. But I fully believe that He wished to punish my enemies; and that, if what I have heard be true, it is not to be wondered at, for never were there greater disorders, sensuality and vices seen than now prevail in France, which is horrible to hear described. And if God is provoked, no one can be surprised by it.' Coming from one who had so recently soiled his hands with the blood of hundreds of helpless prisoners, it must have seemed to be a most outrageous piece of cant.

When, at last, the column reached Calais, the conquerors received a disappointment. They had expected a heroes' welcome, with the brokers vying with one another to purchase the captives. After all, having destroyed so much of their merchandise on the field of battle, they had created a shortage. There should, so to speak, be a sellers' market.

But the brokers of Calais were in no mood to do business. A large supply of foodstuffs was overdue from England, and the town was in a state of near famine. A shortage of accommodation did little to help matters. The victors of Agincourt found themselves unwanted, and hard pressed to meet the inflated prices that the expatriate English citizens were charging for food and lodgings. As a result, they were compelled to ransom many of the captives for sums that, under happier circumstances, would have been laughable – simply to raise the price of one or two square meals.

Nevertheless, some investors were able to declare a profit after the Agincourt campaign. A knight named Sir Rowland Lenthall used his gains to build a house named Hampton Court in Herefordshire. Sir Walter Hungerford took eight prisoners, and with their ransoms rebuilt his castle and the church at Farleigh Hungerford in Somerset. Knole in Kent and Hurstmonceaux in Sussex are two other stately homes that owe their origins to the expedition. The speculators were two brothers, James (Knole) and Roger (Hurstmonceaux) Fiennes.

The French soldiers who were freed at cut prices must have considered themselves fortunate. For those that remained in custody, the ordeal was far from over. During the voyage to England, they were confined below decks in overcrowded and horribly uncomfortable quarters. Once clear of the harbour, the ships ran into a gale. The Frenchmen, who had never been to sea before, were wretchedly ill: the stench of vomit did nothing to improve the conditions. Some of the ships were blown off course by the high winds and had to run for the safety of ports in Holland. For day after day, the nightmare dragged on until, nearly a week later, the fleet docked at London.

At last, these sick and depressed characters, who had once been the cream of the French army and who were now uncertain of when (if ever) they would see their homes again, set foot on English soil. Eventually, they would be distributed around the country – the lesser fry sold off as slaves, the noblemen quartered in fine houses that were, nonetheless, prisons. But, before this could be done, there had to be a final ritual.

Whatever the townsfolk of Calais may have thought, Agincourt had been a great victory. The French army had been virtually destroyed, and there were some who said that Henry should have completed his conquest by marching on to Paris. Such a feat of arms deserved to be suitably celebrated by a victory parade through the streets of London. But it was not sufficient for the victors to march on their own: the victims had to be present as well, dragging their feet before the exultant crowds, trying to close their ears to the mockery and wishing themselves back in France.

Some never returned. The Duke of Bourbon was one who died in captivity. Twenty years later, the Duke of Orleans was still in England, having been moved about between the Tower of London and Windsor and, later, confined to Pomfret Castle. The price of his freedom now included a promise never again to bear arms against England. Still proud, despite all those years in captivity, the Duke refused. He was eventually released in 1440 for a payment of £40,000.

The French learned at least one lesson from Agincourt. A part-time army composed of nobles and peasants, farmers and town-dwellers, would not do. Instead, a well-disciplined force of professionals was formed, with a predictable improvement in performance. The English were less ready to change their ways. One hundred years later, the army was much as it had been on that victorious day in 1415 and was using more or less the same tactics.

So far as prisoners of war were concerned, the next few centuries saw little change in their treatment. Their fate was still left to their captors: ransoms were charged, the poor were sold into slavery and a fortunate few were exchanged. The increased use of mercenaries had certain advantages, for these men seldom knew whom they would be fighting next: their victims in one battle might be their victors in the next. Consequently, it was prudent to be merciful.

Hugo Grotius who, in 1625, published *De Jure Belli et Pacis* ('On the Law of Peace and War'), was the first statesman to advocate an end to what might be described as chemical warfare. He insisted that the use of venom on arrows and the pernicious poisoning of wells should be condemned. He also (echoed by the political philosopher Montesquieu in 1748) stressed that the only right of a captor over his captive was to prevent the latter from doing any harm. In 1648, the Treaty of Westphalia concluded that prisoners taken on the battlefield should no longer be sold to the slave masters.

During the eighteenth century, there were attempts to introduce compassion into warfare. If the German historian Girtanner (1793) is to be believed, Louis XV was approached by one of his officers after the Battle of Fontenoy in 1745. 'Your Majesty,' he asked, 'how shall we treat the enemy wounded?' 'Why, like your own,' the king replied, 'for they are no longer our enemies once they are wounded.'

The debate continued – though not, unhappily, in Britain. The French philosopher, Jean-Jacques Rousseau, suggested that it would be appropriate to remove the captives from the scene of hostilities – to put them, as it were, in quarantine. He made no specific recommendations, however, on how they should be treated. Despite this weight of learned opinion, the tendency was for one side to handle its captives in a manner similar to that of its opponents. The sorry truth is that, when a man has been taken in combat, there is very little he can do. There is a great deal of difference between a soldier who is armed and a soldier who has been disarmed. Sometimes, it may have seemed better to have died gloriously in battle, than to become an unwanted relic of warfare, a man of no use to either side, a creature that could only hope for mercy. Perhaps those vanquished warriors of the Middle Ages were more fortunate. They, at least, were worth money. Freedom did not depend on the fortunes of war: it could be bought.

2

DURANCE VILE

Whatever else may have been to the glory of Britain in the second half of the eighteenth century, the treatment of prisoners of war had no part in it. The overcrowding of captives aboard hulks that had once been men-of-war; the malnutrition; and the utter disregard for human dignity – these had few parallels elsewhere in the supposedly civilised world. It was not, perhaps, surprising. In English criminal law, forgery and the theft of linen were among innumerable offences punishable by hanging. Members of the country's own armed forces were treated roughly and sometimes with brutality. Even lunatics were bedded down in straw, exposed to the mockery of 'sane' visitors in institutions that would have done discredit to a zoo.

If the nation's own citizens fared no better than this, what hope could there be for the king's enemies? Prisoners of war were encumbrances. They required men to guard them who might be better employed fighting. They had to be accommodated and fed in no matter how inadequate a manner. If a POW were not paroled (which, in the main, was the privilege of officers) or, better still, exchanged for an enemy captive, he languished in goal or in one or another of the hulks. In either case, his circumstances did not exceed the most basic needs for survival. In many cases, they were insufficient even for this.

During the first three years of the Seven Years War (1756–63), the French king gave money from his own purse to those of his subjects that were held captive in Britain. Known as 'the Royal Bounty', it was distributed by French agents in London. The amount a man received depended on his rank. For all French prisoners, it produced a rather better diet, ensuring that, if a man were exchanged, he would return to France fit enough to fight again. When, in 1759, the king withdrew his support (partly due to reports that it was not being distributed properly), the conditions of French POWs in England became so miserable that a public subscription was launched at the Crown and Anchor in the Strand to raise funds for them. A total of £7,000 was contributed. It was spent on 3,131 greatcoats, 2,034 waistcoats, 3,185 pairs of shoes, 3,054 pairs of breeches,

6,146 shirts, 3,006 caps and 3,134 pairs of stockings. There is no mention of food, though the British authorities protested that their captives received exactly the same rations as their own fighting men.

For a Frenchman in England, conditions were bad enough. When, in 1775, the American War of Independence broke out, cruelty was taken to the extremes. This, it must be acknowledged, was partly due to lack of space. The forces of King George III did not control the interior of North America for long. They were mostly confined to certain coastal cities, such as New York for all the time, and Newport, Philadelphia, Charlestown and Savannah, for some of it. The British and Hessian troops were crammed into barracks that had not been built to hold so many: there was no room to accommodate prisoners.

A solution might have been a greater willingness to grant parole or, better still, to exchange. George Washington, sympathetic though he may have been to the plight of his men in captivity, was apt to oppose the latter. The British, he argued, had everything to gain from it. The services of professional soldiers would be restored to them, which did not seem fair dealing for a bunch of demoralised amateurs. Nor, once they had been in British hands for any length of time, were his own men physically fit for active service. Many of them, indeed, died in gaol. Matters became particulary serious after the Battle of Long Island and the taking of Fort Washington on Manhattan in the summer of 1776. Suddenly, 5,000 captured American troops, plus a number of civilians whose attitudes suggested that they were best interned, had to be accommodated. A fire that broke out in September of that year added to the problems by destroying about one-third of New York city. The only buildings that could be spared for the housing of POWs were a couple of warehouses (one of them used for the storage of sugar), some churches and a Quaker meeting-house (employed as a hospital), and two gaols. One of these was the headquarters of the city's provost marshal; the other had been used for the imprisonment of debtors in peacetime.

There were also a number of hulks, which were mostly used to accommodate personnel captured from privateers, though these, too, were populated by captive soldiers. The American Commissariat of Prisoners, headed by a gentleman named Thomas Boudinot, was responsible for seeing that reasonable humanity was exercised. Its work cannot be accounted a success. When, for example, Mr Boudinot, accused that most infamous of provost marshals, Captain William Cunningham, of ill-treating his captives, Captain Cunningham cheerfully agreed that all the charges against him were correct. But he made no apology and gave no promise that the conditions would be improved.

Boudinot, dissatisfied by Cunningham's attitude, took his list of complaints to the Commandant of New York, General James Robertson. The general grudgingly accepted the evidence and agreed that Cunningham should be punished. Considering the immensity of his sins, Boudinot may well have taken Robertson's next action as an insult. The evil captain was moved to Philadelphia for a shortish spell. Afterwards, he was posted back to New York, where he resumed his cruelty with renewed barbarity. If the accounts of prisoners are to be believed, he burned captives with hot irons, poisoned the food and, in a grim series of midnight rituals, hanged 250 of them without trial.

To give him his due, however, General Robertson does not seem to have been entirely lacking in compassion. On 5 November 1777, accompanied by the Mayor of New York and his ADC, he visited the provost gaol to investigate complaints personally. One result was that he ordered six men, who had been tailors in peacetime, to be brought ashore from the hulks and set to work making clothes. A few days later, one hundred loaves and a quarter of beer were delivered to the captives. It is fair to assume that they received them, for the dastardly Cunningham was enduring his period of exile in Philadelphia at the time.

In April 1777, Elias Cornelius was a young surgeon serving with General Ward's Connecticut Militia. His unit was running short of medical supplies. To make good the deficiency, he resolved to raid the enemy lines and help himself.

Accompanied by a small scouting party, he rode off in the direction of Eastchester a small town in Connecticut. According to his information, the town was still in the hands of the Americans. As he soon discovered, however, the reports were out-of-date. At first it seemed as if Eastchester was completely deserted. Ward's men, it seemed, had pulled out. Unfortunately, the British had moved in. As he rounded a corner, four redcoats ran from behind the shelter of a shed. One of them grabbed Cornelius's horse and two of them pulled him down to the ground. They seized his pistols and suggested that he had best give himself up. Cornelius refused. The odds might appear to be somewhat uneven but he had no intention of yielding without a fight.

He must have been a strangely innocent young surgeon, for the redcoats quickly disabused him of any such ideas. As the NCO in charge pointed out, he recalled afterwards, 'If I didn't at once surrender, he would order his men to blow a brace of pistols through me. I surrendered.'

The soldiers promptly helped themselves to all his possessions including

Agincourt; mistaken judgement caused Henry V to order the slaughter of the French prisoners (*Popperfoto*)

The *Old Jersey*: prisoners confined in her during the American War of Independence regarded her as a hell ship

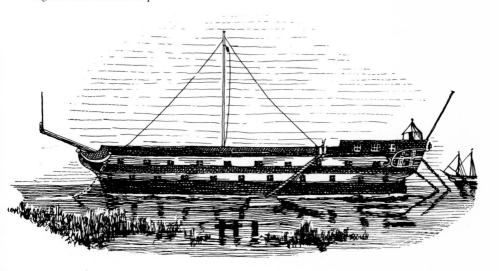

(*Above*) Sissinghurst Castle in Kent was used for the accommodation of captured French sailors during the Seven Years War (*Nigel Nicholson*); (*left*) somebody mistakenly decided that the meeting of three roads marked the parole limits of POWs in Sissinghurst Castle. In fact, the old inn has always been called the Three Chimneys. Contrary to local myth, the name is not a corruption of 'trois chemins'

his pocket book, which contained notes to the value of £30 – and took him to Westchester. On the way, they captured a second prisoner. That night, the two captives were lodged in a tavern, surrounded by thirteen guards and forbidden to speak to each other. Cornelius demanded that his belongings should be returned to him. After much argument, he was given back his pocket book (minus the money) and a pair of silver buckles.

Next morning they began the journey to New York in custody of a squad of Hessian mercenaries. At about 11 am, they halted and a British army surgeon wandered across to the group. He offered Cornelius a copy of the day's newspaper and said that he would probably be given parole when he arrived in New York. Cornelius hoped it was true: his experiences of captivity so far had not been encouraging. The guards were rough, and he and his companion had received no food on the previous evening. Now, one of the soldiers produced 'some mouldy bread, a pint of rum put in a bucket of water and some sour apples'. He threw the apples on to the ground 'as he would among so many pigs'.

The escort was changed, and the journey continued. The next stop was in Harlem, which seems to have been the headquarters of this particualar Hessian battalion. At all events, they were taken to a colonel's quarters. The guards mocked them and went through a pantomime of drawing their swords across their throats. One of them, an NCO, said that they would soon be hanged. An assistant of the regiment's medical officer was more merciful. He saw that Cornelius was very weary indeed, and gave him a glass of wine.

Cornelius and his fellow prisoner were now handed over to an English detachment. The last few miles of the march were carried out at a brisk pace, with the escort changed frequently. Other captives were now in the procession, some of them so exhausted that they seemed to walk in their sleep. Nevertheless they were not allowed to stop, even for a drink of water, until they were within sight of the city.

When, at last, they were permitted a brief rest, they were well rewarded. The halt took place outside the shop of a Mrs Clemons, a lady about thirty years old, who had moved to New York from Boston. She took pity on Cornelius and his forlorn fellow captives. With no opposition from the guards, she quickly produced four loaves of bread, some cheese and several pails of beer. She even, Cornelius noticed, gave money to some of his companions.

The other inhabitants of the neighbourhood were a lot less friendly. A collection of youngsters, with several negroes among them, mocked them and threw stones at them. The guards made no attempt to drive the youths off: indeed, they seemed to approve of such conduct.

When the march was resumed, and despite the good deeds of the amiable Mrs Clemons, two of the prisoners became so exhausted that the others had to carry them.

At last they reached their destination, Livingston's Sugar House, a peacetime warehouse that had been hastily transformed into a prison for private soldiers. A sergeant named Walley from the 20th Regiment of Irish Troops was in charge of the establishment. He was, Cornelius recalled, 'the most barbarous cruel man that I ever saw. He drove us into the sugar-house yard like so many hogs. From there, he ordered us into the sugar house itself, which was the dirtiest and most disagreeable place that I ever saw, and the water in the pump was no better than that in the dock.'

Furthermore, the building had no proper roof. Whenever it rained heavily, the water seeped through to every floor and it was impossible to keep dry. For diet, the prisoners were divided into groups of thirteen. Each syndicate was given 4lb of poor quality Irish pork and 4lb of mouldy bread to last four days.

On the following morning, Cornelius asked the irascible Walley for pen and paper. He wished, he said, to appeal to the general for parole. His request was refused. Might he, then, be allowed to send a letter to his father? Again, it was turned down. This time, Walley gave vent to his impatience by striking Cornelius across the face with a swagger cane that he used for beating prisoners.

In this instance, the sugar house seems to have been used as a transit camp. After his unfortunate experiences with Walley, Cornelius and a captain named Bissel were taken to the gaol that also served as headquarters for the provost marshal and his guard. In captivity, as in so many other aspects of life, some men were more equal than others. Captain Bissel was taken away to an upper part of the building: the luckless Cornelius was thrown into the dungeon, where respectable prisoners of war shared the accommodation with thieves, murderers and other members of the city's criminal fraternity.

One of his fellow prisoners was a quartermaster from the 1st New Jersey Battalion, who had been condemned to hang for the crime of deserting from a British regiment seven years before the outbreak of the rebellion. He had been in this particular prison for six months, waiting for sentence to be carried out.

A Captain Chatham, who had been arrested for refusing to pilot a British ship up the Delaware River, was seriously ill. As Cornelius pointed out to one of the guards, he was bound to die if he did not receive any medicine. Might some be sent for? The man agreed to take the matter up with his superiors. Some while later, Cornelius was informed that the prisoners 'are sent here for that purpose [to die], and His Gracious Majesty will forgivingly bury them in Potter's Field'. His Gracious Majesty would not, however, provide any panacea to make the journey towards the grave more endurable.

But Chatham was not the only inmate who was close to death. No arrangements had been made to care for the wounded, who were refused medical attention, and the food was just as bad as at the sugar house. Each man received 2lb of meat and 2lb of bread a week. 'Often,' Cornelius ruefully recorded, 'neither was fit to eat.'

When General Burgoyne, that strange mixture of playwright, politician and soldier, surrendered to his American opponent, Horatio Gates, at Saratoga on 17 October 1777, conditions improved a little. The food was still of poor quality but there was more of it. Butter and a gill of rice per week were added to the diet. At about this time, too, Cornelius was able to send a letter to his father, who shortly afterwards came to see him from his home on Long Island. The encounter was not a happy one. Cornelius Senior was a fervent loyalist, who abhorred his son's decision to enlist with the rebels. However, he suggested that the war would not last long and that Washington's whole crew would soon be in the same situation as his heir apparent.

The rigours of prison life were beginning to affect the health of the young surgeon. By January 1778, he was suffering from scurvy. He was moved back to the sugar house for a short period, and thence to the Friends' Meeting House, which was being used as a hospital. Conditions were not very much better: there were no medical supplies, although a surgeon did his best to alleviate the suffering. He noted Cornelius's qualifications and said that he could use an assistant. On 16 January, he took matters a stage further by promising him parole in return for his help in caring for the sick.

Cornelius was non-committal. The offer was attractive but conditions at the meeting house were more relaxed and he had decided to escape.

He made his getaway during a snowstorm on the following night. While the sentry's attention was distracted, he perched himself on a tombstone in the yard and jumped over the fence. He satisfied a couple of guards by pretending to be a drunken civilian and eventually reached a safe house on the edge of the city.

Elias Cornelius was, perhaps, fortunate despite his unhappy experiences. Bad though conditions were, he does not appear to have suffered the extremes of cruelty meted out to prisoners by the dreaded Cunningham and his equally unpleasant side-kick, Sergeant O'Keefe. Cunningham had been born in Dublin. When he was old enough, he enlisted in the dragoons, where he rose to the rank of sergeant. After the Seven Years War, he seems to have left the service and set up in business as an emigrant agent. In this capacity, he was a fairly typical example of a villainous breed that made fortunes from the trade. Provided they survived the passage, his clients (most of them Irish) eventually arrived in North America. But, by this time, Cunningham and his colleagues had robbed them of pretty well everything they possessed.

When he had amassed enough money, he decided to cross the Atlantic – though in a good deal more comfort than his clientele enjoyed. In New York, he set himself up as a horse-breaker. Here, again, his transactions were a great deal less than honest. When, at last, a crowd of dissatisfied customers turned upon him, he beat a hasty retreat to the harbour and sought sanctuary aboard a British frigate. The outbreak of the revolution found him eager for revenge. General Gage provided him with the means by appointing him Provost Marshal. When General Howe took over, he retained Cunningham's services.

Conditions in the prisons were bad enough, without Cunningham's contributions to the suffering. In summer, the heat was so intense, and the overcrowding so abominable, that the prisoners, six at a time, took it in turns to stand beside the windows for brief gulps of fresh air. In batches of twenty, they were allowed exercise for half-an-hour a day in the pitifully small yard. Fuel for cooking purposes was supplied at intervals of three days – and then in insufficient quantities – and the only means of making bread was by pounding up ship's biscuits (usually infested with weevils). Some inmates became so hungry that they really did eat old shoes, and there are also accounts of rats, mice and even insects being eaten. Turnip peelings were regarded as a delicacy. In one gaol, the hospital doctor found that his patients had eaten grit from the walls and pieces of wood.

The sanitary conditions were fearful. Lice, bed-bugs and fleas abounded. It was impossible to keep clean and, not surprisingly, there were epidemics of smallpox, yellow fever, dysentery and flux. No lights were permitted at night. The only chance to escape from these dreadful places was to yield to the blandishments of the recruiting sergeants who sometimes called – to swallow one's pride and enlist in the enemy's ranks.

Cunningham's more personal refinements to the system were to throw prisoners into the dungeons for even the smallest deviations from the rules – and to leave them there for several weeks. He insisted that drinking water should be supplied in latrine buckets; and, when he made one of his periodic tours of the premises, he either beat the captives with his cane or else, by way of a change, knocked them senseless with his fists.

Considering the conditions, which might have been designed to sweep away the last vestiges of morale, it is surprising how many prisoners resisted the recruiting sergeants' promises. When Colonel Ethan Allen was captured after an ill-considered attempt to take Montreal, he was eventually put on parole. He was confined to the limits of New York and seems to have spent most of his time touring from one prison to another. He afterwards recalled how one emaciated victim described the temptation to him. He wrote:

> I made the other prisoners stand a little off and told him, in a low voice, to enlist. He then asked whether it was right in the name of God. I assured him that it was, and that duty to himself obliged him to deceive the British by enlisting, and deserting at the first opportunity.
> The integrity of these suffering prisoners is hardly credible. Many hundreds, I am confident, submitted to death rather than enlist in the British service, which (I am informed) they most generally were pressed to do.

Ethan Allen was born in Connecticut. Before the war, he had explored Vermont – though it was unsafe to settle in what was still wilderness. With his brothers, he had founded a force of part-time soldiers named the Green Mountain Boys. In popular imagination, they represented the backwoodsman's claim to justice. On 10 May 1775, Allen and his irregulars overcame and captured the British fort at Ticonderoga. Perhaps the success went to his head. Having achieved one victory, he determined to win another. This time, it was to be far more impressive. In his pride and in his rashness, Allen dared to throw his small force against the defences of Montreal.

Inevitably, he failed, and he was among those taken prisoner. He reminded his captors of 'the kind and generous manner of my treatment of the prisoners I took at Ticonderoga'. They seem to have been unimpressed. Colonel Allen was fitted with handcuffs and leg-irons (some 8ft long and weighing 30lb), and put into the lowest part of a ship. He was guarded day and night by sentries with fixed bayonets – a precaution that appears to have been rather unnecessary, for his movements were so constrained by his litter of ironmongery that he could do nothing more than lie on his back.

However, one of the officers, a man named Bradley, was kinder to him. He used to send him grog and food. Nor, according to Bradley, was the ship's captain ill-disposed to his unwilling passenger. He was merely carrying out instructions. Someone unnamed had ordered him to be treated with 'the utmost severity'.

Eventually, Allen was transferred to a merchantman named *Adamant*, which was bound for England. The vessel was crammed with prisoners. According to his calculations, thirty-four men, each of them handcuffed, were crammed into a confined space measuring 20ft by 24ft. Two latrine tubs were placed in the middle: the food, as always, was abominable.

The crew appear to have gone out of their way to mock and humiliate the prisoners. Eventually, when an unkindly sailor spat in his face, Allen's patience broke down. With a commendable agility, when one remembers that his wrists were manacled, he managed to knock the man down. Two soldiers with fixed bayonets immediately appeared on the scene.

Ethan Allen was by no means the simple backwoodsman that his no doubt carefully created image suggests. He was shrewd, occasionally eloquent, and capable of much charm. On this occasion, he needed all these virtues. Unless he did some fast and persuasive talking, he would soon be dead from a bayonet thrust.

He described the British guards as 'prejudiced, abandoned wretches from whom I could expect nothing but death or wounds'. Nevertheless, 'I told them that they were good honest fellows; that I could not blame them; that I was only in dispute with a calico merchant, who knew not how to behave towards a gentleman of the military establishment.'

The soldiers seem to have been impressed. At all events, they pushed him back into the ship's dungeon without doing him any injury.

After a voyage of forty days, during which – and much to Allen's surprise – nobody died, the *Adamant* docked at Falmouth. The prisoners were taken to Pendennis Castle, about a mile from the town. The commandant of the castle was a decent fellow, a youngish lieutenant named Hamilton, who looked after Allen well. He made sure that he had a good breakfast each morning and entertained him to dinner. The food was good and he always treated his captive to a bottle from his personal store of wine.

Perhaps Lieutenant Hamilton's attitude was influenced by his knowledge that, in London, the politicians were debating whether or not to hang Ethan Allen. The charges are not very clear. It may have been because, at the time of his capture, he was wearing Canadian uniform; or it might have been intended as a gesture, to discourage the rest of the 'rebels'. The general opinion was that he should be executed. From a Tory point of view, it amounted to vengeance for an act of treason against the king. As the Whigs saw matters, his presence was an embarrassment. Embarrassments to the political scene are best swept under the carpet. A quiet job on the gallows would dispose of the tiresome Colonel Allen for ever.

Twice, he was on the verge of being executed, and twice he was reprieved. Eventually, the politicians decided to send him back to America and he was put on board the frigate *Solebay*. The voyage was a considerable improvement on the dismal journey in *Adamant*. By applying his not inconsiderable panache to the ship's captain, he was allowed to take exercise on deck, provided he confined his walks to the windward side. He was also, upon occasion, allowed to share the captain's table at mealtimes.

Over in the purlieus of New York, there had been a plague of executions. One oak tree on Long Island had received the doubtful privilege of having five men hanging from its branches simultaneously. The worst offenders were the Hessian Guards, who were as unpleasant a gang of thugs as ever wore military uniform. But Allen was fortunate. Not only did he escape the noose: he was also given parole, provided he remained within the limits of New York.

His parole came to an end on a pettifogging charge concerned with some minor infraction of the rules, and he was thrown into the provost gaol. He was refused a trial and, for the first few days, food. His quarters were now a minute cell above the prison's dungeons.

Using a small penknife, he managed to cut a hole in the floor. Through it, he was able to communicate with a Captain Travis from Virginia. He never discovered Travis's appearance, for the hole was too small to reveal more than one of his eyes. In any case, Allen's life in captivity was coming to an end. Thanks to negotiations carried out by Boudinot, he was exchanged for a Colonel Archibald Campbell.

He had, however, seen enough of life in the New York prisons to realise how bad the conditions were. Cunningham and O'Keefe were villains but, in Allen's opinion, an even worse offender was Joshua Loring, the Commissary of Prisoners. He wrote:

This Loring is a monster...! There is not his like in human shape. He exhibits a smiling countenance, seems to wear a phiz of humanity, but has been instrumentally capable of the most consummate acts of wickedness ... murdering premeditatedly (in cold blood) near or quite 2,000 helpless prisoners, and that in the most clandestine, mean and shameful manner. He is the most mean spirited, cowardly, deceitful, and destructive animal in God's creation below; and legions of infernal devils, with all their tremendous horrors, are impatiently ready to receive Howe [the British Commander-in-Chief] and him, with all their detestable accomplices, into the most exquisite agonies of the hottest regions of hell fire.

Loring had an additional sin to those of Cunningham and O'Keefe. He was an American and, therefore, a traitor.

Ironically, Cunningham received his deserts in 1791, though not for his ill-treatment of POWs. On 10 August of that year he was hanged in London for the crime of forging a draft for £300. Nevertheless, in the end, he seems to have repented of his wartime misdeeds. His last words were 'I beg the prayers of all good Christians, and also the pardon and forgiveness of God, for the many horrid murders I have been accessory to.'

Conditions in the prison ships were no better than those in the gaols. The most infamous was a retired ship of the line named *Jersey* (commonly referred to as 'the Old Jersey'). Her masts, spars, rigging and sails had been removed and sold: she now lay ingloriously at a berth off Long Island. Her crew amounted to a captain, two mates and a dozen sailors, who lived in quarters in the afterpart of the vessel. None of them had any responsibility for the POWs, who occupied the remainder of the ship. Eighteen guards, serving for periods of one week at a time, were provided by each of the four regiments stationed on Long Island.

Between eight hundred and 1,100 prisoners were quartered in *Jersey*. Most of them were crewmen from captured privateers, though soldiers were sometimes sent there too. Cleaning the ship took precedence over personal hygiene. The working parties were commanded by officer prisoners, who received extra rations for the duty. In day-time, the inmates were allowed on deck, and were able to buy fruit and other foodstuffs from the so-called 'Dame Grant' boats that came alongside. All captives were confined below decks after sunset: lights-out was at 9 pm.

Nobody was allowed to smoke below decks, mainly out of consideration for the sick. Not surprisingly, in view of the inadequate food and the overcrowding, there were many ill men on board. One new arrival noted that, on his first morning on board, he met 'a man suffering from smallpox; and in a few minutes I found myself surrounded by many others labouring under the same disease in every stage of its progress'. And, from the owner of a 'Dame Grant' boat, comes 'It was distressing to see the faces of hundreds of half-famished wretches, looking over the side of the ship into the boat, without the means of purchasing the most trifling article'.

In the autumn of 1781, a young seaman named Christopher Hawkins was taken on board the *Jersey*. He had been serving under Captain Christopher Whipple in a sixteen-gun privateer brig, when he was captured. Had he realised it, the war was dragging towards its conclusion many miles to the south, at the siege of Yorktown. But no matter: Christopher Hawkins was an adventurous lad, and he determined to escape.

There had been several such attempts, some of them successful. A captain and four mates had hijacked a yawl that came alongside and sailed to freedom, despite heavy musket fire from the sentries. Thirty men got away one night, when their leader was allowed on deck for a drink of water. He overpowered the guard: his companions ran up the ladder and dived overboard.

An officer who was due to be exchanged, left the ship with a cabin boy hidden in his sea chest; and four other officers cut their way through to the outside world by hacking a hole in the vessel's side with their jack-knives. One of them was wounded in the arm by a bullet and, when recaptured, slashed by a cutlass. He died later that night: the others got away.

Hawkins had noticed that, whilst the gunports were covered with iron grilles bolted to the hull, it should not be too difficult to remove them. When he mentioned this to Captain Whipple, Whipple advised against the idea. To swim to the nearby shore would be to invite recapture. He would have to make his way to a point on Long Island about two miles away. Since it was October and the weather was turning cold, he'd probably die of exposure. 'It's only throwing your life away,' Whipple said, 'for there is not a man on earth that can swim from the prison ship to that point as cold as the water is now.'

But Hawkins had no such misgivings. He was a strong swimmer; and, when he put the idea to a friend named William Waterman, Waterman agreed to accompany him.

A convenient thunderstorm enabled them to hack loose the iron bars without arousing suspicion. They put them back into place and covered the marks of their handicraft with old rags. The idea, Hawkins recalled, was 'not to draw the attention of the British gentry if they should happen to visit the lower deck before our departure'.

Before setting off on the following evening, the two men bundled up a few possessions, which they packed into home-made haversacks. Hawkins selected a thick woollen sailor jacket, a pair of thick pants, one vest, two shirts, two pairs of stockings, one pair of shoes, two silk handkerchiefs, four silver dollars and a bottle of rum that he'd managed to smuggle on board. Two garters were sewn on to hold the knapsack on his shoulders, and a length of string was supposed to secure it across his chest.

Waterman made similar arrangements. Between them, they filched a length of rope from a cable that somebody had left on the ship's forecastle. If they slid down it, their departure would cause no splash: nothing, that is to say, that might alert the guards. 'Thus equipped,' Hawkins wrote, 'we were ready to commit ourselves to the watery element, and to our graves as many of our hardy fellow prisoners predicted.'

The weather was ideal: warm and hazy, and the night was very dark. To make sure that they swam in the right direction, they depended on the lights of ships and the responses of sentries on the shore. There was a house on the far side, with what seemed to be a barn a few yards away from it. This, they decided, should be their objective.

Both men slid down the rope without arousing any suspicion. They kept close to the ship's side, swimming towards the stern, and then set off on their journey. To begin with, they swam slowly, keeping as deep in the water as possible until they were far enough away to escape attention. At half-hourly intervals, the sentries shouted 'All's well', which was, perhaps, an over-statement. Hawkins and Waterman were now some distance away from the vessel that the former described as 'a floating hell'.

At some point, the two men lost contact with each other. Hawkins never saw his companion again, though, some days later, he heard that he had made good his escape. Hawkins himself was going well until, after nearly two hours, his knapsack broke loose. For a while, he tried to swim with it tucked under one arm, but this was no good. It slowed down his progress and tended to drag him off course. For a while, he tried carrying it in his teeth but this was no better. He decided to let go of it.

'The land sentinels sang again "All's well",' he recalled. 'Thinks I, that is a lie, for I have lost my apparel and a bottle of rum.' Nevertheless, 'In this balancing state of mind and subsequent decision, I was cool and self-collected as perhaps at any period in my life.'

He was also very cold and uncertain about how much farther he had to go. Twenty-five minutes later he reached the shore. His legs were so chilled that, at first, he found it impossible to stand up. After a few minutes, he managed to struggle to the shelter of some bushes, where he promptly fell asleep. There was no sign of the house and barn that, or so he had hoped, would provide more comfortable accommodation.

Christopher Hawkins was now in a serious predicament. His clothes, presumably, were somewhere at the bottom of the water: he was naked except for a small hat that, oddly, he had worn for the swim. The local inhabitants could not be considered friendly. Most of them were 'Tories', which was another way of saying that they were loyalists. If any of them happened across this nude escaper, they would hand him over to the soldiery. To make matters worse, he was now very hungry. He had, he reckoned, swum two-and-a-half miles in two-and-a-half hours, and such achievements tend to give a man an appetite.

When he stumbled across a pile of melons, he found that they had been tainted by the first frosts and were horribly bitter. A Dutch family took pity on him briefly, to the extent of giving him some bread and butter, and allowing him to 'steal' a shirt and a pair of old pants from a washing line (As they pointed out, if they actually handed the garments over to him, and if he were recaptured, they'd be in dire trouble from the English). An English doctor was even more generous. But, despite these acts of kindness, he was recaptured. Fortunately, he was confined to a house, where the guard was more interested in a girl who was preparing food in the kitchen. While the soldier's attention was distracted by her maidenly charms, he sneaked out through the window and, this time, he was not retaken.

The plight of American prisoners in British hands had not gone unremarked. On 2 April 1777, Benjamin Franklin and Silas Dean, who were in Paris trying to drum up French support for the rebellion, wrote an angry letter to Lord Stormont, the British Ambassador. In the light of such conduct, they suggested, severe reprisals would be appropriate. Commenting on it, the *Gentleman's Magazine* pointed out that it was obviously difficult to dispose of such large quantities of prisoners. 'What then,' asked the writer, 'is to be done? Not indeed to load them with chains, or force them with stripes, famine, or other cruelties, as the letter charges, to enlist in Government service; but to allow them the same encouragement with other subjects to enter on board the King's ships, and then they would have no plea to complain of hard usage.'

It was a similar argument to that put forward by recruiting sergeants in the New York prisons, though the latter were more specific. They promised each man who enlisted a sixteen-guinea bounty, and the guarantee that he would not be compelled to fight against his fellow countrymen (conveniently overlooking the fact that, by serving elsewhere, these reluctant warriors would release British troops for the North American war).

Lord Stormont had little to contribute to the argument. He asserted that all possible was done for the prisoners, that they were permitted to receive charitable donations and that complaints were attended to promptly.

Messrs Franklin and Dean were mainly concerned with the fate of American prisoners in England. At the height of the war, there were 924 of them, mostly crews captured from privateers. As Lord Stormont said, they were, indeed, entitled to charity and sometimes they received it. But the prison system was riddled with graft and there was no guarantee that the sums raised would eventually benefit the captives. The Contractors Bill of April 1778 attempted to improve the situation; but, after its first and second readings had sailed through the Commons with comfortable majorities, it was thrown out by the Lords.

Presumably, too, Lord Stormont was unaware of the situations of men such as Ebenezer Smith Platt, a Georgia merchant who had been taken prisoner at sea. Mr Platt was interned in Newgate, put in irons, and confined to the part of the prison that was occupied by thieves, highwaymen, housebreakers and murderers. The authorities gave him no food and no clothes. If it had not been for private benevolence, he would certainly have died.

In their protest, Franklin and Dean spoke of reprisals. This has always been the safeguard of prisoners of war; the assurance that, if one side treats its prisoners badly, its opponents will do likewise. In fact, the Americans seem to have been remarkably generous in their attitude to English prisoners. There was, admittedly, the case of some loyalist civilians, who were interned in a copper mine at Semsbury, Connecticut, but this was an exception.

Part of the reason, no doubt, is that – during the early days of the war, at any rate – the tally of Americans in captivity far outnumbered that of the British. It is, perhaps, significant that the fortunes of the former took a small turn for the better after the surrender of Burgoyne and his army of six thousand at Saratoga. Afterwards, the British general found much to complain about, though such shortcomings were largely due to the fact that his opponents were completely unprepared for such large numbers.

Certainly, when the general arrived at Cambridge, Mass, to await (as he supposed) transport back to England, the local commander instructed his ADC to 'wait on General Burgoyne and acquaint him with this my order, and full determination to do all in my power to make his situation as easy and agreeable as circumstances will permit'.

In fact, it was not so easy. Cambridge was overflowing with captured British troops and there was a desperate shortage of accommodation. Burgoyne and his generals, von Riedesel and Phillips, were quartered at a notoriously gloomy inn, named the Blue Anchor, at which the prices were prohibitive. He was quick to express his resentment. In a peevish letter to Washington's chief-of-staff, he wrote: 'After being pressed into Cambridge through bad weather, inconvenience and fatigue, without any preparation made to receive the superior officers, I was lodged in a miserable public house.' It seems to have worked. One week later, he was being entertained at General Schuyler's luxury town residence at Albany – after which he rented a house. But he continued to complain:

> I was only at last relieved by consenting to pay upon a private bargain, a larger sum for an unfurnished house out of repair, than would have been required for a palace in the dearest metropolis of the world.

His juniors fared less well. The officers were quartered in a barracks, seven of them to a room 10ft square, with no discrimination so far as rank was concerned. Their men were confined to the same establishment.

That November was bitterly cold. The accommodation, wrote one officer (Ensign Anbury of the 21st Foot), was 'bare of everything; no wood and a prodigious scarcity of fuel insomuch as we are obliged to cut down the rafters of our room to dry ourselves.' In another hut, forty men, women and children were crammed together without warmth. Since the building was in a sorry state of disrepair, the interior was always thick with snow after a blizzard.

But these discomforts were shared by their guards. As Colonel Lee, the officer in charge of them, wrote:

> This morning rode round the lines and found field officers and some others walking by their barracks to keep themselves from perishing with cold; not one stick of wood to put into the fire, and if some other method cannot be found to supply them, we must either perish or burn all the public buildings.

In view of the excellent treatment that had been meted out on their march from Saratoga, the British had expected something better. Nor did the fact that the barracks had previously been used as an isolation hospital for smallpox cases improve their spirits.

At first, they had tolerated the circumstances, for they had expected to receive parole within ten days. When it did not materialise, they ran up enormous debts in the town in attempts to improve matters. According to one estimate, these totalled £10,000. The money would eventually be repaid by General Clinton in New York. But, as winter progressed, the local traders became anxious.

The cold weather continued. From Captain Cleve, one of Burgoyne's staff officers, comes: 'I never felt so cold before in my life. I can't go a step from my fire-place, and the ink has frozen on my pen. During the recent snow storm, accompanied by a high wind, the snow was a foot deep in my room.'

Nor was the food situation very much better. As Ensign Anbury recorded:

> Every species of provision was very dear, and to add to our misfortune, could hardly be procured for money. You do not, I believe, in England, rank milk in the catalogue of luxuries; yet we are obliged, *ourselves*, to traverse a deep snow for a full mile, to get a small quantity for our breakfast, as our servants are not permitted to pass the sentinels.

One doubts whether Ensign Anbury and his companions would have received any sympathy from the prisoners in New York gaols and in the hulks. In any case, their own Commander-in-Chief was partly to blame for their plight. Sir Henry Clinton, who had taken over from Howe, refused to allow the free passage of ships carrying food from the south.

The south, indeed, was to be the salvation of these men. After about a year at Cambridge, it was decided to move all the prisoners to Virginia. Since the fighting had not penetrated that far, food would be more plentiful and the climate was certainly milder. General Phillips was left behind as a pledge that the debts would be repaid and Burgoyne was allowed home to England. The remainder, under General Riedesel, set off on a march that was to cover 680 miles and take three months to accomplish. The column was lightly guarded: sometimes, indeed, there were no guards at all.

A small town named Charlottesville was their destination. When they arrived, they discovered that the buildings had not yet been completed and that the promised supplies of food had not been laid in. To make matters worse, for it was now November, it started to snow. It was all horribly reminiscent of Cambridge.

But General Riedesel had matters under control. There was nothing wrong, he suggested, that a little hard work could not put right. Eventually, a kind of farming community was created, with the Germans quartered among the hills a few miles to the west, and the English in Charlottesville itself. About two hundred men deserted, married local girls and became settlers. When, in October 1781, Cornwallis surrendered at Yorktown and the war more or less came to an end, his army joined the, by now, thriving English community, which had spread to the town of Frederick in Maryland and Winchester, Virginia. The last prisoners (which is a sombre word for a far from intolerable situation) were not released until the early summer of 1783.

It would be nice to record that the reasonably generous attitude of the Americans, contrasted with the appalling conduct of the British, had taught the latter certain lessons in humanity. This, alas, is not the truth. In 1812, when Britain found herself at war with the now fully fledged United States, the treatment of captives once more gave cause for complaint. It was the old story of overcrowded conditions, lack of food and fearful punishments. A number of Americans were quartered in hulks on the River Medway. In theory, their rights should have been a matter of concern for the American agent, Reuben Beasley, thirty-two miles away in London. But Beasley did nothing. He made only one visit to the captives. Not surprisingly, he was jeered and hissed, which may have influenced his decision never to call again.

3

ENGLAND'S GREEN AND PLEASANT LAND

Napoleon, despite the many claims upon his attention, found time to take an interest in prisoners of war. He was concerned with the conditions of his own men unwillingly residing in Britain and, just as much, with that of the British captives in France. Predictably, he believed that the latter enjoyed very much better treatment and he did not hesitate to make political capital from it. On the eve of Waterloo, when he wished to whip up hatred of the enemy among his troops, he told them: 'Soldiers, let those among you who have been prisoners of the English describe to you the hulks, and detail the frightful miseries they have endured.'

As so commonly in this very unequal world, a man's fate as a prisoner of war depended upon his status. If he was an officer, he was entitled to parole: if he was an 'other rank', he was condemned to captivity in the hulks, or else in one of the land-based prisons.

Very occasionally, there were exchanges of captives, though the system seldom worked. Each side habitually accused the other of cheating. Four months after the depot for prisoners at Norman Cross in Huntingdonshire was opened in 1797, 305 Frenchmen were sent home via King's Lynn, and 305 British prisoners returned from the Continent. It may have seemed a promising start but when, in the following year, a general exchange was mooted, the outcome was less satisfactory. The release of 201 French captives produced a return of only seventy-one British servicemen.

The original idea had been that prisoners should be released in the order in which they had been captured, those who had been longest in captivity having priority. The method was considerably abused. In Britain, certainly, an impoverished character due for exchange would sell his rights to a wealthier internee. There were also instances of mortally ill men, who were high on the list, selling their identities to well-to-do officers who were perfectly fit. The idea was that, when they were back in France, their clients would pay the money to their widows and family. There were, no doubt, several Frenchmen interred in English graves under false names. In 1801, for example, a prisoner named Batrille was taken to hospital, where he eventually died of consumption. But, by this time, he had assumed the name of François le Fèvre, an officer who had hoped to be repatriated, masquerading as an invalid. This particular deception was discovered but many were not.

Exchange, when it happened, was a matter for bargaining. In April 1810, there were about 10,000 British prisoners in France and about 50,000 French prisoners in Britain. The deal proposed by an official named Mackenzie was that they should be swopped, rank for rank, until the supply of British POWs in France had been used up. After that, Spaniards and Portuguese of equal rank to their French captors should be exchanged.

Napoleon disagreed. He counter-proposed that the exchange should be carried out on the basis of four Frenchmen for every one British serviceman. The balance should be made up of three other nationals. As the astute Mr Mackenzie quickly calculated, at this rate, 20,000 French soldiers and sailors would be back in France and fit for service in the French forces, by the time 5,000 expatriate Britons had come home. As for the other nationalities, they were of little value. As Napoleon himself admitted, 'Whilst as a fighting unit, you might set against *one* Frenchman *one* Englishman, you would require *two* Prussian, Dutch, or soldiers of the Confederation.'

Inevitably, the negotiations fell through, and the captives of both sides had to bide their time in idleness – and, often, in discomfort – until Napoleon abdicated and retired to Elba in 1814.

Eventually, for want of any workable alternative, exchanges were confined to very old prisoners, invalids, and boys aged twelve or less.

On rare occasions, captives were returned home as a reward for feats of valour or humanity. A French surgeon, who was detained in the prison ship *Assistance* at Plymouth, was allowed back to France in recognition of his services to sick British soldiers of the 8th King's Regiment aboard HM Transport *Spence*. A captain in the French army was sent home 'for his meritorious conduct in saving the life of a British officer'. A naval lieutenant, on parole at Oswestry, won his freedom 'for saving a child's life from a lion'; five French officers were released from Andover for their work in putting out a fire in the town; and the captain and clerk of a privateer were granted liberty 'for saving the lives of seventy-nine British seamen wrecked on the coast'.

There were several other examples. In France, the authorities were equally ready to reward good deeds. Indeed, at least three incidents are recorded when Napoleon himself interceded on behalf of British prisoners.

Most fortunate of all, however, were the French prisoners taken during the Egyptian campaign of 1801. There were so many of them that the

During the American Civil War, conditions in the Federal prison at Fort Lafayette in New York harbour were relatively good (*Mary Evans Picture Library*)

By comparison, the Confederate Andersonville camp resembled the German concentration camps of World War II (*Mary Evans Picture Library*)

Karl Niemeyer, a notoriously unpopular German prison camp commandant in World War I, modelled his appearance on the Kaiser (*Norman Insole*)

administrative machine felt unable to cope with the situation. As a result, they were packed aboard English merchantmen and shipped home to France.

When it first became apparent in Britain that prisoners of war were a sufficient problem to require some proper authority to care for them and to regulate their conditions, the matter was handed over to the Admiralty. An organisation named The Commissioners for Taking Care of Sick and Wounded Seamen (more commonly known as 'the Sick and Hurt Office') was set up in London. Its object was 'to see that sick and wounded seamen and prisoners were well cared for, to keep exact accounts of the money issued to the receiver, to disburse in the most husbandly manner, and in all things to act as their judgements and the necessities of the service should require'.

The first three commissioners were the diarists John Evelyn and Samuel Pepys, and a playwright and one-time tutor to the Prince of Wales named John Home. In December 1799, the responsibility was taken over by the Transport Office (a branch of the Admiralty, housed in Dorset Square, Westminster). It remained there until 1817, when the Victualling Office took it over.

For on-the-spot representation, the Transport Office appointed agents at the various towns approved for the accommodation of officers on parole, and in the hulks and prisons. At first, these officials were recruited from the ranks of local civilians. Tradesmen were not eligible: lawyers, and other gentlemen of standing in the locality, were. So far as parole were concerned, the agents were required to make sure that the officers fulfilled all their obligations - such as mustering twice a week for a roll-call and being back in their lodgings by sunset. They had also to minister to their needs; to pay their allowances and generally to act as their financial agents; to listen to and deal with complaints; and to make sure that all their correspondence passed through the Transport Office for censorship.

The zeal with which they conducted their duties varied. Some of them employed spies to report breaches of parole and to thwart attempts at escape. It was probably a sensible precaution but it was frowned upon as 'un-English'. Fair play, even in these circumstances, sometimes mattered. The parole agent at Hambledon received a rebuke from the Transport Office for the quality of his letters.

As the person who writes your letters does not seem to know how to write English [he was told], you must therefore in future write your own letters, or employ another to write them who can write intelligibly.

Presumably, this man, a Mr Tribe, did as he was instructed, but it does not seem to have produced any improvement. Soon afterwards, he was instructed, 'If you cannot really write more intelligibly, you must employ a person to manage your correspondence in future, but you are not to suppose that he will be paid by us for his trouble.' Does this mean to say that the wretched Tribe had been writing them himself all the time, or was there a shortage of literate clerks in Hambledon? We are not told.

A Mr Smith, the agent at Thame, seems either to have been surprisingly innocent, or else not above accepting money for misleading his colleagues. In 1809, he was concerned with the conveyance of a prisoner named Kermel to Portsmouth. Before Kermel was sent on his way, Smith told the guards that he was a man of excellent character and a gentleman to boot. Such a glowing reference caused the soldiers to relax their vigilance, with the result that the Frenchman escaped. In fact, he was a notorious villain and the very fact that he had been sentenced to a term in one of the hulks should have put Smith on his guard.

No doubt the experience taught him a lesson, though he over-reacted to it. Not long afterwards, he received another reprimand – this time for being over-zealous and employing spies.

The agent at Tiverton was brought to book in 1809 for assisting a prisoner to sell a contraband article (Agents were forbidden to have anything to do with commercial transactions by POWs which may have been one reason why tradesmen were excluded from their ranks). In 1812, the agent at Reading was dismissed for helping a perfectly fit French general to pose as an invalid and thus become eligible for repatriation. Also in 1812, the agent at Leek in Staffordshire was fired for withholding money due to prisoners and for consistently failing to send in his accounts.

Some agents were popular with their charges and, at the same time, satisfied the requirements of the Transport Office. But, as time went by, the feelings of the prisoners seem to have hardened against them. They were accused of being tactless and, a grievous sin among the officer classes, ungentlemanly. According to a Captain Moriarty, who was employed at the Valleyfield prison near Edinburgh, 'the men chosen were attorneys and shopkeepers [sic] for whom French officers have no respect, so the latter do just what they like.' He urged that serving officers should replace civilians in this role.

His remarks do not appear to have gone unheeded. But there was other evidence as well. A justice of the peace at Wantage took the trouble to write to the Transport Office about the local agent, a chemist named Crapper. 'Being' he said, 'a low man himself, he assumes a power which I am sure is not your wish, and which he is too ignorant to exercise.' It was, perhaps, an unjust accusation, for it concerned two French senior officers who had greatly exceeded the limits of their parole by travelling ten miles to dine with a local dignitary.

Quite properly, under the circumstances, Crapper arrested them. The local magistrates refused to support his action: the Transport Office, however, confirmed it. A spate of angry letters from Wantage citizens followed, each of them inveighing against the unfortunate Crapper. He was, some of them suggested, unable to control his charges, a drunkard who was totally unfit to have responsibility for the 340 prisoners in his care. He survived the incident, though his days and those of his colleagues were coming to an end. Eventually, they were replaced by Naval lieutenants with no less than ten years' service to their credit. Captain Moriarty had won his point.

Eligibility for parole varied from time to time, though only in the minutiae of the regulations. In 1796, the privilege was largely confined to naval officers. A captain, a lieutenant, an ensign, a purser, a chaplain, a master, a pilot, midshipmen, surgeons, boatswains, gunners, carpenters, master caulkers and master sailmakers were all permitted reasonable freedom. The fate of privateers depended on the size and armament of their ships. Captains of ships registering not less than eighty tons burthen, and which had no fewer than fourteen carriage guns (all of them four-pounders or more), received the same treatment as their opposite numbers in the regular navy. Masters of anything smaller were confined to the prisons or to the hulks.

In 1804, the rules were revised. Under the new regulations, all commissioned army officers down to and including the rank of sous-lieutenant were eligible; all commissioned officers of the navy down to the rank of midshipman; three officers from any privateer that had a crew of one hundred or more, and mounted a minimum of fourteen guns; and captains and mates of merchantmen that registered fifty or more tons.

Before receiving parole, an officer had to sign an undertaking drafted by the Transport Office, putting him on his honour to obey the rules. It stipulated that:

1 He might walk for one mile and no more along the great turnpike road – this distance to be measured from the edge of the town in which he was lodged.
2 He must not trespass into fields.
3 He must not be from his lodgings after 5pm between 1 October and 31 March. During the spring and summer months, the hour was extended to 8 pm.

4 He must behave decently and observe the law.

5 He must not write home to France unless he handed his letters to the agent, who would then send them on to the Transport Office for censorship. This regulation, which seemed to be an infringement of their privacy, was particularly disliked by the prisoners.

Failure to observe any of these conditions was punishable by a spell on board a hulk or in one of the prisons. The penalty for attempting to escape was particularly severe, for it involved a spell of ten days in the Black Hole.

The Black Hole was the prisoner's nightmare. In the hulks, it was a minute cell measuring 6sq ft, situated in the bottom of the hold. The only ventilation was through tiny holes ('too small to admit a mouse'), and the unfortunate captive received no more than one visitor every twenty-four hours – when a guard appeared briefly with food and to empty the latrine bucket. The meal itself was a meagre affair for, in theory, these men had to repay the cost of being recaptured. The price, in fact, was recouped by halving their diet.

Some men went mad during their captivity in Black Holes, others died. But the cost of an attempted escape was ten days in this hellish place, plus a longer period in prison. There was no appeal. This, indeed, was one of the few points upon which both Britain and France agreed. If a POW broke his parole and managed to get away, he could expect no more than a chilly welcome. Just as if he had been recaptured in the land of his captivity, he would be sentenced to a spell in gaol.

Agents who employed spies to keep an eye on their charges may have been criticised by officials of the Transport Office as unsporting. In fact, this was hypocrisy, for they themselves financed such trade. Anybody who sneaked on a paroled officer who was out after curfew received a reward of 10s 6d (52½p). But the jackpot, namely, ten guineas, went to the citizen who was responsible for the arrest of an escaped officer.

Provided he behaved himself, an officer on parole had a reasonably pleasant time. The attitude of the inhabitants in towns selected as centres for these prisoners varied. At Wantage, for example, it was apt to be hostile, though there may have been some excuse. Under the unhappy Crapper's management, the prisoners did almost as they liked, which was not always to the liking of the local citizenry. Nevertheless, thirty of them are said to have given a supper party and a ball to the town's tradesmen. The details of the occasion depend upon whose version you accept. One of Crapper's critics alleged that the festivities went on until three o'clock in the morning – thereby breaking the rules by several hours. Crapper, on the other hand, denied the whole business. The prisoners had, he agreed, asked for an extension of their liberty until 10 pm but he had refused it.

At Odiham in Hampshire, the atmosphere seems to have been very much more peaceful. In 1806, a young French naval officer named Baron de Bonnefoux had been serving aboard the *Belle Poule* in the West Indies. His ship was captured by HMS *Ramilles*, and, after many adventures, he found himself on parole at Thame. By a happy coincidence, a wealthy Englishman whom he had known when stationed at Mauritius, had taken a house nearby for the summer. The friendship was renewed and de Bonnefoux looked forward to a busy social life.

The local gentry were certainly hospitable, and the young ladies of the town appear to have enjoyed the company of the French officers. There was, however, a manufacturing element that took less kindly to these guests that were not of their inviting. One day, when he was walking in the street, de Bonnefoux was rudely pushed out of the way by one of them. He retaliated: each called up his allies and a brawl occurred. When the fighting was over, the Baron reported his assailant to the agent, a worthy named Smith. Smith seems to have sided with the local roughs. During the row that followed, he attacked de Bonnefoux with his cane: de Bonnefoux seized a poker and there was further mayhem.

Receiving no satisfaction, the Frenchman eventually complained to the Transport Office in London. After inquiring into the case, the commissioners decided that it might be as well to remove him to Odiham.

He liked Odiham very much better. The agent, Shebbeare, was a good fellow who was prepared to bend the rules occasionally. The prisoners had formed a philharmonic society and a Freemasons' Lodge, and had refurbished the local theatre. The local people were amiable and de Bonnefoux who, despite the affray at Thame, was a young man of considerable charm, made many friends. He also revealed a generous side to his nature. One of his fellow officers had made love to a local girl, who was about to have a child by him. This was strictly against the rules: the offender would either have to pay 500 francs to support the infant, or else serve a term in prison. Since this particular young man was hard up, the prospect looked bleak. When de Bonnefoux heard about it, however, he immediately paid what was, to all intents and purposes, the penalty of his friend's misconduct.

The quality of accommodation varied from place to place. In some towns, prisoners on parole were provided with almost luxurious quarters; others were less fortunate. A marine artist named Louis Garneray had fallen into British hands. After an uncomfortable period in the hulks, he was granted parole. The reality, alas, did not quite come up to his expectations.

When I arrived in 1811 under escort at the little village of Bishop's Waltham [he wrote] which had been assigned to me as a place of residence, I saw with some disillusion that more than 1,200 French of all ranks had for their accommodation nothing but some wretched tumble-down houses which the English let to them at such an exorbitant price that a year's rent meant the price of the house itself. As for me, I managed to get for ten shillings a week, not a room, but the right to place my bed in a hut where already five officers were.

Garneray was an early riser who, under happier circumstances, enjoyed a walk before breakfast. On his first morning on parole, he rose at five o'clock and began to get dressed. He wrote:

'What are you going to do?,' asked one of my room mates.
'I am going to breathe the morning air and have a run in the fields,' I replied.
'Look out, or you'll be arrested.'
'Arrested! Why?'
'Because we are not allowed to leave the house before six o'clock.'

The prisoners at Kelso in Roxburgh seem to have been particularly fortunate. They enjoyed the company of the local people, who were glad of their society. As one gentleman said, 'The time of their stay was the gayest that Kelso had ever seen since Flodden.' They, too, brought the local theatre back to life and put on regular entertainments. When the Duchess of Roxburgh said that she would attend a performance, they covered the streets of the small town with red carpets.

Amateur theatricals have long been a diversion for those deprived of their liberty. In this case, the Government began to shake its collective head in disapproval. Such goings-on, the politicians suspected, brought the prisoners and the people who had, perforce, become their hosts, too closely together. Whilst they did not actually say that it might discourage the view, so necessary for the prosecution of a war, that enemy servicemen were brutes beyond the pale of humanity, they doubtless took the possibility into consideration. They certainly said that such pleasurable events corrupted morals. Consequently, they must cease.

To misquote a saying about American servicemen in World War II, British soldiers may have felt that the French were overpaid (which was not true), over-sexed (which they may have been) and over here (which they certainly were). Several young women offered to assist in escapes to France, at a price. The soldier or sailor concerned had to promise that he would take his fair accomplice with him and that, once on the far side of the Channel, he would marry her. A young lady from Tiverton in Devon actually succeeded in both particulars.

On a more innocent note, a number of marriages were contracted between prisoners and British girls without any infringement of parole. According to the parish records of Ashby de la Zouch, no fewer than fifteen such ceremonies were carried out between 1806 and 1814.

Some prisoners on parole, such as the Baron de Bonnefoux, had respectable private incomes. Others depended entirely on their allowances, which were not very much. Indeed, this was a continual bone of contention. In the early years of the war, anyone with the rank of captain, or above, received the sum of 10s 6d ($52\frac{1}{2}$p) a week: below that, the rate was 8s 9d ($43\frac{1}{2}$p). After receiving many complaints, which apparently escaped the blue pencil of the Transport Officer's censor, an official of the French Admiralty named Rivière, filed a formal protest. Since M Rivière had, nine years earlier, denied the British Government any right to investigate the treatment of British prisoners in France, he might not have seemed to be the ideal negotiator. But his plea that the cost of living in England was higher than in France was accepted.

The matter was taken a stage further when a Lieutenant Wallis managed to escape from France. He was summoned to the Transport Officer and asked to compare typical prices of a British market place with those of a French. When he had completed his sums, he was able to prove that Rivière's assertions were correct. The commissioners were satisfied, and the allowances were increased to 14s (70p) a week for senior officers; and 11s 8d ($58\frac{1}{2}$p) for lieutenants and others of lesser rank.

Some added to their small incomes by giving lessons to local families in music, drawing, dancing and fencing. In one town that was short of doctors, a captured French surgeon more or less set up in practice; and the more talented captives, in or out of prison, manufactured model ships and other works of art that have long since become valued antiques. Many of them took the opportunity to improve their own education and some planned escapes, despite the severe penalty for being caught.

The amiable Baron de Bonnefoux found himself in trouble due to a misguided act of kindness. At Odiham, an English friend suggested that he should break the terms of parole and accompany him on an excursion to Windsor. Nobody, he said, need know. The day passed pleasantly, and de Bonnefoux caught a glimpse of the King, which delighted him. Some while later, he was overheard describing his outing to a young lady of the town. The eavesdropper was a personable widow who had, one suspects, taken a liking to the handsome young officer. In a moment of jealousy, she placed an advertisement in a newspaper, drawing attention to his escapade. The local agent felt compelled to investigate the matter. Despite his English companion's admission of responsibility, de Bonnefoux was arrested and taken to Chatham for a spell in one of the hulks. He escaped on the night before he was due to go on board, was recaptured, and was compelled to serve the statutory ten days in the Black Hole. Eventually, after nearly two years in the hulk *Bahama*, he was paroled once more and allowed to go to Litchfield.

He remained there for a while and then decided to make another attempt at escape. This time he was more fortunate. Wisely, perhaps, he put his fate into the hands of the professionals. These men, who toured the parole centres in search of clients, were basically smugglers. They charged an extortionate price for taking a prisoner to France. Once on the far side of the Channel, the spent their fees on contraband goods, which they smuggled back into Britain. Baron de Bonnefoux and another naval lieutenant, Colles, who went with him, were charged £150 each for the journey from Litchfield to Rye in Sussex, and another £50 for the sea crossing.

Baron de Bonnefoux was ever correct. Before departing, he wrote to the Transport Office, saying that his health required him to return to France. He promised, however, that he would never take up arms against England again.

Another naval officer, Lieutenant Rousseau, who had been captured in an action off San Domingo in February 1806, was equally punctilious. He had heard that his mother was dying of grief. Since the sight of him was the only thing that might restore her health, he determined to go home to France. He refused, however, to break his parole.

Taking up his pen, he wrote to the Transport Office, giving a kind of ultimatum. If he were not arrested and put in prison within eight days, he said, he would consider his parole cancelled.

Inevitably, he was arrested and taken to Portsmouth. Poor Rousseau! He made three attempts to get away, and failed on each occasion. He, too, ended up in the horrible interior of the *Bahama*.

Although, on the whole, courteous to their captors, the officers sometimes became obstreperous. At Alresford in Hampshire, for example, there were so many outbreaks of violence, that the Marquis of Buckingham observed that 'They certainly serve their country better here than they could at sea or in France.' In some instances, colonies of men on parole had to be broken up into smaller units, distributed over the country. There were even fears of an invasion by the French army via Ireland – which would be the cue for all paroled officers in the West Country to rise up against their captors. A similar scare occurred in Huntingdonshire, when a mass break-out from the Norman Cross depot was feared.

There were also efforts by officers to be transferred to towns where their friends were quartered. The purpose, usually, was to plan an escape. To justify the move, they invariably pleaded ill-health. More often than not, the doctors saw through such ruses. There was, for example, the case of a paroled prisoner in Cornwall. He had, he said, a severe infection of the lungs, and he felt sure that a sojourn in Reading would improve his condition. Since Cornwall was widely recommended for such sufferers, and Reading had nothing at all to commend itself in this respect, the application was turned down.

A man had to know his place in society and, if he were an 'other rank', or a member of the lower deck, it lay either within the interior of a hulk or else in the only moderately less uncomfortable confines of a prison. Here, too, came the officers who, in one way or another, had defaulted against the terms of their parole. But, in their case, the sentence was finite. Once they had been purged of their sins, they were allowed back into comparative freedom. For lesser mortals, who had not received commissions, there was no knowing when the ordeal might end.

The hulks were ex-warships that had been stripped down to the barest essentials. There were fifty of them moored at Chatham, Portsmouth and Plymouth. Between them, they accommodated 35,000 prisoners of war. Vessels such as these were also used for the confinement of British criminals. The total capacity, in this respect, was considered to be 400 convicts. For French POWs, however, 800 was considered to be acceptable – and 1,200 was by no means out of the question. If their inmates were to be believed, they were manned by the scum of the Royal Navy. On one occasion, two crewmen from a captured privateer were observed playing a game of écarté surrounded by a crowd of onlookers. When somebody asked what the stakes were, one of them explained that they had been chosen by lot to murder the vessel's captain, a loutish mariner of great unpopularity, named Linch. The winner was to have the privilege of carrying out the deed. Presently, the game came to an end and, five minutes later, Linch was discovered lying on deck – dead with a knife between his shoulder blades.

On another occasion, a prisoner named Charles Manseraux was elected to do away with a villainous master's mate and an equally detested sergeant in the Marines. This Manseraux seems to have been a tender-hearted individual. When he discovered that the sergeant was a married man with several children, he spared him and murdered a private soldier instead.

Captain Milne of the infamous *Bahama* tried to prevent men from escaping by reducing rations until they were only just sufficient to maintain life. In fact, this merely aroused the prisoners' anger, and the climax came one stormy morning, when the boats from the shore were unable to deliver the supply of bread. For food that day, they were told, each would receive one ship's biscuit.

This was too much. The prisoners assembled on deck and said that they would not disperse until they were provided with a decent meal. Milne flew into a fury and ordered an ensign in the marines to open fire. The young officer refused. A more moderate approach, he said, would be in order.

Eventually, a French officer who had been confined on board for trying to escape, told the gathering to break up. He then had a brief interview with Milne. There were, he pointed out, some 800 Frenchmen on board. Any violence would result not only in the loss of French lives, but of a good many English as well. Milne realised the truth of this and, for a short while, his attitude was more reasonable.

Even at the best of times, the food was bad. The Admiralty contractors cheated abominably and no ship ever received its full quota. Fish was stipulated for two days a week – Wednesdays and Fridays – but it was never eaten. It consisted of herrings that had long become rotten but they, at least, had some value as a kind of currency. The prisoners sold them at a penny a piece to the purveyors, who then resold them to another ship. According to one estimate, some herrings were in service, going the rounds from hulk to hulk, for ten years before they eventually disintegrated.

With the money they made from these small transactions, the captives bought butter and cheese. When they complained about the fare, their remarks were ignored.

For those with money, extra rations could be bought from the vendors who came alongside and offered their goods for sale. At times, the decks of a hulk gave a passable imitation of a market place, for many of the prisoners were also in a small way of business. Some repaired shoes, others blended tobacco, and there were craftsmen who produced such wares as small ornaments and wooden bowls.

Much of the administration was left to the prisoners. A committee of fifteen, which was re-elected at frequent intervals, was responsible for overseeing the fair distribution of rations. The cooks were also elected: the men ate six to a mess, but they were allowed neither spoons nor forks. The only tableware consisted of bowls and small metal drinking vessels. It did not make for elegant manners, but this did not dismay the bottom end of the prisoner scale, the Rafalés.

These men were mostly ratings from captured privateers. They might reasonably be regarded as the underworld of the prisoners. Many of them were naked: they had sold their clothes either to buy food or else to pay their gambling debts. Gambling was the consuming passion of the Rafalés. When a man had a run of bad luck, it was apt to consume everything.

Whilst most members of a hulk's captive population slept in hammocks, the Rafalés slept on deck. They adopted what became known as the 'spoon system'. In other words, they lay so close to one another, that when one man turned over, all the others had to follow his example In some cases, this was carried out by words of command. The senior member, becoming, perhaps, cramped in one position, would cry 'Prepare to tack' and then 'Tack!' Just as a sailing ship might go about, so would the line of these ruffians heave itself over.

Similarly, the hammocks were crammed close together, though a prisoner with fastidious tastes, and who had the money to indulge them, could occasionally buy himself a more comfortable position. Sometimes, in a particularly overcrowded hulk, a newcomer had to pay for any location at all. Otherwise, he was compelled to join the Rafalés on the deck. When an officer was sentenced to a spell aboard the *Canada* for attempting to escape, he was forced to hand over 120 francs for a spot in the middle of what had once been a gun battery. It was not, he protested, 'near a port. Just big enough to hold my dead body.'

The most severe penalty for misconduct was confinement to the Black Hole, though the captives themselves could be harsh. In their eyes, the worst sin was that of betraying an attempt to escape. But the very experience of living in these vessels was punishment enough for the crime of being captured. As a senior French officer, Colonel Leberte, who was imprisoned in the hulk *Canada* for breaking his parole, wrote:

> Would you know the full horror of their condition, come without giving notice beforehand; dare to descend before daylight into the tombs in which you bury living creatures who are human beings like yourselves; try to breathe for one minute the sepulchral vapour which these unfortunates breathe for many years, and which sometimes suffocate them; see them tossing in their hammocks, assailed by thousand of insects, and wooing in vain the sleep that would soften for one moment their suffering!

Remarkably, however, the incidence of sickness was less in the hulks and in prisons on shore, than it was among officers on parole. In 1814, for example – when there were more French prisoners in Britain than at any other time – 320 of the 45,940 men held captive in these dreadful institutions were in hospital. Of the 2,710 officers, who were enjoying the much more comfortable life of parole, 165 were on the sick list.

During the Seven Years War, Britain found herself faced with a problem that had never troubled her very much before, how to accommodate a large number of prisoners of war. It was, perhaps, the price for winning battles: the human debris from these clashes of armies had to be kept alive. In 1756, there were 7,261 POWs in Britain; by 1763, the number had become 40,000. They were housed in borough gaols, common prisons, country houses, barracks, castles and even farms. Millbay Prison at Portsmouth was the only purpose-built establishment. Escapes were frequent, which was not surprising. With such a sudden and huge addition to the nation's captive population, there had been a good deal of hasty improvisation.

But now the Government decided that a more systematic approach was required. To begin with, a list of possible properties that might be adapted to this purpose was considered. In Warwickshire, Kenilworth Castle had what can only be described as a narrow escape: in Scotland, if it had not been for the campaigning of Viscount Dundas, the Royal Palace at Linlithgow would have been taken over.

At Sissinghurst in Kent, the owner of a dilapidated Tudor mansion had been more accommodating – no doubt because he was in financial difficulites at the time. The word 'Castle' was added to 'Sissinghurst' and, in 1756, the premises became a prison for French seamen taken from prizes captured by the Royal Navy. Detachments from militia regiments were used to guard the captives. Among the officers was Edward Gibbon, who had not yet related the downfall of the Roman Empire, but was serving with the Hampshire Militia.

Mr Gibbon described the duty as 'hard, the dirt most oppressive ... The inconceivable dirtiness of the season, the country and the spot aggravated the hardships of a duty far too heavy for our numbers.'

Possibly because of this, Sissinghurst had a bad reputation, and the threat of being sent there was used to enforce discipline at other POW camps throughout the country. Moreover, the militiamen seem to have been unusually trigger-happy. When one sentry threatened to shoot a captive unless he put out a light, he was peevishly told to 'fire and be damned'. The soldier took the suggestion literally, and the sailor was killed in his hammock.

A party that tried to escape by crawling along a drain fared only moderately better. The first to emerge was shot in two places and then slain by a bayonet thrust; the others were recaptured.

When the prisoners complained about their treatment, the Court of Enquiry decided that 'while the person in charge [a civilian named Mr Cooke] was not so much to blame, the behaviour of the common centinels, whose understanding did not enable them to distinguish between the letter and the meaning of their orders, arose from a lack of printed orders.' Mr Cooke was replaced; and, in 1763, Sissinghurst Castle was abandoned as a prisoner of war camp.

The end of the Seven Years War brought a brief respite, but it did not last for long. By 1795, 13,666 French captives were kicking their heels unhappily in England. The officers, 1,357 of them, were allowed parole. Of the other ranks, 4,769 were confined to Porchester Castle in Hampshire – the others were scattered about as before.

In the following year, however, the authorities at last showed some signs of getting to grips with the problem. A large depot at Norman Cross near Peterborough was opened. Built to accommodate 7,000 prisoners of war, it was intended to be a model institution. Quarters for the garrison were based on the assumption that there should be one guard for every twenty prisoners. Cells measuring 8ft by 7ft and 11ft high were built for individual prisoners; and there were larger rooms that could, if need be, become partitioned to provide nine cells in each.

Norman Cross served as a prototype, and formed the basis of specifications that were used for planning other such establishments. By 1814, there were eight of these large prisons: at Norman Cross, Millbay, Stapleton, Valleyfield (about nine miles south of Edinburgh), Forton (in Hampshire, Porchester, Chatham (nowadays St Mary's Barracks) and finally Dartmoor.

Dartmoor was the most dreaded of a collection of unpleasant alternatives. The other prisons were reasonably close to towns. In contrast to the harsh attitude of the authorities, the local people were reasonably sympathetic, and the tradesmen were glad of the opportunity to sell their wares to such inmates, admittedly not very many, as could afford to buy them. But there was also the feeling of being reasonably close to civilised surroundings; the sight of rooftops glimpsed from a cell window, smoke rising from chimneys – evidence, surely, of people living normal lives; and the feeling, however slight, of living on the fringe of a more congenial and better-ordered world.

On Dartmoor, there were no such comforting sights. The premises, which were opened in 1806, occupied thirty acres on a site 1,400ft above sea level. It was exposed to the north and east winds, which made it abominably cold, and the desolate moorland landscape surrounding it did nothing for the morale of the inmates. As any other prison, it was enclosed by a high wall, 16ft tall. To the ingenious escaper, walls were not necessarily obstacles. At one place, for example, two prisoners tunnelled their way to freedom. The episode had an unfortunate sequel: one of them was shot, the other was severely wounded and taken back into captivity, but the fact remained that it was possible to burrow a way out.

Up here on the moor, however, the prisoners often wondered whether life within the walls was safer than the precarious conditions outside. When the fog came down, which it frequently did, and suddenly, too, it was dangerously easy to lose one's way. There were rumours, no doubt encouraged by the guards, of swamps that sucked unsuspecting wayfarers into the depths below. People, it was said, had died of starvation on the cruel plateau, so thinly populated and so full of menace.

The prison was built with accommodation for 5,000 prisoners. There were five self-contained barracks, each two storeys high and housing 1,000 men. Each had its own exercise yard, its own supply of running water, its own quarters for the guard and, inevitably, its own Black Hole. The captives slept in three tiers of hammocks slung from cast iron pillars, apart from the Rafalés who, as was their custom, preferred the floor. Here, for no reason that has been sufficiently explained, they were called 'the Romans'. Their elected leader, who was changed at frequent intervals, was known as 'the General'. He was the only one to enjoy the comparative luxury of a hammock. The men appear to have practised some early, very basic, form of Communism. For most of the time, there was only one pair of breeches among the lot of them. These were issued to whoever was appointed as spokesman for negotiations with the rest of the community. Most of this man's excursions were concerned either with begging for food or else with stealing it.

Once, when the Romans held a parade to mark some anniversary or other, an unusually plump rat strutted onto the scene. This was too much for the men who, as usual, were famished. They broke ranks and chased the rodent into the kitchen, where they were intercepted by the guard. The 'General' assured the NCO in charge that he had nothing to worry about: his companions were 'quiet now as sheep'. As a reward for such instant obedience, he suggested, double rations might be issued. As for the rat, according to one observer, it was caught and eaten raw.

In Dartmoor, as in other prisons, there were several classes of inmate. At the top were *les lords*, who were officers who had been confined for breaking parole. Next came *les labourers*, men who made money from the sale of articles they had manufactured and who were regarded as the most respectable of the rank and file. *Les indifférents* were the idlers who did nothing to pass the time; *les misérables* were the mischief-makers, who were regarded as untrustworthy; and, at the bottom of the scale, came *les romans*.

Despite its situation, there were escapes from Dartmoor. Two naval officers made uniforms sufficiently like those of the guards for them to be able to tag on to a squad marching off duty. On the following evening, three more men repeated the trick and, again, it worked.

But the most celebrated escape from Dartmoor was that of a privateer named Louis Vanhille. He formed a friendship with a young woman who visited the prison with the traders who came to sell or barter their goods. With her assistance, he disguised himself as an old woman, mixed with the merchants and walked away to Tavistock.

After a long journey, during which he travelled 1,238 miles, mostly on foot, but sometimes in boats and occasionally in carriages, he reached Bristol (quite why he chose such a very devious route has not been explained). He took passage in a ship bound for Jamaica, where he was arrested and sent back to England. He had hoped to reach America: instead, he spent the rest of the war at Forton prison and, later, in a hulk.

As far as the less-robust captive's plight was concerned, it is probably best summed up by John Holmwood, the Transport Office's agent at Porchester. In a report written during August 1800, he observed:

The prisoners are reduced to a state of dreadful meagreness. A great number of them have the appearance of walking skeletons. One has been found dead in his hammock, and another fell out by mere debility and was killed by the fall. The great part of those sent to hospital die in a short time, others as soon as they are received there.

Such men were not criminals. They had once been proud members of an army that had conquered much of Europe or sailors who manned well-equipped fighting ships. Their only offence had been to fall into the hands of a ruthless enemy and to be too low on the social scale to receive parole. Louis Vanhille may have journeyed a long way, only to end up in yet another place of detention. But, at least, he had been able to rediscover the pleasures of freedom, if only for a limited period. For that he had to be grateful. For the majority such delights would not come until 1814, when Napoleon's retreat to Elba brought the war to another temporary halt, and everybody was able to go home.

4

THE UNINVITED GUESTS

If you had been a neutral during the Napoleonic Wars, you would have found it hard to make up your mind which side, France or Britain, treated its prisoners worst. Each, and neither without reason, accused the other of brutality. In Britain, the captives came under the control of the Transport Office with the Government as the ultimate court of appeal. In France, there was something more personal about the arrangement. The final authority was Napoleon himself. Since a dictator is less predictable than a government department, his decisions were as various as his moods. They ranged from the surprisingly generous to the downright ruthless.

Looked at from the viewpoint of history, it seems probable that the fortunes of Britons in French custody were marginally better than those of Frenchmen in British. At least they were spared the evils of life aboard a hulk. Officers on parole were quartered in the town of Verdun. Other ranks were housed in prisons at Givet (on the banks of the Meuse amid the Ardennes), at Valenciennes (in the north of France) and in fortified towns extending as far south as the Pyrenees. The general idea was to site them as many miles from the coast as possible, thereby putting plenty of obstacles in the way of an escape back to England.

By no means all the locations met with Napoleon's approval. Once, when commenting on the prison at Arras, he remarked sarcastically, 'I do not know why English prisoners have been placed there; no doubt to be near home so that they may escape.' Verdun was pleased to be chosen as the centre for parole, for it meant good business for the local traders. A French newspaper likened the captives to 'sheep enclosed in a field to manure the soil'. The price of lodgings for officers, which had been thirty-six francs a month when the war began, rose quickly until the asking price was 300 francs a month. At this point, Napoleon intervened. Unless charges were kept within reasonable bounds, the prisoners would be sent elsewhere.

The people of Metz, if they heard about this threat, must have been delighted. Rapacious merchants that they were, they had watched with envious eyes the prosperity brought to Verdun by these vagabonds of war.

Indeed, the mayor of Metz had encouraged the commander-in-chief of prisoners and head of the gendarmerie General Wirion, to consider his town's claims as a parole centre. Wirion had been sympathetic. He considered it his duty to reside wherever the paroled officers lived, and he did not enjoy the company of the Verdun citizens. A move, he felt, might do him good. He put the proposition to Napoleon, who snapped back, 'Tell him it is a lie, for in my notes on population, Metz is a village compared to Verdun. Verdun shall keep the prisoners.'

But, in the final reckoning, Metz enjoyed a small revenge. When, in 1812, the prefects and mayors of France were asked to procure signatures of those in favour of elevating Napoleon to the title of Emperor, the mayor was unable to send in more than a dozen names. The mayor of Verdun, on the other hand, canvassed every household and compiled an impressively long list.

As in England, the penalty for breaking parole and for other offences was imprisonment. For comparatively minor misdeeds, officers were dispatched to cells in the local citadels. For major crimes, such as attempting to escape, they were taken to a fortress named Bitche on the Rhine. Prisoners of war used to refer to it as the 'Castle of Tears'. It was built upon an immense rock with innumerable subterranean caves. From a military point of view, it was considered to be completely bomb-proof. From the viewpoint of anyone who had the misfortune to be incarcerated there, it was as unpleasant as anything that Britain had to offer.

Life in Verdun seems to have been a tolerably pleasant experience. Some officers, who had sufficient money, were even able to be joined by their families. This was not so difficult as it may sound. Once the peace of Amiens had been declared in 1802, a great many British civilians, hungry for a glimpse of the France they loved so well, and of Paris in particular, swarmed across the Channel. But when, in the following year, it turned out to be no more than a truce, and when suddenly the war began all over again, many found themselves trapped.

Between 1803 and 1814, officers on parole, providing they were the fortunate possessors of private incomes, had regular remittances sent from England to France via a firm of bankers named Perregaux in Paris. The more well-to-do lived comfortably and ate well. Wirion proved to be a considerate individual, who allowed a good deal of latitude. In theory, there should have been a roll-call every morning and evening. In fact, it became sufficient to put in an appearance once every five days – just to show that you were still there.

There was, however, a much darker side to this apparently easy-going custodian of enemy officers. General Wirion was the son of a pork butcher who had done well for himself. If the citizens of Verdun were making money by the comparatively innocent art of, so to speak, fleecing the tourists, the commander-in-chief of prisoners of war was making a small fortune. The gaming tables of the town were flourishing, and Wirion was receiving a cut of between 600 francs and 1,000 francs a month as his price for non-interference. If a paroled prisoner found it inconvenient to turn up to roll-call, a small fee of three francs was sufficient to make amends. Alternatively, you could, for twelve francs, buy a sort of season ticket that excused you from all such gatherings for one month.

Upon occasion, he invited himself to dine with some of the wealthier prisoners. The meals were followed by games of cards, and Wirion was always allowed to win. Admittedly, he repaid his handsome gains by granting favours great and small – even to the extent of quashing a charge that might, otherwise, have sent the malefactor off to the inner darkness of Bitche.

Nor was this the end of this saga of corruption. Now and again it becomes necessary to invest a small sum to reap a very much larger return. Throughout Verdun there were servants and British officers' mistresses, housekeepers and landlords, receiving modest but regular payments for spying. When they turned up some gem of information about an illicit affair, or a planned escape, they would pass it on to him. He would then use the information to blackmail the unfortunate individual.

With their commander-in-chief practising corruption on such a grand scale, it would have been surprising if his underlings had not followed his example. These iniquities took the form of lotteries organised by the gendarmerie. Admittedly, there were no prizes to be won, but the purchase of a ticket might buy a favour or two and, likewise, refusal to invest would probably ensure a trip to Bitche on the smallest excuse.

By 1810, Wirion's extortions were provoking a clamour of complaints. Eventually, they reached the ears of General Clarke, who had recently been appointed Minister of War. The result was that the hero of Verdun's racketeering was called to Paris to account for his actions. The probability was that he would have to face a court martial.

At ten o'clock on the night of 8 April, he hired a hackney carriage and told the driver to take him to the Bois de Boulogne. He alighted a few yards from the Porte Maillot, took a pistol from his coat, and blew out his brains. A letter to his wife was found in one of his pockets and another, to a doctor, asking him to attend her. According to the police report, 'It appears that impatience at the apparent tardiness of the commission deputed to investigate the complaints against him was the reason for the suicide.'

He was succeeded at Verdun by a Colonel Courselles, who was more cautious in his transactions and more moderate in his demands. Nevertheless, he managed to monopolise the town's supplies of wine, and exploited it by charging exorbitant prices. He, too, was asked to explain his conduct but he managed to shift the blame on to his subordinates. He was, perhaps, fortunate. His story was given ill-deserved authenticity, when one of them followed Wirion's example and shot himself.

The days, weeks, months and years of the semi-captives at Verdun passed not too unpleasantly, despite the dishonest transactions of their custodians. Sometimes a newcomer arrived. He was invariably surrounded by a host of his fellow countrymen, eager to hear the latest news of the war and of affairs at home. Prisoners on parole were allowed one newspaper a week, *Bell's Weekly Magazine*, which was published every Sunday. The authorities considered its contents sufficiently harmless to be suitable reading. Occasionally, however, some more forthright journal managed to evade the ever-alert French postal authorities, and was smuggled into the town.

For amusement, the captives indulged themselves in amateur theatricals, cock-fighting and, occasionally, horse racing. As one Frenchman remarked, 'You Englishmen are much the same, whether prisoners or at home – playing, driving, and shooting each other ... one might fancy oneself in London.'

His reference to 'shooting each other' is hard to follow, though at least two duels were fought. The first was between a British doctor and a man named Balbi, who ran the gaming tables. The doctor, named Gold, wounded his opponent. He was arrested and confined to the town's fort. When the news reached Napoleon, however, he ordered Gold's release. 'A prisoner of war may fight a duel', he said.

The other had a more tragic outcome. In this case, it was fought between two naval officers, Captain Walpole and Lieutenant Miles, who had quarrelled when playing cards. Miles was killed – which was, perhaps, taking things too far. Walpole was removed to Bitche to reflect on his rash conduct.

At Orleans, an internee challenged the local prefect to a fight but the matter seems to have been smoothed over without recourse to violence.

Prisoners of war, as any other community, tend to form clubs and associations. In Verdun, there were two gathering points on the social round, the English Club and the Irish Club. Membership of the latter was obviously confined to those who had been sufficiently convinced of the British cause to enlist in the forces. There is no record of the French authorities attempting to suborn them, though this must be considered a

possibility. An expedition to Ireland, followed by an attack on England
from the west, was one of Napoleon's more fanciful projects. In return for
co-operation, he promised Ireland independence as one condition of any
peace treaty he might be in a position to dictate.

Since there were innumerable Irish refugees living in France, they
seemed to be a natural source of recruits. When the proposition was put
to them, 20,000 enlisted. The Irish Legion, as it was called, received an
eagle and colours. At the parade held to mark Napoleon's elevation to
Emperor, it lined up alongside the French regiments.

On one occasion, when the Irish Legion was on the march, it had to pass
through Verdun. With praiseworthy tact (or, possibly, for fear of arousing
violence), the column was scheduled to pass through the streets very early
in the morning. Inevitably, the tramp of feet awakened many of the British
inhabitants. Faces appeared at windows, and one or two people called out.
But there was no hostility in their remarks. They merely wanted to know
what all the noise was about, and why it was impossible to enjoy a good
night's sleep without the interruption of martial footsteps.

At one time, the parole population of Verdun is said to have numbered
ten thousand. Among them were innovators, eccentrics, men of fierce
national pride who were fretting to get back into battle, and men who were
merely anxious to while away the time as pleasantly as possible.

Their circumstances varied considerably. The rich, as ever, remained
rich though many squandered their wealth in the gambling rooms. The
poor, as always, were poor. In 1807, the Quakers in Birmingham opened
a subscription on their behalf and, in the same year, the British Government,
in a rash moment of charity, sent the sum of £2,000 to be spent on their
welfare. In 1811, the London Quakers followed Birmingham's example.
Throughout most of the war, a Dr Davis ran a dispensary at which he
provided free medicine for the less well-to-do.

No doubt the most ingenious captive was a Captain Molyneux Shuldham,
who set up a small workshop in the town. His object seems to have been
to explore more economic means of transport. His first invention was a
carriage propelled by sails. Given sufficient breeze blowing in the right
direction, it could travel at eight miles an hour. However, it frightened the
horses (just as, many years later, farmers and those in authority feared that
the motor-car might). When one of these beasts bolted and a cart overturned,
the commandant decided that all further work on the vehicle must stop.

But Captain Shuldham was not yet done. If the roads were out-of-
bounds, surely the large areas covered by ice in winter could be put to
good purpose. He accordingly built a vehicle mounted on huge skates.
Technically, it was a masterpiece but, again, he ran into trouble. This

time, it was the anglers who complained. Shuldham's monstrosity, they said, terrified the fish and there was nothing to catch.

Precisely how they expected to catch fish when the ice was thick enough to bear the Shuldham flier is not explained. Nevertheless, the inventive genius was ordered back to the drawing-board with the daunting suggestion that he should apply himself to the creation of something that was proof against panic in any sector of the animal world.

The gambling tables were probably the most popular feature of the leisured (which meant 'captive') classes in Verdun. In the gaming room, there was a large notice that announced, 'This bank is kept for the English; the French are forbidden to play at it.' Some, such as Lord Blayney, profited from it. During the course of one evening, he enriched himself to the extent of £50,000. But many did less well and, when chronic gamblers began to run up excessive debts, the tables were closed down.

A young officer named Chambers was playing for stakes far beyond his means. When he had lost all his money, he asked the management for a loan. Knowing his history of bad luck, the directors insisted that he must supply some form of security. 'But,' protested the young man, 'I have nothing to give but my ears.' He was assured that he need not part with both: one would suffice.

The unhappy Chambers took out his pocket knife, and actually cut off the fleshy part of one ear. Then, to the astonishment and admiration of the other players, he threw it on to the table. In return, he was rewarded with two dollars. He resumed his game. When, however, the matter was reported to a senior French officer, he was condemned for exceeding his means and packed off to Bitche.

Gambling debts were punishable by a spell in prison, but not all victims of chance were sent to the dreaded Bitche. An officer named Waring Knox overstepped the mark in 1811, and was carted off to Valenciennes. Once inside the prison, he tried to do a deal with the French authorities. He had, he said, been brought up with the Prince Regent, and their childhood friendship had survived the years. If he were to be given 200 louis (gold coins valued at about twenty francs each) and a passport back to England, he would use his influence to obtain a confidential post. He would then, he promised, act as a spy for the French Government, sending back priceless scraps of information about secret projects. He did not convince the authorities, and the idea was turned down.

Inside prison, Knox seems to have undergone a change of heart and of fortune. At all events, he made amends for his promise of treason by standing the poorer prisoners a square meal each day.

The ultimate crime, as in Britain, was planning to escape. But there were lesser offences that guaranteed trouble for those who committed them. As a French official said, 'Restless spirits do their best to compel the French to treat the prisoners harshly.' One such restless spirit was a peevish Captain Hawker, who visited a jeweller's shop on the pretext of being about to pay a bill. Instead of handing over the money, he struck the trader. The assault earned him six months in the cooler.

An officer named Brodie was sentenced to a term at Bitche for writing a letter to the commandant, in which he had some harsh things to say about Napoleon. Another of Napoleon's critics, a Lieutenant Simpson, was observed hissing a bust of the Emperor at the theatre. When taken to task next day, he said that he had been drunk. It was possibly true, and the matter was forgiven. Two naval lieutenants were not pardoned for striking a French officer. They were put in prison for fourteen days, which was a very moderate punishment.

Captain Nanney was less leniently treated, when he was arraigned for seducing the wife of a Verdun citizen. He was taken away to the prison at Arras. Another officer fared even worse, when he was observed behaving in an 'indecent manner' with his mistress at the theatre. When a French officer walked over to reprimand him, the excessively ardent lover stopped whatever he was doing and struck his accuser. He was sent to Bitche, and so was an officer of more criminal intent, who was indicted for forgery and for swindling his fellow captives.

Lord Blayney, who fared so well at the tables, eventually quarrelled with a colonel named Whaley. Despite the fact that Napoleon decreed that it was in order for prisoners of war to fight duels, he resolved to use a more subtle method of revenge. He charged Whaley with being a British spy, and of having procured plans of French forts. The accusation was investigated, but it was found to be totally without foundation. Whaley went free: thereafter, Blayney was regarded with suspicion by his fellow captives.

Now and then, the calm routine of Verdun was interrupted. In July of 1812, the French authorities suspected that some of their fellow countrywomen were helping the paroled officers with escape plans. There were others who were trouble-makers; their very presence seemed to cause rows among the captives. To travel from one department of France to another required a passport. Now, they decided, all suspicious women should be banished from the town, and no new civilians admitted unless they had a very good reason.

In 1810, an exchange was arranged for all personnel suffering from incurable illnesses. Eventually, 3,000 Frenchmen in English prisons were released in return for 1,000 British and 2,000 Spanish prisoners. The British

Government had hoped to receive 17,000 Hanoverian troops as part of the deal but Napoleon, very sensibly, rejected the proposition.

Verdun tradespeople always became anxious when there was any talk of moving their, by now, very profitable guests. When, on 7 August 1808, a roll-call was held (it was known as *appel*), 124 midshipmen were suddenly arrested for violating their parole and dispatched to the citadel at St Vannes, a building that, in peacetime, had served as a monastery. As they were led out of the town, a sizable number of local citizens turned out to bid them goodbye. It seemed a rather nice gesture, until it was discovered that they were all merchants anxious to have their debts paid or else to receive some security in lieu.

Towards the end of the war, when there was a large exodus in an attempt to remove prisoners of war away from the advancing Allied armies, bad debts to the value of half a million francs are said to have been left behind. However, since the worthies of Verdun had been profiteering for years on a captive market that had nothing else to do but spend such money as it had, it seems unlikely that anyone was really out of pocket.

In many ways, the French system was similar to the British. The officers, provided they behaved themselves, enjoyed a restricted form of freedom; the rank and file went to prison. Some of the places of confinement were large establishments such as those at Valenciennes and Givet; others were citadels in fortified towns. In whichever case, the prelude to captivity was often a long journey. One POW recalled an overnight stop at a former convent on the road to Givet. 'We were all indiscriminately huddled together in the different apartments, upon the planking for the night, and at dawn of day the drum summoned us to muster.'

Most of the trip was made in horse-drawn wagons, with straw to make the conditions more comfortable. The convoy was escorted by horse gendarmerie and a unit of infantry. He wrote:

Whenever the road passed by a wood, which frequently occurred, we were halted to give the infantry time to occupy its skirts; two gendarmes on each side were posted midway; whilst the rest occasionally displayed their pistols, somewhat ostentatiously, by way of intimidation.

At Valenciennes, the citadel barracks was used to accommodate 1,400 prisoners. It was made up of a collection of small buildings, each of which was divided into six apartments containing three or four beds. Every man (as in other prisons) received an allowance of 10d (5p) a week provided, generously perhaps, by Lloyds of London. The French Government's contribution was the provision of 1lb of black bread, $\frac{1}{2}$lb of meat, a thimbleful of salt, a noggin of peas, a small quantity of wood and $\frac{3}{4}$d a day. Any additions to this somewhat frugal fare had to be bought by the prisoners.

It was not impossible to earn money. At Valenciennes, for example, one-third of the prison population was allowed into the town to work. One of the prison's less-scrupulous commandants had made himself the tidy sum of £6,000 from the arrangement by charging the workers ten sous each for the privilege of toil. His successor, a more reasonable officer named Colonel du Croix Aubert, halved the amount and, later, abolished it altogether. The officers were allowed out to shop, though they had to be accompanied by a gendarme.

Givet prison in the Ardennes was similar in many ways to Valenciennes. Nine hundred and thirty prisoners of war were housed here – accommodated sixteen to a room, and each room equipped with a large kettle, a dish, a ladle and a pitcher. As in the other places of confinement, the POWs were compelled to wear a uniform consisting of a grey jacket and trousers, and a straw hat. It seems to have been part of the French policy to move the captives from one prison to another, often at very short notice. These journeys were ordeals of hardship, especially in winter. Many POWs died on them.

In 1803, a newcomer arrived at Givet who was to make a great deal of difference to the prison's routine. His name was the Reverend R. B. Wolfe, and he came from Stone in Staffordshire. During the lull in the fighting brought about by the Peace of Amiens, he had taken the post of chaplain to a gentleman's family touring the Continent. His young wife and his child accompanied him.

When the truce came to an end, the Wolfes, as became their position in society, were directed to Verdun. But this young cleric was not happy about the situation. He would, he felt, be better employed in one of the prisons housing other ranks. He applied for a transfer and the authorities, in a mixture of surprise and admiration, sent him to Givet. He remained there until the autumn of 1811, when he and his family were allowed to return to England. He wrote:

> On my arrival at Givet I found the depot in the most deplorable state. Anything more degrading and miserable it would be difficult to conceive, and as regards religion, every appearance of it was confined to some twenty Methodists, who were the object of most painful persecution; the bodily privations of prisoners, half-starved by the dishonesty of the French commissaries and their want of the common necessities of life, being equally distressing.

Wolfe applied himself industriously to his new duties. He converted one of the rooms into a chapel and held services there. Unlike the unhappy experiences of the Methodists, they were well attended – though the fact that it happened also to contain the oven used for baking bread may have helped. In winter, it was pleasantly warm.

Having set up his shop, so to speak, he then got to work on his next task. Here was a community of men, living perforce in idleness and doing nothing to better themselves. The place needed a school, he decided. During the following years, 500 POWs were taught both to read and to master the elements of arithmetic. Navigation was also on the curriculum. One of his pupils, a man named Short, became so proficient at it that, when the war ended and he returned home, he set up a school of navigation at St Ives in Cornwall.

But Wolfe's life was not easy. He wrote:

> Traps were constantly laid for me. Spies were everywhere, and I know that, if they could allege anything against me, I should be denounced, and probably without an explanation, marched to the fortress at Bitche in company with deserters and criminals.

The hazards that attended Wolfe at Givet were no doubt the result of a suspicion that he might be helping the prisoners with plans for escape. This was a matter that was continually grumbling beneath the surface of prisoner-of-war life, and which occasionally erupted. When, in Wirion's days, three officers broke their parole and escaped from Verdun, the others were told that, if they were to be treated as men of honour, they must share a collective responsibility for good conduct. If one of them decided to take off, they would all be sent to fortresses as punishment.

Four years later, in 1807, Wirion warned that any officer attempting to escape would be shot. It was, he said, the legal punishment for breach of parole. A similar threat was made at Arras and Valenciennes, though there is no evidence to show that it was ever carried out. In the vicinity of Valenciennes, a reward of fifty francs was offered to anyone who arrested a fugitive; and, in 1811, Napoleon himself reiterated the prospect of a death sentence for a recaptured escaper. He insisted that notices to this effect should be displayed throughout France. Again, it does not seem to have been acted upon – doubtless due to the likelihood that it would cause reprisals among French POWs in Britain. However, a number of men were placed in irons for the staggering period of six years for attempting to break out.

The methods used by escapers varied considerably. The prize for ingenuity (and good acting) must surely go to Captain Charles Cunliffe

Owen who, in 1811, was incarcerated at Valenciennes for some misdemeanour. He had not been there for long when he decided that the best
way of getting away would be to feign insanity. He cut one of his veins
(taking care to select one that would not do too much damage) and then
ran to the commandant's office to denounce an imaginary plot to seize the
Bastille in Paris. The commandant reacted much as Captain Owen hoped
he might, by placing him in the local lunatic asylum. Later, he was
transferred to a private institution in Paris from which he escaped in July
1812.

An officer named Thomas Hudson used forged papers when he attempted
a getaway in 1808, but he was recaptured. He was sentenced to six years
in irons but, on appeal, it was quashed. He was excused on the grounds
that he had been coerced by his fellow prisoners.

One of Givet's inmates, James Emsworth, was away for five months.
Hoping to reach Britain's allies in Prussia, he made his way across France
to Germany and was nearing the Prussian frontier when he was arrested.
It was bad luck, but at least he was more fortunate than the master's mate
of HMS *Alfred*, William Haywood, who was also held captive in Givet.

Haywood had been allowed out on a shopping expedition with a
midshipman named Gale. Somehow, the two men managed to evade their
escort and go to earth in a cave on the edge of the town. They had not been
in hiding for long, before they heard the sound of the cannon that was used
as an alarm signal. Presently, they heard the sound of search parties in the
vicinity but they were not detected.

After a few hours, the coast seemed to be clear but the two men decided
to remain under cover until dark. Later that afternoon, they heard the
sound of a squad of men marching up to the entrance to the cave. An
officer shouted 'Surrender!' and Haywood and Gale came out with their
hands up. The officer promptly took a swipe at Haywood with his sabre
and knocked him to the ground. Not content with this, he plunged the
blade into his body and killed him. He then took a cut at Gale, whom he
wounded but did not take matters to a conclusion. The unhappy midshipman, bleeding profusely, was frog-marched back to the prison.

How, when the earlier search had failed, had the French guard been so
successful on the second occasion? It was not as if the soldiers had
discovered the cave after a search: they had marched up to it without
hesitation, as if knowing that the escapers were inside.

The villain of the piece turned out to be a marine named Wilson who
had been captured when HM Frigate *La Minerve* was taken by a French
warship. Wilson had lost a leg in the action, and considered himself eligible
for a pension. The money, however, had not been sent to him from Britain,

and he had become embittered. He had overheard Haywood and Gale planning their escape: after the failure of the first search, he had betrayed them to the commandant. As, presumably, a reward for his services, he was made a warder in the hospital. Afterwards, he never appeared in the prison unless accompanied by an armed guard.

But perfidy such as this was by no means confined to British informers. At Bitche, the fort's commandant was warned of an intended attempt to escape. Instead of preventing it, he allowed the two sailors concerned, Marshall and Cox, to go ahead. Without suspecting that their plan had been discovered, the two men made their exit and reached a point some yards beyond the walls, when they ran into a carefully prepared ambush. They were both killed in what can only be described as cold-blooded murder.

An attempt to tunnel a way out of Givet was betrayed by another informer, in this case, by the armourer of a captured East Indiaman named *Sir William Douglas*. The man's motive was never explained: it was, one has to assume, the hope of better treatment.

One of the few successful escapes was that of Captain Edward Boys, RN. In 1810, Boys was quartered at Arras. Accompanied by two companions, he managed to negotiate the prison wall by means of a rope. He and his accomplices carried with them a supply of pepper, which they intended to throw in the faces of any guards who might pursue them.

Some hours before their break-out, Boys afterwards recalled, 'We amused ourselves with writing a letter to the commandant, in which we thanked him for his civilities, and assured him that it was the rigid and disgraceful measures of the French government which obliged us to prove the inefficiency of *"locks, bolts and fortresses"*.'

After innumerable adventures and a payment of £80, Boys reached England in a fishing boat from Flushing. His return was something of an anti-climax. When, eventually, he arrived in Dover, after being refused permission to land at Ramsgate, the time was eight o'clock in the evening. Since it was now dark, he was not allowed to go ashore until the following morning.

Napoleon was generous in his treatment of prisoners who interested him. Perhaps because he had found the Channel an impossible barrier, he admired what he regarded as virtually suicidal attempts to cross it.

Two sailors who escaped from Arras prudently decided to march by night, using the moon as a guide on their journey to the coast. In a wood close to Boulogne, they chopped down some trees and built a small boat. They then waterproofed it with a layer of suet.

Soon after completing their work, they were discovered. The authorities were intrigued. Did they really imagine that their craft would float? The men were asked to give a demonstration. It behaved perfectly, and there were no leaks. Napoleon happened to be in the vicinity. When he heard about the exploit, he ordered one of the seamen, a mariner named Wright, to be brought before him. Why, he wanted to know, had Wright decided to escape? Had he, perhaps, a mistress in England whom he wished to rejoin?

Wright told him that he had no mistress. His mother was ill, and he was determined to visit her. Napoleon seems to have been impressed. He commended the young man on his dutiful attitude, and gave him and his companion permission to make the trip. He even handed him a small sum of money to buy comforts for the ailing Mrs Wright.

A similar story is told of a packet-boat captain who had been interned in Verdun. He and a friend walked to Boulogne, where they had hoped to steal a boat. Unfortunately, Napoleon was planning his invasion of England, and pretty well everything that floated had been commandeered. But the two men were undaunted. If they couldn't find what they wanted, they would manufacture it. They built a wooden frame, 3ft wide by 4ft long, and covered it with sailcloth. It floated well enough and they paddled out into the Channel.

They had not gone far, however, when they were challenged by an officer in a French customs pinnace. Their reply obviously did not satisfy him, for they were promptly taken in tow back to Boulogne and put into the town gaol.

But, in this case, too, Napoleon intervened. He ordered the men and the craft to his headquarters. 'Is it really true,' he said, 'that you thought of crossing the sea in that thing?'

'We'll show you, if you'll let us go', one of them said.

Napoleon laughed and, to their delighted surprise, he agreed. He even arranged their departure in such a way that they were bound to be picked up by a British ship.

An Irish packet-boat captain named Flynn and some of his crew escaped from a fort in Holland, and rowed nearly half way across the North Sea before being taken aboard an English merchantman. But the record, although it has never been confirmed, belongs to an Italian, serving with the French army, who was imprisoned in England. His name was Jean-Marie Salatti. If the story is to be believed, he made his escape to France by swimming the Channel. Captain Webb was the first to do it officially in 1875 but it seems likely that Salatti beat him to it by a good sixty years.

5

THE UNCIVIL FACE OF CIVIL WAR

On 12 April 1861, the Confederate forces began the bombardment of Fort Sumter, an isolated Unionist strong-point in Charleston harbour. The ordeal lasted thirty-four hours – at the end of which, the United States flag was hauled down, and the fort's occupants departed for New York in a steamship. The American Civil War had begun.

Both sides were too preoccupied with organising and equipping their armies to spend much thought on the fate of those unwanted relics of victorious battles, the prisoners. Nor, initially, had they believed that any very elaborate arrangements would be necessary. The Confederates, despite the fact that they fired the opening shots, had not believed that, when it came to the crunch, there would *be* a war. For their part, the Unionists thought that the matter would be concluded in ninety days. The question of providing accommodation for a more prolonged spell in captivity did not arise.

Both sides were to be surprised by the immensity of the problem, and it would certainly have been better for the prisoners if their respective leaders had taken a more realistic attitude. There are no accurate figures – one estimate suggests that 211,411 Federal soldiers were taken, of which 30,218 died in captivity. The same source refers to 462,634 captured Confederates and lists 25,976 as having ended their days in northern prisons.

A more cautious assessment hazards a total of 400,000 taken by both sides. But, whatever it was, the numbers caught their captors by surprise, and neither protagonist was prepared for this inundation of helpless humanity. The northern states improvised to better effect than the southern, though this is not an occasion for applause. As the mortality figures suggest, conditions on both sides were a great deal less than good, let alone perfect.

By the mid-nineteenth century, the European powers were working towards the provision of more humane treatment for captured soldiers. The first of several Geneva Conventions took place in 1864 and a delegate from the United States was present. In the previous year, President

Abraham Lincoln had insisted on certain standards, which were listed in *Instructions for the Conduct of the United States' Army in the Field*.

It was generally conceded that prisoners must be properly accommodated, nourished and clothed. Attempts to escape should not be regarded as crimes: they were, indeed, a captive's duty. If recaptured, the worst that should befall a truant was to be guarded with greater severity – which was not to suggest that he should be punished. Enlisted men might be made to work (though not on military projects). Officers, on the whole, should be offered parole in return for a promise not to return to their own lines. This might be given in writing, or orally.

It was clearly too much to hope that such rules would be rigidly observed. When it came to the point, everything depended on the senior officer on the spot. Sometimes there were unintentional infringements; sometimes, intentional. In the case of the American Civil War, however, matters were less simple, not least, because it was a *civil* war. Were, for example, the Confederates to be regarded as honourable enemies or as rebels guilty of high treason? Nor were suggestions that the two sides might come together to discuss such matters as exchanges greeted by the northern statesmen with anything approaching enthusiasm. To hold such a conference would be to recognise (or to *seem* to recognise) the Confederates as a nation in their own right. This was totally unacceptable.

There was, however, a limit to the number of captives that could be accommodated and fed by a system that had not envisaged any problem on such a scale. The battles of Bull Run and Ball's Bluff (1861–2), no matter how sweet the taste of victory, found the Confederate authorities unable to cope with so many prisoners. Pride had to yield to more practical (and, indeed, humanitarian) considerations. For the first time, there was a readiness by commanders on both sides to exchange. Later, on 18 February 1863, the commandants of all major prison camps in the north were permitted to release captives who were not officers, and who were prepared to take an oath of allegiance to the United States. Those who applied for their freedom under these terms had, in most cases, to be segregated in special quarters until they were set free. The fear, which was by no means unfounded, was that they might be treated with violence by their more intransigent companions.

But the problem was not merely one of food and lodgings. A prisoner, by his very nature, had to be guarded. Who were to perform such duties? Were able-bodied soldiers, who would be more profitably employed in the front line, to be used? The very thought was ridiculous. The Unionists relied on men who had either been severely wounded or else whose health was not sufficiently robust for active service. Such units were referred to as the Invalid Corps and the fact that the initials IC were stamped on the backs of their uniforms did little to enhance the wearers' self-respect. Nor did these somewhat sickly soldiers appreciate it when their charges called them 'condemned Yankees'.

Such insults were not, of course, one-sided. A Confederate interned on Johnson's Island in Lake Erie wrote:

> Our treatment by the officers was, as far as I know, courteous enough; and as to the enlisted men who guarded us, my principle objection aside from their propensity to shoot, lay in the fact that most of them could not address us a 'rebels' without qualifying the term with the adjective 'damned'.

The Confederates, too, had problems over the provision of guards. The most satisfactory arrangement was at Castle Pinckney in Charleston harbour, where a well-drilled unit of boy soldiers, known as the Zouave Cadets, served this purpose. The lads did well – there were no escapes, though this may be explained by the fact that Castle Pinckney was the only fortress used by the southern states as a prison. If, by design, it was hard to enter, it was, presumably, equally difficult to make an exit.

In other camps, there were simply not enough guards to go round. Since they were far removed from the Unionist lines, the captives were required to assist in the policing by providing their own custodians. They were divided into groups of about ninety men, and a leader (who was responsible for their good behaviour) was elected by each. He was rewarded for his trouble by small privileges. If he failed to please his charges, he could be broken and another elected in his stead.

The commandants of the camps and prisons were as varied a collection of officers as ever donned uniform. Many of them were civilians hastily given military rank to fit them for their new responsibilities (The commandant of Johnson's Island, for example, was the mayor of the nearby town of Sandusky on the mainland). Others, such as the notorious Captain Wirz of the Confederates' Andersonville, were officers who had been severely wounded in action.

Lieutenant-Colonel William Hoffman, the Commissary General of Prisoners for the Federal Forces for most of the war, had, himself, been briefly in Confederate hands. He was a member of a Unionist force that, in the very early days, had surrendered in Texas without firing a shot. By all accounts, he seems to have been a conscientious officer, though his instructions were not always carried out by his men on the spot.

No doubt, he wished there were more like Colonel Martin Burke, commandant of Fort Lafayette, who had a collection of privateers, officers and political prisoners in his charge. Previously, Colonel Burke had served in the field as a staff officer. His obedience was such that, according to a general, 'If I had told him at any time to take one of my ADCs and shoot him before breakfast, the aide's execution would have been duly reported.'

The Confederate General John H. Winder, Provost Marshal of Richmond, Va – and, therefore, responsible for the safekeeping of prisoners – incurred much of the odium for the subhuman conditions experienced by most of his captives. In fact, General Winder had so many other things on his mind, that he had little attention to spare for the physical needs of his unwelcome guests. Nor did he occupy the position for long. He was appointed on 21 November 1864 and he died in February of the following year. Nevertheless, his much-vaunted misdeeds made good copy for the Federal newspapers. Indeed, atrocity stories about the prisons on either side of the front line were useful fuel for the respective propaganda machines. The press exposed such infamies in bold headlines: parsons in their pulpits thundered about man's (ie the other side's) inhumanity to man.

Initially, the Federal high command relied on existing prisons and military establishments to house the captives. The penitentiary at Alton, Illinois, was used for such purposes – Forts Lafayette and Columbus at New York were adapted and, likewise, Fort Warren in Boston harbour, Fort Delaware on the Delaware River and so on. But, as the war progressed, these places became so overcrowded that the authorities had to extemporise.

Camp Morton, near Indianapolis, became one of the larger prison camps controlled by the northern states. According to Colonel Hoffman, 'it is a very favourable place for a prison, but occupies a large area. It has a stream of water running through it, and many shade trees standing'. In peacetime, it had, in fact, been the state's fairground. In 1861, it was requisitioned as a camp for troops recruited in Indiana. In 1863, after a couple of substantial Federal victories, it was converted into a prison camp. What were somewhat euphemistically described as 'barracks' were gimcrack buildings, 120ft long by 20ft wide, which had originally been built to accommodate livestock and collections of agricultural implements. On the whole, the animals seem to have had the best of the deal. They were certainly not crammed into them, 700 to a hut, which was the fate of POWs when Camp Morton's population was at its peak.

To fit the establishment for its new role, a stockade, about 14ft high, was erected around it, with platforms for the guards sited at suitable points. Within the stockade, 20ft from its base, there was a low fence. It was known as the 'dead line' for the very good reason that any prisoner who crossed it was liable to be shot.

Nearly all the camps, no matter whether Federal or Confederate, had similar arrangements for containing their inmates. They also had in

The Holtzminden tunnel (seen exposed in the foreground) established a record as the longest constructed by captives in World War I (*Imperial War Museum*)

For German officers in British custody, the accommodation at Donington Hall was by no means uncomfortable (*Imperial War Museum*)

Russian officers held captive in Germany. Those who elected to return home were shot by the Bolsheviks (*Literary Executor of the late J Stuart Castle*)

common an abysmal indifference to sanitary arrangements. The sewage coursed away through open ditches. Few had proper latrines, and the effect on the health of the captives was predictable. This, certainly, was the main reason for the high mortality rate. The record, if such it can be called, probably belonged to Camp Douglas (near Chicago), where in February 1863, 387 of the 3,884 inmates died. No doubt the harsh winter contributed to this grim toll of 10 per cent, though the climate was a source of sickness and discomfort no matter which side you were on. Warriors from the warmth of the southern states found the rigours of a northern winter intolerable: northerners found the southern summer a great deal too hot for their liking.

On the whole, the Federal authorities fed and sheltered their captives better than the Confederates treated theirs. But there were exceptions. In St Louis, a medical school in Gratiot Street and another building in Myrtle Street were hastily converted into prisons. Both were horribly overcrowded. At one time, the erstwhile academy for aspiring doctors could spare little more than 35sq ft for each captive.

Nor were the medical services sufficient for this undernourished and insanitary collection of humanity. It was estimated that something like 10,000 doctors were employed by the forces of both sides. But these men were considered essential for duties in the neighbourhood of the front line, to repair wounded soldiers for further action. There were few to spare for the useless warriors who populated the prison camps, and this applied to medical supplies as well. The worst equipped in this respect was probably Libby Prison run by the Confederates. The entire contents of the hospital's so-called dispensary added up to a box of Dover powders (a blend of opium and ipecacuanha) and a few bottles of castor oil.

The ordeal began as soon as a soldier was compelled to lay down his arms. Giving evidence before the House of Representatives after the war, a clergyman named the Rev J. T. Van Burkalow described the kind of treatment a Federal captive might have expected after being taken prisoner. He said:

The general story I have gotten from them was to the effect that, when captured and before they got to Richmond, they would generally have been robbed of their clothing, their good US uniforms, even to their shoes and hats, taken away from them, and if anything was given to them in place of them, they would receive only old worn-out Confederate clothing. Sometimes they were sent [to prison] with nothing but old pants and shirts. They generally had their money taken from them, often with the promise of its return, but that promise was never fulfilled.... They remained in some places for weeks, some of them for six or eight weeks, without tents or any kind of covering.

The captives at Castle Pinckney must have counted themselves fortunate. At least they had a roof over their heads. There is even evidence to suggest that they were able to retain their sense of humour. Above one of the fort's casements, somebody erected a notice reading 'Music Hall, 444 Broadway'. It was inspired by an enlisted man in the 69th New York Irish Regiment who, in peacetime, had played at a theatre on Broadway with Christy's Minstrels. There is also evidence to suggest that the Castle Pinckney inhabitants engaged themselves in good-natured repartee with their boy guards.

Sometimes, however, life even here took on a grimmer aspect. Captain Walter W. Smith, the prizemaster of the Confederate schooner *Enchantress*, had been captured on 22 July 1861. He was tried by a court in Philadelphia and sentenced to death for piracy. In an attempt to prevent Captain Smith's execution, the Confederate authorities decided that one of Castle Pinckney's inmates must serve as hostage. He must be a senior officer but this was the only stipulation. In true democratic fashion, the captives might elect the unfortunate man themselves. They did so by drawing lots and the role fell to Colonel Michael Corcoran, commanding officer of the 69th New Yorkers. Colonel Corcoran was removed to a condemned cell in readiness for the gallows.

Happily, the Colonel's life was spared. On appeal, Captain Smith's sentence was quashed. The judge very wisely wondered why men captured at sea should be considered fodder for the hangman, whilst soldiers taken on land were either treated as prisoners of war, or else released in an exchange.

Libby, too, had senior officers among its inhabitants – at one time, there were three generals incarcerated in this former tobacco warehouse. The food was abominable, and the conduct of the commandant brutal. One captive recalled the fate of a coloured soldier, who asked how soon he might expect to be paroled. 'The captain became so infuriated,' he wrote, 'he drew a pistol and snapped it at him. It missed fire; he struck him over the head with it, and kicked him, venting his fury in the most profane language.'

The only person who had anything good to say of the prison was a Lieutenant-Colonel James M. Sanderson, who issued a statement to the effect that the rations were really not too bad. Since the general verdict (as stated by another prisoner) was that the food 'was of the coarsest kind, and not suitable for a dog to eat', Colonel Sanderson aroused the anger of his fellow captives. A meeting was held to deny his remarks and he was ostracised. Eventually, as much for his own safety as for anything else, he was removed to a camp in the south, where, not long afterwards, he was exchanged for General Robert E. Lee's nephew, who was in Federal custody.

For the enlisted men at Libby, the conditions were terrible. Like the French rafalés in the Napoleonic wars, the men slept spoon-fashion on a damp floor with no blankets. The idea was that, when the exposed sides of their bodies became unbearably cold, the sergeant in charge would call out, 'Attention, spoon!' and then: 'Right about face, spoon!' The line turned over and, presumably, dozed off until the next word of command.

Some men could not endure such conditions, and spent the nights walking about. Each room, admittedly, had a stove installed in it, but only two armfuls of pine wood were allowed every twenty-four hours. This was quickly used up and, since there were 500 men to a room, only the hardiest and most aggressive got anywhere near the stove. One inmate of Libby recalled, 'I never felt the warmth of the stove the whole time I was there.' He also said, 'It was impossible to keep clean. We were filled with vermin and filth. I did not wash my clothing in six months.'

If Libby was bad, the camp named Andersonville was several times worse. It became a symbol of all that was most terrible in the Confederates' treatment of captives. That there may have been mitigating circumstances was disregarded. Andersonville stood for hell and, when the war was over, the officer in immediate charge of it, Captain Wirz, was hanged. He was accused of personally murdering thirteen inmates, either by shooting or by clubbing them to death. But death at Andersonville was on a much larger scale. It was caused by overcrowding, lack of food and the usual disregard of sanitary arrangements.

Robert H. Kellogg was one prisoner who described his first impressions of the camp. Upon arrival, Kellogg and his fellow captives were greeted by a captain (probably Wirz), who 'swore at us and threatened us'. He estimated that the camp occupied between twelve and fifteen acres. It was, he noticed, surrounded by 'a high stockade of pine logs, with sentries in elevated boxes'. He wrote:

> As we entered the place a spectacle met our eyes that almost froze our blood with horror, and made our hearts fail within us. Before us were forms that had once been active and alert, *stalwart men*, now nothing but walking skeletons covered with filth and vermin. Many of our men, in the heat and intensity of their feeling, exclaimed with earnestness 'Can this be hell? God protect us.'

The men were divided into messes – each of ninety, with a sergeant in charge. These NCOs had to conduct a roll-call every morning and draw the rations, such as they were (one-and-a-half pints of coarse corn meal, two ounces of bacon and a little salt per man per day). Since there was no ready-made accommodation, the inhabitants had to do the best they could. Kellogg recalls buying eight small saplings, each about 9ft long, which cost him $2. They were bent into arches and both ends were embedded in the ground. This provided a frame, over which they draped their blankets.

On the first night in the camp, Kellogg recalled, there were ten deaths.

The old prisoners called it *being exchanged*, and truly it was a blessed transformation to those who went from such a miserable existence on earth to a glorious one above. The policy of the Confederate authorities respecting us seemed to be, to unfit as many as possible for future service; and, to secure the object more speedily, they cut down the rations to half the usual quantity, so the old prisoners, who had been in the notorious Libby at Richmond, declared it was even worse than at that place.

The dead were buried without coffins in trenches, 4ft deep, in a rough-and-ready cemetery, a quarter of a mile from the camp. Outside the stockade, there was a hospital but this was no more comfortable than the crude shelters fashioned by the prisoners. The tents were badly torn, there was no bedding – not even any straw – and no medical supplies.

Andersonville had been created in 1863 to ease the strain of feeding both Confederate soldiers and Federal prisoners of war in Virginia. A site was selected at Anderson, a railroad station twelve miles north of Americus in Georgia. It was chosen by Captain W. S. Winder, the Provost Marshal's son.

Originally, it had been intended to accommodate between 8,000 and 10,000 men, and the stockade was erected with this number in mind. It was built from the trunks of trees, each 20ft long and sunk 5ft into the ground. At first, it encompassed 17 acres: later, it was extended to enclose 27 acres. Part of this area, however, was occupied by a swamp.

Colonel A. W. Persons, the first commandant, went about his work half-heartedly. Using slave labour, he built one or two huts, and then his enthusiasm for the project seems to have exhausted itself. To make matters worse, lumber, nails and labour were all equally hard to obtain. When the camp was opened in March 1864, it was filled with 7,500 prisoners.

But the tide of the war was going in the Confederates' favour. By August of that year, the population of Andersonville had increased to 32,899. This provided an area of 36sq ft for each man, in which he was compelled to do everything from cooking his meals to sleeping, from attempting to keep himself clean to relieving himself.

The situation was obviously beyond the control of Persons. General Winder, who was now Provost Marshal in Richmond, assumed overall responsibility for the camp; and Captain Henry Wirz was appointed to take charge of its day-to-day affairs. Wirz, who had been born in Switzerland, had practised medicine in Louisiana before the war. In the Battle of Seven Pines, his right arm had been shattered. Since no American doctor was able to repair the damage, he made a trip to Europe in 1863. The surgeons there were no more successful. They failed to cut out the diseased bone, with the result that he was never free from pain. The agony may not have been reason to forgive his brutality but it must surely explain it.

Nor were matters improved as the Federal blockade of the south tightened its grip. When Wirz applied for tools, such as picks and shovels, he was told that there were none available. Rations became more and more difficult to obtain: supplies of vegetables ran out completely. Eventually it became impossible to serve food properly for want of adequate vessels.

So far as the positioning of the home-made bivouacs was concerned, there was a complete lack of planning. As a Dr Joseph Jones, who spent a miserable two months at Andersonville, noted, 'the tents and huts are not arranged according to any order, and there was in most parts of the enclosure scarcely room for two men to walk abreast between the tents and huts'. Scurvy (sometimes mistaken for pellagra), diarrhoea, dysentery and hospital gangrene were commonplace. Wrote Dr Jones:

From the crowded conditions, filthy habits, bad diet and dejected depressed condition of the prisoners, their systems became so disordered that the smallest abrasion of the skin from the rubbing of a shoe, or from the effects of the hot sun, or from the prick of a splinter, or from the scratching of a mosquito bite, in some cases took on rapid and frightful ulceration and gangrene.

Nevertheless, and despite the long distances that separated Andersonville from the Federal lines, some prisoners managed to escape. These were mostly men employed on duties beyond the stockade. There were one or two attempts at tunnelling, though they seldom succeeded. The idea was to seem to be digging a well. It might have fooled the Confederate guards, had it not been for the so-called 'tunnel traitors' within the camp. These men, according to an apologist, were guilty of disloyalty to their comrades for psychological reasons created by the environment. The mixture of fear, anxiety, anger, loneliness and so on was too much for them. To let off steam, so to speak, they informed on prospective escapers, usually just after the tunnel had been completed and the men were ready to leave.

In mid-June 1864, thirty men were on the point of departure through a tunnel, when they were betrayed. The 'tunnel traitor' was identified. His head was shaven bare and a T was branded on his forehead. Once this had been done, he was marched round the camp in a ritual of disgrace.

On another occasion, according to Kellogg, 'A lame man, for telling of a tunnel was pounded almost to death last night. Next morning, he claimed the protection of the guard. The guard didn't protect worth a cent, but shot him through the head. The rebel had only saved our men the trouble of killing him.'

The number of traitors is unknown but, in Kellogg's opinion, there were enough of them to make any organised break-out an impossibility.

Once an escaper was clear of the stockade, he was hunted by bloodhounds. (The northern authorities took pride in the fact that they did not employ dogs.) If he was recaptured, he was either placed in irons or in the stocks.

Methods of escaping varied. At Camp Morton, there were attempts to scale the stockade at night. This could either be done with the help of a home-made ladder or else by using one of the planks from the accommodation barracks. No more than twelve men would embark on such a venture at any one time. The records show that, on at least one occasion, the bid was successful. The guard was overpowered and 'several' (the exact figure is not given) got away. Once beyond the confines of the camp, the local inhabitants were inclined to be helpful. They were mainly small farmers who were sympathetic to the rebel cause.

But, at Camp Morton, the prisoners were in much better physical shape than those at Andersonville. The daily ration was fourteen ounces of bread (or sixteen ounces of cornmeal) and fourteen ounces of fresh beef (or ten ounces of pork or bacon) per man. Twelve pounds of sugar, five pounds of ground coffee, six quarts of beans, fifteen pounds of potatoes and one quart of molasses were issued per 100 men.

The prisoners received clothing and blankets to keep them warm. In winter, extra blankets were issued, but the more handy inmates usually made them into cloaks or capes. To pass the time, they manufactured jewellery and wood carvings (the former included rings, shirt studs, collar buttons, cuff links and masonic insignia), which they sold either to the guards, or else to the local townspeople, with the soldiers acting as middlemen.

At Andersonville, it was problem enough to survive. The main preoccupations of prisoners were the prospect of parole, rations, the weather and their health. Such energy as they had to spare was consumed by well-digging for water, and by making and mending clothes. There was nothing left for such leisurely exercises in craftsmanship.

In any case, Colonel A. A. Stevens, who commanded the Invalid Corps guards at Camp Morton, was a much more kindly individual than the irascible Captain Wirz. From the moment of his arrival in 1863, conditions improved. The only thing that Colonel Stevens seems to have been incapable of putting right was the sanitation. The camp's sewer remained an open ditch.

Elmira, a hutted camp almost midway between New York and the Niagara Falls, was opened on 6 July 1864. One of its outstanding features (or, perhaps one should say, *characters*) was a negro named John W. Jones. Mr Jones was in charge of the dead. He recorded each passing in neat handwriting: indeed, his records became a source of pride to the camp. He also treated the late, and doubtless lamented, Confederate prisoners with a gentle courtesy amounting almost to reverence. Since he had once been a slave and his supine clients were, it might have been argued, represen-tatives of the slave masters, it was considered to be a fine example of Christian conduct.

In most respects, Elmira does not seem to have been an unduly harsh camp and its security arrangements were by no means infallible. Two men escaped by scaling the fence (though one was recaptured on the bank of a nearby river). Ten men took the underground route through a tunnel and were never seen again.

The exploit of the tunnel so impressed a sergeant named Womack that he felt that he, too, must attempt to remove himself. We know much about Sergeant Womack's adventure, but there remains a mystery which has never been explained – and, presumably, never will be. Did a Federal officer de-liberately assist it, or was that unnamed officer unusually careless?

Womack was responsible for one of the huts and his duties included calling the roll at the appointed hour. Once he had done so, he was required to report to the camp's headquarters, to reassure the commandant that all was well with his men and that none of them had escaped. During these visits, he struck up an acquaintanceship with one of the officers who, now and then, loaned him a book to read.

Shortly after the tunnelling venture, Womack found, to his surprise, that a precious piece of camp stationery had been slipped between the pages of a volume. It was a printed form which, if correctly filled in and signed by the commandant, would entitle the bearer to walk out through the camp gates without let or hindrance.

The idea of completing it was an attractive one. Nor, as one of his companions suggested, need the problem of supplying the commandant's signature be impossible. There was an engraver named Miller among the prisoners. He was also, as it happened, an expert forger.

Womack considered the idea for some time. Although the temptation was great, there were two objections. One was that, if he were honest with himself, he had to admit that he was afraid. The other was that he did not trust Miller. He read the book and returned it with the printed form still between its pages.

A week or two later, the officer lent him another book. This, too, had a blank pass between its pages. A man should not make a habit of rejecting opportunities. In any case, Womack was becoming restless, and restlessness is a good antidote to fear. He had also come to the conclusion that it was not necessary to trust the counterfeiting Miller. If he applied himself diligently to the task, he might manage to produce a suitable facsimile by his own efforts.

He practised hard, tearing up piece upon piece of paper, until he had produced what he considered a very passable likeness of the required signature. Prisoners at Elmira were allowed visits from friends who resided in the northern states, and Sergeant Womack had a distant relative who lived in Baltimore. At one of these meetings, the sergeant remarked that he would be very grateful for a suit of civilian clothes. Next time the relative called, he smuggled the suit into the camp. Meanwhile, Womack had been adding to his wardrobe from another source. On the way back from one of his visits to the camp's orderly room, he had managed to steal a complete Federal uniform from the store. He was now ready to depart.

He had made out the form in the name of Reynolds, a fictitious soldier in the 110th New York Volunteers. 'Reynolds' was given permission to pay a visit to the town of Elmira – to do whatever he liked provided he was back in camp by 9 pm.

The date was now 26 October 1864. Anyone who knew Sergeant Womack well might have remarked that he had become a more rotund figure, a man who, suddenly, it seemed, had put on rather a lot of weight. It was not surprising, for he was wearing the uniform of a private in the Federal Army and, beneath that, a complete set of civilian clothes.

As his hesitation to escape may suggest, he was a cautious man. He did not believe in taking chances and, right up to the moment when he committed himself, he took none. As he walked towards the gate, a friend followed in his wake, carrying his blankets. It was a very sensible precaution: if he were caught, he would immediately be put into the camp's cooler, a cell that justified its description. If this occurred, the friend had instructions to throw him the blankets. They would at least provide a little warmth under these unpleasantly chilly circumstances.

A sentry opened the gate: a sergeant took his pass and disappeared into the guard room, presumably to clear matters with the officer on duty. Womack became nervous, but the NCO came back and told him that he might go on his way. He even strolled with him to the outer line of sentries, chatting about the pleasures of night-life in Elmira.

For a man who had taken such pains over his arrangements to escape, Womack had been uncharacteristically careless. He had been so relieved when the sergeant told him that his outing had been approved that he forgot to take back his pass. It was now in the orderly room – being studied, or so his anxious imagination told him, by an extremely suspicious officer.

He muttered something to the sergeant of the guard, and walked back to the gate. The lieutenant emerged from his office to meet him, holding the vital document in his hand. Womack gave up hope. This, he told himself, was the moment he had feared. Somebody would be told to grab him and, none too gently, he would be marched off to the cooler.

In fact, the lieutenant affably handed him the pass, chided him on his forgetfulness, and said, 'You might have got into trouble without it.'

The way was clear. In an alley-way in Elmira, he discarded the Yankee uniform and made for the station. He was now a civilian with ten dollars in his pocket and a train to catch. His immediate destination, he had decided, should be New York.

He reached the station only to find that there was not another train to New York for two hours. He dared not hang around for so long. His escape would have been noticed and the resulting hue-and-cry would give the railway station a high priority. Rather than risk recapture, he spent the night walking 18 miles along the line to a place named Waverley.

Waverley's station-master was a friendly Irishman, who told him that there would be a train for New York at eight o'clock. Womack suspected that he realised that he was an escaped POW, though he seemed to think none the less of him for that. There was, the railway employee explained, a tavern not far away. He might as well take breakfast there while he waited.

The owner of the inn was no less friendly. He offered Womack a drink. For anyone else, it might have been a little early in the day but, after spending all night plodding over the permanent way, the invitation was most agreeable. Did the publican, too, suspect that he was a prisoner of war on the run? And was he, too, tactful enough not to voice his suspicions? The people in this part of the world were really extremely kind. It was difficult to see how it was possible to wage a civil war with so much goodwill in the air.

Womack reached New York, where he spent two weeks in the guise of a tourist. After that, he made his way south and eventually reached the Confederate lines.

Impressions of captivity vary from person to person. To judge by the recollections of a Lieutenant Cunningham, life on Johnson's Island was, with certain reservations, not entirely bad. This was a lozenge of land in

Lake Erie, three miles to the north of Sandusky and half-a-mile south of Marblehead. The camp had been built at a cost of $30,000 to relieve the overcrowded prisons at New York. From June 1862, it was used exclusively for the accommodation of officers. There were thirteen two-storey frame buildings, each designed to accommodate 250 POWs.

When Cunningham was there, the captive population of Johnson's Island amounted to 2,500. They slept in wooden bunks arranged in three tiers. For want of sufficient space, they were compelled to share the bunks but, as he remarked, this was not unacceptable. During winter, it meant that there were two blankets for each berth.

The severity of the northern winters came as an unpleasant surprise to these southerners. On one occasion, Cunningham remembered, 'So intense was the cold that the sentries were taken from the walls, and the ice king kept watch and ward for Uncle Sam.' During the summer months, excursion steamers came out to give tourists a glimpse of the captives. Rather unkindly, the trippers shouted and jeered, but the small ships did not remain in the vicinity for long. A more permanent vessel was the USS *Michigan*, which remained on station between the island and the mainland to guard against escapes, presumably by strong swimmers.

Cunningham and his companions saw little of the officers in charge of the guard. An NCO, assisted by a private, conducted roll-call every morning and made sure that each prisoner was back in his quarters by sundown. Anyone whose absence was discovered was liable to be shot (one officer, who overspent his time visiting friends in another building, was killed on his way back). They also enforced the rules that all lights must be extinguished when 'Taps' was sounded. On several occasions, trigger-happy guards vented their impatience by discharging their rifles into the rooms of offenders.

But the biggest burden of these prisoners was, in Cunningham's words, 'the terrible ennui of prison life'. It was, he wrote, 'an infallible sign of surrender when the men became listless and no longer cared for the things that had hitherto been either their work or their recreation'. He recalled the case of one officer who 'murmured, "I shall never see home again"; and, steadily sinking, turned his face to the wall and died.'

To pass the time, they engaged themselves in manufacturing trinkets, somewhat in the manner of the captives at Camp Morton. They attended lectures, and enjoyed afternoon concerts by a group of theatrically talented inmates, who had formed a minstrel band and called themselves the 'Rebellonians'. The performers sang popular songs, with the words doctored to give them a more topical and local impact.

Letters from the outside world were permitted and so were newspapers and magazines, provided that they bore the stamp 'Examined,' which meant to say that they had been censored. For other news, they depended on 'the grapevine', though Lieutenant Cunningham was sceptical about its value. 'The main feature of this prison telegraph,' he said, 'was its complete unreliability. As I remember it was never correct – even by accident; but it sang songs of exchange and release and, whilst feeling the notes to be false, we yet liked the music and hoped it was true.'

The picture of Johnson's Island painted by Lieutenant Cunningham is of a tolerably well-ordered community, with most of the captives doing their stoic best to come to terms with unpleasant circumstances. A report by the Acting Medical Director of the commissary, Charles T. Alexander, however, gives a somewhat different impression. 'Seeing the camp,' he wrote, 'you would not know whether to be most astounded at the inefficiency of the officer in charge of the prison camp, or disgusted that men calling themselves gentlemen should be willing to live in such filth.'

As remarked earlier, the commandant (a graduate of Yale), combined these duties with those of mayor of Sandusky. Perhaps, it might have been better if he had spent more of his time on the island. Or was the Acting Medical Director giving vent to his dislike of Confederate officers?

6

THE WRONG SIDE OF THE LINE

So far as improving the human predicament is concerned, nations are apt to crawl through history, sniffing suspiciously at anything that might be labelled progress. Before the question 'Will it do any good?' is answered, another must be posed: 'Will it do me/us (meaning the ruler or government concerned) any harm?'

Individuals are more dynamic. Henry Dunant, who was born in 1828, was the son of a Geneva business man. In 1858, he moved to the French colony in Algeria, where he founded a company named the *Société Anonyme des Moulins de Mons-Djémila*. True to its name, it possessed a mill. It did not, however, own any land upon which to grow wheat. When Dunant applied to the authorities for a few acres of Algerian soil, they ignored his request. A lesser man might have been defeated by this display of official indifference. Dunant, on the other hand, saw it as a challenge. If these jacks-in-office were not prepared to help him, the French Emperor might be more accommodating.

He travelled to Paris, only to discover that Napoleon III was many miles away, campaigning with his soldiers on the Plain of Lombardy in an attempt to free Italy from Austrian domination. Dunant packed his bags again, and set off for a corner of the earth that, as he soon discovered, had been ravaged by the war. He did not find the Emperor: instead, he happened upon the Battle of Solferino on 24 June 1859.

The Austrians were thoroughly thrashed, which was no doubt a matter of satisfaction to Napoleon III. For Dunant, it was an awesome and profoundly disturbing experience. The medical arrangements, he quickly noticed, were more or less non-existent. There were only six French army surgeons to cope with the 9,000 wounded who had been brought into the nearby town of Castiglione. But these men were, perhaps, fortunate. Many more were left lying on the battlefield without care or shelter – a prey for the looters, who crept out from beneath their stones to rob them.

As one Frenchman said to Dunant, 'Ah, Sir! We fought well, and now we have been left to die.'

Henry Dunant did what he could to help. He abandoned his mill in Algeria and, in 1862, he wrote down his impressions in a short book entitled *Un Souvenir de Solferino*. The work was both vivid and angry. How could humanity reconcile its conscience to such things? 'Would it not be possible,' he asked, 'in time of peace and quiet, to form relief societies for the purpose of having care given to the wounded in wartime by zealous, de-devoted and thoroughly qualified volunteers?'

Un Souvenir de Solferino achieved all that its author could have hoped. In England, Charles Dickens drew attention to it in his weekly journal, *All the Year Round*. In France, one of the Goncourt brothers remarked, 'One puts down this book, cursing war'. Among other appalled readers was a jurist, two years older than Dunant, named Gustave Moynier. In Moynier's view, to protest was not enough. Something must be done to alleviate the sufferings of war wounded. In February of the following year, five men – among them Dunant, Moynier and two doctors – met in Geneva to discuss the problem.

One of their earlier preoccupations was to devise an emblem that could be worn by doctors and nurses, and displayed on hospitals and ambulances, as a symbol of those who, whilst they might be part of an army, were non-combatant. Ideally, it would confer a kind of neutrality upon them, making them immune from attack.

They chose a red cross on a white ground.

In 1864, Dunant and his colleagues achieved what the world's statesmen ought to have done many years earlier. They arranged the first Geneva Convention, at which delegates of the leaading powers gathered to discuss 'the amelioration of the condition of the wounded in armies in the field'. The Red Cross emblem was accepted. The conference, as a member wrote, 'was important and unique since it aimed at regularizing in a permanent manner a situation which until then had only been haphazard'.

Prisoners of war did not become the subject of a Geneva Convention (and there were several) until 1929. Nevertheless, Dunant's evangelism for a more humane attitude towards the victims of hostilities inevitably affected them. When, in 1870, the International Committee of the Red Cross established an office in Basle, one of its departments was known as the 'wounded and missing section'. During the Franco-Prussian War, a bureau was set up in Berlin. Staffed by eleven people, it answered 60,000 inquiries about personnel missing from the French army, and handled 186,000 letters to and from French prisoners of war. But the lists its members so diligently compiled were confined to the sick, the wounded and the dead. Those who had come through the ordeal of capture undamaged were not (officially, at any rate) a matter for concern.

The nations were edging towards a state of affairs in which a captive's plight could at least be made tolerable. It might have been considered progress when a prisoner's alternative to an unpleasant death was no longer the prospect of being sold into slavery. But, as all previous wars had made very clear, it was no occasion for pride. In 1899, another Geneva convention urged the wider use of bureaux such as that which had functioned so effectively in 1870. Unfortunately, the Dutch republics of South Africa were not represented among the delegates. Consequently, in the Boer War, the British saw no reason to abide by its resolutions. The Russians and the Japanese, on the other hand, had been among the signatories. During the Russo-Japanese War of 1904, an office was established in Tokyo with a major-general in charge. It dealt with 70,000 prisoners, sending the information to the Russian Government via the French Embassy. It also handled correspondence to and from the captives, and took scrupulous care to return the personal effects of men found dead on the battlefield. Among them were several wills, 418 articles of clothing, 77 notebooks, 1,257,300 Japanese yen and 2,249,890 Russian roubles.

Yet another convention, held in 1906 at the invitation of the Swiss Government, carried the business of tidying things up a stage further and, in the following year, a conference was held in The Hague. What with the Red Cross as an international instrument of mercy, and the nations taking a more reasonable attitude, conditions were as good as anyone could have hoped when World War I broke out in August 1914.

If such hope were tempered by cynicism, it was hardly surprising; nor can 'good' mean very much more than 'better than bad'. One of the first letters received by the Prisoner of War Information Bureau in London during August 1914 was from a German woman who had heard that her husband had been taken prisoner. It was, perhaps, significant that she asked, 'Should I consider myself a widow?'

The early days of any war produce a certain amount of confusion about the fate of prisoners. World War I possibly incurred less than most. Nevertheless, the Germans were embarrassed by the number of captives taken during the autumn of 1914. As one Prussian officer remarked, 'We were surprised that the Allies had so many troops to surrender, and that they surrendered so readily.' He admitted that the German general staff had, in fact, been so confident of a quick march to Paris that few arrangements had been made for their reception.

No doubt this officer was exaggerating. In the event, far more British troops were captured during the final German offensive in March 1918, than in all the previous months and years put together. Until the Battle of Cambrai in November 1917, there were 40,000 British officers and other ranks in German hands. Cambrai added 9,000 to the score; and then, during that dreadful March, when the Allies came very close to defeat, another 100,000 were taken. When, on 11 November, the Armistice was signed, there were 6,577 British officers and 161,026 other ranks in German prison camps, plus more than 10,000 soldiers from the colonies, nearly 1,100 officers and ratings of the Royal Navy and 3,073 from the Royal Naval Division.

In *Prisoners of War* (1924), Herbert C. Fooks writes, 'In war, as elsewhere, there are often circumstances under which it is difficult to determine one's duty exactly.... It has been said that many of the troops of the World War [I] were instructed that it was better to die fighting than to be captured. This is, however, an idealistic view of a soldier's standard of bravery.' For Lieutenant Herduin, who commanded a company of French infantry before Verdun in 1916, surrender might have saved his life. After five days' fighting, with neither food nor water, he had only nineteen men left. Rather than allow them to fall into the enemy's hands, he pulled back to his regimental headquarters.

To most people, this might have seemed a prudent act. The brigade commander, however, took a different view. He ordered Herduin to be shot for deserting his post. The unfortunate lieutenant was detailed to command his own firing squad; and, ten minutes after his execution, an order arrived quashing the sentence.

But this was exceptional. For those who were taken prisoner, there were at least establishments to record the very fact that they were still alive. Under Article 14 of the Hague Convention signed in 1907, each of the belligerent states was compelled to set up a bureau as soon as hostilities erupted. Its staff had three responsibilities:

1 To reply to all inquiries concerning prisoners, even down to supplying the names of any who had been fortunate enough to escape.
2 To render a return of all prisoners' names – their numbers, ranks, units, whether or not they were wounded, the places at which they had been captured and the camps in which they were interned.
3 To gather up and keep together personal effects found on the field of battle, and those of men who had died in captivity.

It was a considerable task. Indeed, what with supplying extra food and keeping the records straight, the clerical work entailed by prisoners of war was almost as impressive as the more dramatic side of captivity.

Britain responded commendably quickly to the requirements. Before the outbreak of war, there had been no such organisation. Nevertheless, within a week, 49 Wellington Street, which is off the Strand in London, had been taken over by the War Office, and the Prisoners of War Information Bureau was in business. It was staffed by fifty civil servants, most of them women, who had been selected for their knowledge of German. Soon they were answering 400 inquiries a day from Germany, and others from neutral countries.

Inevitably, the information provided by the bureau was somewhat basic, and gave little idea of how captive Germans were faring in their enemy's hands. Similarly, the British Government was anxious for reports on its own soldiers. Atrocity stories, most of them false, had been published in a propaganda campaign so effective that, years later, the Nazi mouthpiece, Dr Goebbels, used it as an inspiration for his own efforts. In a world dominated by lies, how does one discover the truth? There had been rumours of the maltreatment of Allied prisoners in transit to permanent camps. Officers who had managed to escape brought back stories of a serious lack of clothing, and there were grim accounts of some camps where acute food shortages prevailed.

Nor did the German Emperor reassure anyone when he addressed German soldiers on the way from Bremerhaven to German colonies in China. 'As soon as you come to blows with the enemy,' he said, 'he will be beaten. No mercy will be shown. *No prisoners will be taken!*' [Author's italics]

The British Government protested to the German Government, filing its letter at the American Embassy in London and hoping that it would be transmitted via the American Embassy in Berlin. Clearly, there was a need for some sort of inspection by a neutral power. Not only would it pierce the fog created by propaganda, it would also enable retaliatory measures to be taken when instances of brutality were observed.

Several months of negotiation went by until, in early 1915, the German Government agreed to a system of inspection by members of the American Embassy (The Swiss Government assumed the responsibility when the US entered the war in 1917). It had, of course, to be a two-way affair. If American diplomats in Berlin were to have the run of German prison camps, it followed that their colleagues in London must be permitted to visit captive Germans in Britain. The reports that followed suggested that conditions in German POW camps holding soldiers taken on the Western Front were, on the whole, tolerable. On the Eastern Front, matters were very much less than good. The administrative machine had, it seemed, broken down under the sheer volume of surrendering Slavs.

German infantrymen taken on the Western Front (*Imperial War Museum*)

The theatre was a popular feature of most POW camps in Germany. This scene is from an Oflag VA production of *Gas Light* directed by the author of this book (*Richard Garrett*)

In World War II (as in World War I) the arrival of Red Cross parcels to POWs in Germany made all the difference between a reasonable diet and starvation (*From the collection of Don Bruce*)

In Britain, the fate of German prisoners gave no cause for concern. Soldiers who, in peacetime, had belonged to the labouring classes, were, it appeared, being better fed than their meagre wages had previously permitted. At the end of 1914, the American Ambassador in London was able to report that there had been only five deaths among the UK prison-camp population. Three had been heart cases, one man had died of dropsy, and one of typhoid – a disease that, or so the doctors said, he must have contracted before being captured.

The men were adequately provided with food and clothing: money could be sent to them from Germany. In the latter case, the camp commandant took possession of it and acted as a banker. The captives were allowed to send two letters a week (more, in an emergency). Specially ruled paper was provided for this purpose, and there could be no writing between the lines. The correspondence could be in either English or German – though, prisoners were warned, it was in their interest to use English. Those in German took longer to censor, and this was liable to produce delays.

By all accounts, the system worked. When, in late 1914, the German cruiser *Emden* was sunk by ships of the Royal Navy, the German Red Cross Society raised a fund for the comfort of survivors in captivity. The money was sent to England via the Dutch post office and eventually paid out by the GPO.

In Germany, the blockade was already starting to bite and, inevitably, the sufferers were POWs. While still negotiating the matter of inspection, the German authorities agreed that parcels of food and other necessities might be sent to prisoners in their camps. This, as soon became apparent, was not an entirely disinterested gesture. Under the guise of charity, contraband materials (in one case, rubber) were being smuggled out of Britain. Other packages were found to contain messages intended for German military intelligence. They were, presumably, the work of agents, who discovered that addressing a parcel to a fictitious prisoner of war was a convenient method of sending dispatches.

By the spring of 1915, several sources of comfort for captive Britons had been established. Most regimental depots had been reinforced by teams of ladies and gentlemen, packing parcels of food and clothing. The so-called Prisoners of War Help Committee had been formed to extend the work of these volunteers, and to provide a link between them. At one point, it submitted a plan to the War Office by which it would concentrate all POW parcels in one place. The War Office turned it down. In addition to these activities, many families and firms that had employed captured personnel in civil life were anxious to send packages to Germany – or, at least, to pay for them to be sent.

In most cases, the intentions were worthy, though the results were by no means satisfactory. A large proportion of prisoners were still receiving insufficient food, whilst others were receiving too much. According to one estimate, there was enough surplus food adrift in the Fatherland to feed one German division. In some instances, the confusion was made greater by the address on the first postcard received by next-of-kin. This was merely intended to indicate that the man in question was a prisoner: it was not to be assumed that he would be detained at the place printed on the card. For example, many relatives received cards posted from the camp at Limburg. In a great many instances, the POWs to whom they referred had never been to Limburg at all. The second card gave a more accurate idea of a captive's place of internment but was unreliable. Prisoners were moved from camp to camp and it was difficult to keep track of them.

The public was becoming anxious that its captive sons and husbands were half-starved. The War Office mistrusted a system that seemed to be haphazard. After many debates and investigations, the Army Council decided to replace all voluntary organisations by a single unit to be run by the Red Cross. Operating from two houses in Thurloe Place, South Kensington, it would have more power than the Prisoners of War Help Committee. All told, it was to have nine responsibilities:

1 To authorise the work of the various committees and associations concerned with the welfare of POWs, and to approve shops (such as the Army and Navy Stores, Selfridges and Harrods) for the packing and dispatch of parcels.

2 To control the work of 1.

3 To give financial assistance to regimental care committees and, later on, to local associations.

4 To provide a care committee to look after personnel from regiments that had not formed such organisations. This responsibility also applied to civilian internees and (after October 1917) to officer prisoners.

5 To pack and distribute food and bread for dispatch to those prisoners who, otherwise, might have gone without.

6 To administer, in whatever way required by the Military Intelligence branch of the War Office, a form of censorship concerning parcels sent to POWs.

7 To organise the transport of supplies that could not be entrusted to the parcel post.

8 To provide food, packing materials, clothing, etc.

9 To deal with inquiries on all matters concerning POWs in enemy countries.

Eventually, 750 people were employed at Thurloe Place. Between them, they packed a quarter of a million parcels – working on the basis that a prisoner should receive a 10lb parcel and 13lb of bread each fortnight. A special label was designed for use on their packages; and post office officials were instructed not to accept any that did not display it.

Despite more grumblings from the public, more dissent from the military authorities, and more arguments (resulting in the formation of a Joint Parliamentary Committee in 1917 to take another look at the problem), these precious cartons of relief got through to the camps, and the prisoners' hunger abated.

When, in September 1918, workers at a firm of box-makers named Stevenson went on strike, the operation continued without interruption. Impervious to accusations of scab and blackleg (which, admittedly, were less freely bandied about in those days), a team of twenty Red Cross workers marched into the factory and took over the idle plant.

The good deeds of the Red Cross on behalf of POWs in World War I were far too many to be described in detail. Its members published a monthly journal entitled *The British Prisoner of War*, which was distributed to the relatives of men in German hands. Offices were set up at points along the coast of northern France to assist in the tracing of missing personnel. There were depots for the dispatch of bread and parcels at Copenhagen and at Berne.

Initially, Lady Evelyn Grant Duff, the wife of the British Minister, was in charge of the bread supplies. Lady Grant Duff was a remarkable woman. She applied herself to the task with an almost evangelical fervour. Much of the flour was imported from Marseilles. Vans departed from the Swiss capital en route to Frankfurt and thence to the various camps. It took five or, at the most, six days for a loaf to reach anywhere in Germany. Prisoners were given an opportunity to complain if the quality was below a certain standard. In fact, there were few grumbles and a great deal of applause.

Parcels from Berne were also sent to prisoners in Austria, Bulgaria and Turkey. But the ultimate compliment to the Red Cross was made on Christmas Day, 1917. Officers and orderlies interned in a camp at Holtzminden, grateful no doubt for favours received, decided to hold a subscription on its behalf. The considerable sum of £2,289 was collected.

Officers, warrant officers and NCOs down to the rank of Corporal, were not required to work. Private soldiers could be employed, though the rules of this particular game insisted that they should not be assigned to military projects. This rule was broken on at least two occasions and probably on many more. Roumanian prisoners were drafted to Alsace and made to dig trenches. The men were so badly fed that, on one occasion, a party of them broke into a nearby camp, holding French POWs, to beg for bread. While there, they also made a tour of the garbage cans used to store food for the camp's pigs. When, later on in the war, the services of Russian prisoners were required in Alsace, many refused to go. They were kicked and beaten: some were pushed over on to the ground, and boiling water was poured over them. Ten men were killed and fifty severely injured.

But many Russian prisoners never travelled far from the Eastern Front. According to a German soldier who returned to Berlin after being wounded in October 1914,

> Above the terrible thunder of the cannon could be heard the heart-rending cries of the Russians; 'O Prussians! O Prussians!' But there was no mercy. Our captain had ordered: 'The whole lot must die; so rapid fire.' As I have heard, five men and one officer on our side went mad from these heart-rending cries. But most of my comrades and the officers joked as the unarmed and helpless Russians shrieked for mercy while they were being suffocated in the swamps and shot down.'

The soldier was writing to a representative from the American Embassy, but the letter was unsigned. 'I would give my name and regiment,' he wrote in a PS, 'but these words could get me court-martialled for divulging military secrets.'

French prisoners were set to work trench-digging on the Eastern Front, under scarcely better conditions. So far as the British were concerned, it very much depended upon where a man was sent. Those who worked in the coal mines, or the salt mines, had a particularly bad time of it. But a job in industry above ground was no guarantee of good treatment. According to Dr Daniel J. McCarthy, who was employed at the American Embassy in Berlin, there were 150 parent camps in Germany and 'thousands of working camps'. 'The chances of getting a brute for a commandant or overseer,' he wrote, 'were not few.'

Although guarded by German soldiers – many of them too old for active service – the fate of a working prisoner usually depended upon the civilian management of the industry concerned. The coal and steel barons of Westphalia went to considerable lengths to hinder inspection by the Americans and, in some instances, the military authorities supported them. In one town (Wittenburg), all the users of POW labour banded together and appointed one man to supervise the lot. The individual seems to have been an above-average brute. He ordered the guards to punish the prisoners by the use of whips; he refused all requests from the American Embassy to inspect the conditions; and he frustrated all attempts at communication by the prisoners. 'The guards,' Dr McCarthy observed, 'were put in an uncomfortable situation.'

The men responsible for the working parties were mostly members of the Landsturm, the equivalent of the Home Guard in Britain during World War II. They were usually kind and considerate, and anxious to make their prisoners comfortable. Nevertheless, they were inclined to be rigid in their outlook and to go by the book. At the parent camps, the guards tended to be younger.

Some British prisoners had a rough understanding of the Hague Convention of 1907, and they realised that they need not work on military projects. It was, admittedly, sometimes difficult to discriminate between military work and non-military. How, for example, was one to regard employment on the telephone system? It might be used for military purposes or for the harmless communication of civilians. In many cases, the protests of the POWs who refused to work on what they regarded as unsuitable projects were respected and they were drafted to other tasks. But the authorities were not always so reasonable. When five men were ordered to assist in the building of Zeppelin sheds, they downed tools. This, they said was a military operation and did not comply with the terms of the Hague Convention. They demanded the right of appeal to the kommandant of their parent camp at Celle.

They were returned to Celle but the kommandant was less than sympathetic to their views. He ordered them to be tried by court martial for refusing to work. The five were each sentenced to twelve months in prison. They appealed: a re-trial was ordered, but it confirmed the findings of the first.

Without a sight of the proceedings, it is impossible to judge whether or not these men were treated fairly. Prisoners of all nationalities were subject to the civil and military laws of the host country. In Britain, for example, a German NCO named Johannes Schmidt was interned aboard a ship in Portsmouth Harbour. During a quarrel, he assaulted one of his fellow captives. He was tried and sentenced to six months' hard labour in HM Prison at Bedford. There can be no doubting the justice of this penalty – though the use of HM Prison at Chelmsford for persistent escapers may be questionable.

No doubt the kommandant at Celle would have argued that the verdict was lenient. When more than one man refused to undertake a particular job, a charge of conspiracy was sometimes added. This could result in a sentence of anything between five and twenty years in a civilian or a military prison. Sometimes, the prosecutor even demanded capital punishment, though there is no evidence that this was ever carried out.

But much depended on the kommandant's attitude. In many cases, refusal to work was punishment by confinement to barracks or by being deprived of certain liberties. Every camp had a punishment block, which was isolated from the rest of the huts. In some of these places, blankets were not allowed: a man had to sleep on the floor in his clothes. Parcels from home were also forbidden, though the inmates were taken out of doors for one hour's exercise each day.

A more extreme form of punishment was confinement to a camp gaol – a building made up of minute cells (4ft by 7ft), in which prisoners served terms of solitary confinement. The diet routine was three days on bread and water, with camp rations on the fourth, and back to bread and water for another three. The penalty for a first offence was one or two weeks, with longer periods for subsequent misdeeds.

Most British prisoners in Germany would have been reasonably content to work on the land – though, even in this instance, there was sometimes confusion. When soldiers interned in one camp sent a message back to London via the American legation, asking whether they might volunteer to work on farms, it was referred to the Foreign Secretary, Sir Edward Grey. Sir Edward replied that, 'His Majesty's Government did not wish them to work in the manner referred to.' Not unreasonably, the men concluded that this was a refusal. In fact, the offending word was *volunteer*. They might be *made* to work on farms, but they were not to offer their services.

In many cases, the lot of a private soldier in German hands was far from bad. Mr H. Jeffrey of Edenbridge in Kent was a tanner by trade in peacetime. He was drafted to a tannery from his parent camp at Parchin in Mecklenburg. The kommandant of Parchin had 35,000 prisoners directly or indirectly under his control. He had been recalled to military service after running his own business. He was certainly one of the more humane officers who served in this capacity: on his own evidence, he was determined that his wartime duties should leave him with 'a clean conscience'. As in most other camps, the junior officers and the other ranks took their cue from the top. Consequently, life here was made as easy for the POWs as circumstances allowed.

Mr Jeffrey recalls that they were required to begin work at six o'clock in the morning. Two hours later, they were allowed half-an-hour for breakfast. At one o'clock, they were released for a lunch-break lasting one-and-a-half hours – after which, they returned to their labours until eight o'clock in the evening.

Mr Jeffrey said:

The guard used to take us to the tannery every morning and bring us back at night. It wasn't too bad, because the chaps had received their Red Cross parcels and they had a good lot of food. At night, we used to sleep on wooden bunks.

We were just working, and we were as happy as sandboys. It was something to do. They used to give us soup at lunchtime. Well, the old girl who made it had done her best, I suppose. It was really all potatoes and a bit of horse flesh in it. There were sixteen of us prisoners – including two Poles. One of the Poles I remember, escaped.

Two guards used to take it in turns to watch over us. The head guard came to see us occasionally, but he wasn't there all the time. He'd got a pub down in the village. He'd never been to France fighting at all, though he was a big chap and perfectly fit. The other guards didn't like him much.

On Sundays, they used to take us for a walk, and we played football. The director's son at the tanyard got the ball for us. He liked football, and we used to have a kick-about at lunchtime. After the football games on Sundays, the guards used to take us to the pub and we'd all have a drink. That happened every Sunday.

Work, provided the conditions were reasonable, was a very acceptable alternative to being confined within a camp. A report by a member of an American inspection team referred to 'the serious problem of mental depression and one of its most important underlying causes, ie the uncertainty of the time of imprisonment'. This, the writer observed, 'was very markedly relieved by congenial occupation'.

Mr L. G. B. Eastwood, who was a corporal in the Border Regiment, would no doubt argue that it could also be relieved by a congenial camp. On his arrival in Germany, Mr Eastwood was sent to Worms. He said:

When we arrived there, we had to be disinfested. They had great tubs filled with disinfectant, and you had to climb right inside them – you'd see a chap with his head sticking out. Then they'd shave all the hair off your body – the Russians did that under instructions from the Germans. It was a very rough sort of camp, and the Germans used to knock the Russians about if they didn't do what they wanted

Each wooden hut had two layers of bunks. The rations were very poor. We had barley soup with noodles and awful *ersatz* coffee – which some of the fellows said was made from acorns. We had no parcels here and it was quite a business dishing out the bread. We used to get these big loaves, and we were detailed into parties with a couple of NCOs in charge of each. Then we used to carve the loaf up very accurately. We used to weigh each portion on a pair of home-made scales. You had to eat your bit quickly, otherwise somebody'd pinch it.

Later, Mr Eastwood was moved to a camp at Giessen. Conditions here were very much better. He said:

You can't expect hotel accommodation in a POW camp, can you? I think it wasn't too bad at all really. We had Red Cross parcels, and the camp was well organised. Mind you, there was never a time when we couldn't eat a good meal, and the two main topics of conversation were food and women. But there was a library here, and one of the huts had been fitted up as a chapel. We had a padre who was a prisoner, and he used to hold services.

There was also a nice brass band; and in the evenings they used to dance out there on the parade ground. You couldn't have done that at Worms. At Worms, they gave us wooden shoes – very roughly made – and they were hell to walk in. At Giessen we were given proper boots and clothing. I remember we had dark blue trousers with a yellow stripe about two inches wide, down the legs. We had KG (for *Kriegsgefangner* – Prisoner of War) in red letters on the back of the tunic, and your POW number was stuck on to your chest. At every camp, you got a different number.

I suppose the distinctive uniform was to make it harder to escape, though nobody tried to get away to my knowledge. I think most of the escapes occurred in officers' camps. Officers were able to get stuff from England that an ordinary ranker couldn't very well get. We thought, 'We're well out of it. We're out of it for good.'

Mr Eastwood's only excursions into the outside world were trips to the station to collect Red Cross parcels. Officer prisoners, on the other hand, were allowed out of camp for walks in the surrounding countryside. For these expeditions, they gave their parole. At one camp, the officers objected to their escort carrying a gun on his belt. Since they had pledged themselves not to escape, it seemed to be an insult. After a good deal of argument, they refused all further walks until the offending weapon had been removed. Very reasonably, the German officer eventually capitulated.

Indeed, these gentlemen were fortunate to be able to exercise themselves beyond the wire at reasonable times. In at least one POW camp in Britain, the captives had to take their walks either very early in the morning or else very late at night. Local opinion was so incensed by their presence in the neighbourhood that the guards feared for their safety.

The first camp to which a POW was sent was the worst – on this Messrs Jeffrey and Eastwood were in complete agreement. In the former's case, this was at Kassel. He said:

We used to get up in the morning at about six, and they'd give us a drop of coffee and a little bit of black bread. We had a roll-call, and all we did then was to mooch about until midday, when we had some soup and some sauerkraut. That was the worst time – that first camp. You couldn't do anything – just mooch about. It was awful.

As for escaping:

> Where we were, there was no future in it. One Pole did get home, but Poland was nearer and he could speak fluent German. The last thing I had expected was to be taken prisoner. But I wasn't sorry afterwards – to get away from France. That was terrible. It was a bit of a shock to start with, wondering what was going to happen to us. But afterwards, I said to myself, 'I'm glad I'm out of it.' It was a relief.

Both Mr Jeffrey and Mr Eastwood were taken prisoner during the German push of 1918. Mr Jeffrey was serving as a rifleman with the King's Royal Rifle Corps. He remembers the occasion well:

> We were in the front line, and it was foggy. We had a stand-to at four o'clock that morning, and we couldn't even see the barbed wire in front of the trenches. There were a lot of artillery shells going over, and we stayed in our positions until about eight o'clock, when we went down to the dug-out. We just had time for something to eat, and then we went back again. We left our greatcoats in the dug-out.
>
> We never saw a soul until midday. It was a thinly populated part of the line, and one chap in the next bay to us suddenly said, 'Jerry's at the back of us'. They'd broken through each flank; they'd gone right back and got the artillery. Then they wiped us out afterwards. There were thousands of us taken prisoner.
>
> As we got out of the trench, one of the Germans started talking English. He said he'd been a waiter in England. They rounded us up, and we had to help carry their wounded back. Then we marched for miles and miles until it was nearly dark. We spent the night in some old barn; next morning, we reached a railway station. We were put in some cattle trucks, and that's how we reached our first camp.

In a few instances, there are accounts of wounded prisoners suffering from neglect and ill-treatment. When, for example, a captain named Henderson was hit in the thigh, and the sciatic nerve was exposed, he was left for seven days without attention. Eventually, he was put into a cattle truck, where his injury was examined by a woman doctor employed by the German Red Cross. She refused to put on a dressing on the grounds that it smelt too badly. At Wittenburg, when a typhus epidemic broke out among the Russian prisoners, the authorities withdrew all medical attention – for fear, presumably, of catching the disease.

Mr Eastwood was more fortunate. He was out in the open when, at five o'clock in the afternoon, a bullet passed through his shoulder and punctured his right lung. He remembers:

A German patrol came down the road and picked up myself and a stretcher-bearer who'd been dressing my wound. We were on our own – the battalion had retreated and left us behind. A German officer came up and pointed to us to go down the road. As we were going along, a German doctor came up and looked at me. He made them put me on a stretcher, so I really have him to thank for the fact that I am still alive.

I don't remember much about the next week. I was taken to a dressing station and put on some sort of shelf. It looked to me as if it was in a church, and the first thing I remember was somebody pinching my boots. Of course, boots were at a premium in Germany.

I don't remember anything much after that. I think once we were in a marquee, but I don't really recall anything until we were put into a hospital train. That was a week later – a blank week in my life!

Thus, after a spell in hospital, Mr Eastwood came to Worms. His only possessions at this moment in his life were one blanket and a tunic. But he was grateful. 'I really must say this for the Germans,' he reports, 'I think the German doctors were a great help to me. They literally kept me alive.'

American prisoners confined in a hospital at Dulmen probably took a different view. Those who were fit enough were assigned to work in a corner of the ward under the supervison of a coffin-maker. As the other patients died, so did their output increase. The toil was made even more macabre by the fact that their overseer was perpetually singing a melancholy song. As one of the captives wrote, 'Mere shadows of human beings listened to the coffin song, and its music was understood by all. One captive kept his ears stuffed with cotton, but when he despaired of living he would pull out the cotton and listen to the bracing notes of the Westphalian woodsman.'

Norman Insoll's entrance into captivity was more spectacular; but Mr Insoll was an officer, and what is more, a member of the Royal Flying Corps. If you had to be taken prisoner, the best way to arrive was from the sky.

It was Boxing Day, 1916. Very early that morning, he was ordered to take part in a bombing raid on a German headquarters in northern France. Two squadrons of bombers, totalling twenty-four aircraft, were to be used – covered by twenty-four fighters flying 2,000ft above them. Mr Insoll – like, one must assume, the other pilots – had no observer. With a 104lb bomb on board, the aeroplane was unable to carry the weight of two men. This was a considerable disadvantage, for there was no one to protect the aircraft's tail. As he put it, 'I had only one fixed Lewis gun in front. If you wanted to aim it, you had to turn the whole aeroplane.'

The formation reached the target and dropped its bombs. Soon after-wards, two German fighters approached him from the rear. One of them presently sheered off: the other pilot was more persistent. Mr Insoll said:

He kept on diving at me and I knew that the worst thing in the world was to go into a dive myself. I side-slipped the whole time; first one way, then the other – getting closer to earth the whole time. He shot my petrol tanks rather badly away. Luckily, the aircraft didn't go up in flames and I landed on the target. It was really a rather silly place to land.

There were bomb craters several hundred yards away, but the head-quarters itself had not been hit. He said:

Naturally, with those bombs, it was rather like stirring up a hornets' nest, and a lot of troops gathered around. I should think there were a couple of hundred or more. They came all round the aeroplane, but I'd climbed out by then. One chap, who spoke a bit of English, got into the cockpit and pointed a Very light pistol at me – which I knew was empty, because I'd used it, so that didn't worry me.

After a time, a very young German officer of about my own age came along, and the whole crowd disappeared. He took me to the adjutant's office, where I remained all day. Various people came to see me – including one gentleman, who I think was a general, and who spoke perfect English. He told me that his brother was headmaster of one of our public schools.

He was very pleasant, and chatted. They were very good to me there. They gave me sardines on toast and some cognac. I suppose they were deciding where I should go. Eventually, of all things, a cab arrived – a one-horse cab. We had one man on the box, a sergeant sat next to me, and we set off for Cambrai. It was quite a long way, and we seemed to travel for most of the night. The Germans were very cold; I was much better off, because I was in flying kit, which was beautifully warm. In any case, they pulled up at several estaminets and had a little refresher, and they kindly brought out a drink for me on one occasion. It was a brandy, or something.

We arrived eventually with a very exhausted horse. There was nobody about; it was about one in the morning, and they couldn't find the Citadel where I was to be deposited. After a while, some pedestrian directed them to the civil prison. They took me there, but the man in charge didn't want me – he said I didn't belong there. But they refused to go any farther, and the horse had got its head between its knees by this time. Eventually, the man agreed to take me in, and we sat down in front of one of those continental stoves. He gave me coffee; we tried to talk to each other. Neither of us spoke the other's language but we seemed to manage. Eventually, he pulled out a big bunch of keys, and off we went upstairs to a room on the first floor. In it, there were six Frenchmen in night caps and night gowns, all chattering away. They were all in there for theft and so on – it was a civilian prison. I was told I could sleep somewhere on the floor.

Two days later, Mr Insoll was escorted to the Citadel. A room had been set aside for prisoners, and there were three other fliers in it. He recalls:

The four of us were there for about three weeks. We were taken into an office every day and interrogated by various officers from the German War Ministry. It was rather stupid, really. I mean, they wanted to know where the British Fleet was. How was I, a boy of eighteen in the Flying Corps, to know! And then they wanted to know the number of my squadron. Of course, we weren't allowed to say, and I told them I couldn't reply.

Next day, they got a major in – a very fierce looking man, and they said, 'You must tell the major what your squadron number is.' I just laughed – and *they* laughed, and offered me a cigarette.

After these interrogation sessions, the prisoners returned to their room. On one of its panelled walls, there was a large map of the area. 'After the first day or two,' Mr Insoll said, 'we found a dictaphone behind the panelling. Looking at the map, people would say, "I was here or there" – you were rather interested to show the others where you'd been. Of course, the Germans were listening to every word. But we cut the wires, and lifted it out, and after that, they didn't hear anything more.'

Food was scarce: sauerkraut and black bread was the staple diet. But, on New Year's Eve they were presented with a bottle of schnapps by the German Flying Corps – 'which I thought was very decent of them'.

He said:

A few days later we were paraded, and we found that there were about two or three hundred British Tommies held prisoner in another part of the Citadel. Some of them were very badly wounded, and had lice among their paper bandages. Between us, we arranged with the commandant for them to be de-loused; they took us all down to a laundry, and they baked our clothes and gave us showers. After that, we entrained for Osnabruck. The journey took about two days; there were four of us and one guard in each compartment.

For Norman Insoll, the war (as they used to say) was over. The problem was how to make the best of the next two years though, in the life of a prisoner of war, the sentence was not stipulated. That – for Mr Insoll as for so many others – was the worst aspect of life in captivity. But, with only German bulletins for news, there was no indication of how the war was going. 'It was,' he said, 'rather depressing. But, apart from this and with good companionship time doesn't go too badly when you're young. You can take these things. It helps a lot.'

7
TIME TO GO HOME

Most private soldiers held captive in Germany during World War I were employed by industrialists and farmers; in Britain, they built roads and wooden huts; and in France, they worked on the land (though Austrian prisoners dug much of the Saint Quentin Canal which had, it might have been argued, a military purpose). The American view was that 'as large a number as possible should be constantly employed because their own warfare [sic] and that of the United States demanded it' (Herbert C. Fooks).

Such employment, one must assume, absorbed their energies. In any case, having received one dose of life on the Western Front, many shared the feelings of Mr Jeffries and were not anxious to experience another.

Officers were different. Officers did not work. Many, perhaps, had been weaned on the *Boys' Own Paper* and its diet of adventure stories. Pilots, especially, were anxious to get back into action, to resume their efforts (in the words of several) 'to strafe the Hun'. Having, much against their will, come into a POW camp, the overriding ambition of many was to get out.

By no means were all officers compulsive escapers. One of them (Captain J. R. Ackerly) recalled that he had been confined to three camps, and nobody had attempted to get away from any of them. During the latter part of the war, a system of exchange was arranged. German and British officers could buy themselves journeys to neutral Holland in exchange for a promise that they would take no more part in the fighting. The deal had been arranged out of concern for their health. Too long in captivity, it was quite sensibly argued, might have disastrous effects. Many were grateful for the opportunity, though some refused. Their reason, they professed, was that they did not wish to be disqualified from further combat. They may also have been reluctant to go home by so simple a route. Escaping, if not exactly a sport, was a challenge to their courage and ingenuity.

Conditions at the average officers' camp in Germany were by no means intolerable. The Germans produced one meal a day (at midday), which was poor by any standards. Mr Insoll recalls a particularly dreadful concoction. 'There were,' he said, 'a few potatoes floating about in it, which we used to take out and use – and there was half a horse's head complete with eye. It put you off. Luckily, we had parcels, so we only ate the potatoes.'

For the other two meals, they relied entirely on the Red Cross and contributions from home. The contents were either shared out among a group, or else consumed individually. The camp kitchen could be used for cooking the contents of tins, provided it did not interfere with the preparation of the so-called main meal.

There was also a canteen, run by a committee, at which cigars, cigarettes, beer, light wines and writing materials were on sale. The profits were used to finance the camp theatre, the orchestra and even, at one place, the building of tennis courts.

Early in the war, itinerant salesmen were allowed to visit the camps. Their selection of merchandise does not seem to have been vetted by the authorities. One such vendor did a brisk trade in copies of the *Baedeker Guide to North Germany* – a volume that, since it contained maps, was eagerly snapped up by prospective escapers.

Sometimes, it was surprising how naïve the guards seemed to be. One officer wrote to his tailor in London, instructing him to supply a cap as worn by one of the Guards' regiments. When the wrong item was dispatched, he was allowed to send an extra postcard – demanding the correct version. The reason for this determination to get it right was, or so he believed, that this particular style could easily be adapted to counterfeit a German officer's. It was part of an escape plan.

The German suspicions may have been allayed by their insistence that British officers should salute their superiors in the German Army. Since you cannot salute unless you are wearing something on your head (the Americans salute bare-headed, but they are the exception), it seemed only reasonable that the extra postcard should be sent. A proper regard for the civilities of army life was, after all, understandable.

It is harder to comprehend the credulity of a German sentry who, at the bidding of a British officer, took a trip into the nearest town and bought three female nightdresses. The English may indeed have seemed to be a strange race, but was transvestism to be numbered among their other peculiarities? The soldier would have been less willing to make the purchase, had he realised that they were intended as a source of white cloth to be used as camouflage for an escape when the ground was covered with snow.

Officers were housed in all manner of buildings. At least two cavalry barracks were employed for this purpose, several hotels, a theatre, a former warehouse and a factory. For persistent escapers ('jug-crackers', as some of them chose to call themselves), there were punishment camps, where conditions were particularly rigorous. A warehouse at Magdeburg, the notorious Fort 9 at Ingolstadt and a fort at Zorndorf in East Prussia – seventy miles east of Berlin – were the most commonly used.

If a kommandant had reason to be suspicious that his charges were assembling escape kits, detectives from Berlin might be called in to search the camp. Their delving was not always successful. After one such foray in a camp at Ströhen (to the west of Hanover, 100 miles from the Dutch frontier), several of the sleuths afterwards complained that their pockets had been picked and their identity cards removed. One of them was seen to leave the establishment with the words 'You know my methods, Watson!' pinned to the tail of his coat.

The commandants of the so-called 'strafe camps' were notably severe, though none of them was more disliked than the Neimeyer twins. One of them ('Milwaukee Bill') was in charge of a peacetime hotel at Clausthal in the Hartz Mountains; his brother was at Holtzminden, a former cavalry barracks in the Hanoverian command. It is hard to tell which of the twins was the most hated. The Neimeyer at Holtzminden was described by Lieutenant E. H. Garland of the Royal Flying Corps as 'That notorious Hun bully. His vanity was colossal, and was only equalled by his uncouth manners, crass stupidity and ignorance in dealing with men and officers.' He liked to ape the Kaiser's image, even to the turned-up moustache. If one is to believe another prisoner, even his dog disliked him. The animal, it appears, preferred the company of the captives.

Norman Insoll remembers that 'Milwaukee Bill was supposed to be the worst, though I believe they were both pretty bad. He used to take drugs and get very het up.'

The brothers had lived in America before the war, and spoke reasonably fluent English. The fate of one, the Holtzminden Neimeyer, is unknown. 'Milwaukee Bill', whatever his villainy, came to a tragic end. When the armistice was signed, he departed for his flat in Dresden, where he committed suicide.

Tunnelling had long been the traditional method of escaping. At Clausthal, it was impossible, for the ex-hotel was up in the mountains, firmly planted on rock. Stürm, down in the Hanoverian marshes, was more promising. 'Here, of course, you could tunnel to your hearts content, because it was all sandy stuff', Mr Insoll said. 'Nevertheless, it was most dangerous; not only was it liable to cave in, you also got marsh gas. Some men had to be pulled out, because they were becoming affected by it.'

This particular venture did not come to a successful conclusion. The tunnel had passed beneath the wire and reached a point near the entrance gate. Suddenly, one of the sentry boxes was seen to wobble and then to fall over on its side. The escape route, it appeared, had been dug rather too close to the surface.

So far as records are concerned, the tunnel at Holtzminden broke them all – both in terms of length and the number who escaped through it. Seventy yards long, it took nine months to make. The originator was a Canadian officer named Major Colquhoun. The infamous Neimeyer believed, not entirely without reason, that this former cavalry barracks was escape-proof. According to Hugh Durnford, an officer in the Royal Field Artillery who was employed as adjutant to the Senior British Officer, '"You see, yentlemen", he would say in his Americanised English, "you see, yentlemen, you cannot get out now, I should not try. It will be bad for your health", and we allowed him to think that we agreed'.

But Major Colquhoun believed that escape was possible. He and 249 other officers plus twenty British orderlies (privates and NCOs) was housed in Barrack B, a four-storeyed building, 50yd long, with an entrance and a staircase at either end. The orderlies' quarters were only 16yd from the wall marking the perimeter of the camp. This, obviously, was the place to begin. It was out-of-bounds to the officers, but it was not difficult to penetrate the roughly built barrier – and to disguise the fact.

Some distance beyond the wall, there was a field of rye. Provided the job was complete before the crop had been harvested, it would provide good cover for the exit.

The entrance to the tunnel, which was only 18in in diameter, was at a point beneath a staircase. At first, yellow clay had to be removed; then they dug through a stratum of large stones. Three men were employed on each shift. One, lying on his stomach, did the digging, using a trowel and a cold chisel. He put the earth into a basin (later, a sack was used), which was hauled back by the second man, who was responsible for dumping the contents. The third member of this industrious trio pumped away at a set of bellows in an attempt to keep the air clean, and to provide sufficient oxygen for the candlelight by which the digger worked.

If the length of the Holtzminden tunnel is impressive, the ingenuity displayed by its makers is equally remarkable. The sides were reinforced with boards removed from the beds of Barrack B; the bellows were manufactured from wood and leather; and the air was pumped to the work face through an ever-lengthening tube made from biscuit tins.

Throughout this period, Captain Neimeyer prowled the premises looking for trouble, and promising any officer whose demeanour was less than respectful 'three days [in the cells] right away, cost price'.

At one point, operations were interrupted by reprisals for the supposed ill-treatment of German prisoners in Britain. No walks were allowed; all games were forbidden; and there were four roll-calls ('appels') a day instead of the customary two. Hugh Durnford wrote:

> This was depressing for the tunnellers, as of course it meant a much greater restriction of working hours. So they took two desperate decisions. Henceforth they would work ... through the night ... And they would break surface as soon as they judged the tunnel had reached some beans which were at any rate better cover than bare earth.

From time to time, a stick with a fragment of white rag attached to its end was poked up through the earth. Observers on the barrack roof noted its position. Eventually when it appeared amid the beans, the work was judged to have been completed.

The big break-out took place at 10.15 pm on the night of 24 July 1918, a few minutes after lights-out. The twenty men who had put in the most work were given priority. After they were clear, admission to the tunnel was strictly confined to the inhabitants of Barrack B. The first man through cut his way to the surface with a bread knife. Above ground, it was raining.

At two o'clock, the orderlies reported a snag, and this caused a two-hour delay. A couple of hours later, everything came to an end when the roof fell in. At least one frustrated escaper had to be dragged out feet first.

Norman Insoll was waiting his turn. He said:

> The tunnel when I came to Holtzminden was half-built, and it was very difficult to get on the list. I had a friend who was working on it, a naval engineer, and he was able to help me. Of the twenty-nine who got through, ten got to England, which was a very good percentage. But then a piece of the tunnel fell in, and all the rest of us had to come back.
>
> The Germans found the exit, but they couldn't discover the entrance. They sent a boy down with a piece of string, but he became afraid and had to come back. Then they sent a dog. It didn't like it and came up. Eventually, they made the orderlies dig it up.

When the break-out was discovered, Mr Insoll recalls:

> Captain Neimeyer went off his head. He got *very* het up. I don't blame him really, because he was standing beside the barracks, and shouting. He had two sentries with him, when somebody on the top floor threw a great log out of the window at him. This infuriated him even more. He sent one of the sentries inside – to go and shoot somebody.
>
> I happened to be going innocently upstairs, and this man came up and fired off his rifle just behind me. He wasn't trying to hit me – the bullet went out of the window. He just had to make a noise, but it frightened me to death. I came down quickly, and went back to my room.

After any escape, the guards were particularly sensitive. At one camp, an officer in the Royal Engineers escaped. The sentries became confused, and opened fire on prisoners in the compound. Fortunately, nobody was hit. But, at one point, it seemed as if the POWs might fight back with their fists and with slats of wood. The Senior British Officer (SBO) persuaded everybody to calm down, which was just as well. As one inmate remarked, 'If it had been taken any further, we'd have all been lined up and shot.'

This episode was reported to the inspecting power's representative (American, at the time), who decided that the camp was too lightly guarded. If the number of sentries was increased, there would be less chance that a nervous soldier might become panic-stricken and fire without thinking of the consequences. The British population agreed with him, and the SBO actually applied for more sentries.

If an escaper was caught, he was sentenced to solitary confinement, either in a cell within the camp or else in a civilian gaol. The length of the ordeal varied according to the number of times he had committed the offence. On the first occasion, he might be fortunate and receive no more than a fortnight. After that the term grew longer, and was sometimes as long as three months.

But still these compulsive escapers kept at it. One officer, who tried to swim the moat surrounding a fortress, painted his face white and green in the hope that he might be mistaken for a water lily. At the same camp (Ingolstadt), the particularly harsh winter of 1916 enabled a British officer accompanied by a Frenchman to get away over the ice. They were recaptured 200yd from the fort by a farmer who attacked them with a whip.

At Zorndorf, a Russian colonel fitted himself out with a counterfeit German officer's uniform, and manufactured a saddle and a bridle. His plan was to walk out of the camp, steal a horse and ride the relatively few miles between the fortress and the Eastern Front. Unfortunately, he was unable to find a horse. Since a figure in a rather badly fitting uniform, wandering aimlessly around with everything needed for riding except a mount, is liable to attract attention, it was not long before he was returned to captivity.

In at least two other cases, POWs made their exits disguised as German officers. One of them (he who had ordered the Guards officer's cap from his London outfitter) discreetly modified the badge he had made from buttons and silver paper by painting a minute Union Jack on it. He was afraid that, if he were recaptured and his 'uniform' (which included a greatcoat fashioned from a cape supplied by a Russian colonel) was too convincing, he might be shot as a spy.

One officer remarked that, 'Anyone who thinks too much of what may happen, will never escape from prison.' And, from a captive at Ingolstadt, 'No one cared twopence for court-martials, and nearly everyone in the fort had done considerable spells of solitary confinement.' According to his estimate, an escape attempt took place at least once a week – 'in fact, the camp was nothing less than an escaping club' (A. J. Evans).

But not all of these adventurers were quite so sanguine. One escaper, posing as a German officer attached to the drainage commission, rehearsed his act with considerable care. 'After all, in England nowadays,' he wrote, 'an actor rarely gets shot or put in prison if he fails to give satisfaction; whereas in our case, there was a distinct likelihood of getting shot, and a certainty of being gaoled if we were found out.'

This particular officer was recaptured five days later. He received a month's solitary in a civil prison, and was posted to Zorndorf afterwards.

If you herd together a random collection of men, it is amazing how many talents will reveal themselves. One officer made an imitation officer's sword from wood gleaned from a packing case. It lent greater realism to his Prussian officer's disguise. Another, who planned to walk out of the camp posing as a German sentry in charge of a detail of officers masquerading as orderlies, manufactured a very fair replica of a rifle. When he was arrested, it was not the 'rifle' that gave him away, but one of his 'charges'. The man happened to be his brother – a would-be escaper of such tenacity, that his face was known by pretty well every soldier and policeman in Germany.

Men who, before being taken into captivity, had probably never in their lives handled needles and thread, revealed considerable ability at cutting and sewing garments from the most unlikely materials. Honest citizens showed that they could forge an identity card or a passport with a skill that any professional counterfeiter might have envied. Nor were such criminal talents confined to the graphic arts. As one British officer POW remarked of another, 'Harrison told me he had a weakness for sardine openers when lock-picking. I liked the strong wire that is used for stiffening an officer's cap' (J. L. Hardy).

Occasionally, it was possible to arrange for small items to be smuggled from England in parcels. Those supplied by the Red Cross were strictly taboo so far as this was concerned, but there was no reason why personal gifts should be above suspicion. As one 'jug-cracker' observed, 'Watching a German open a parcel in which you know there is a concealed compass was one of the most exciting things I've ever done.' This particular officer, A. J. Evans, must have created some sort of record. Having, after several attempts, reached Switzerland, he was repatriated. Returning to duty with the Royal Flying Corps, he was posted to Palestine, where he was again shot down and taken prisoner – this time, by the Turks.

Most officers had arranged some sort of code with their families for use under circumstances such as these. Norman Insoll had stipulated that he would mark any letter containing a hidden message 'C. Insoll'. It was not, alas, very successful. After the incident of the tunnel at Holtzminden, he decided to give a short account of the undertaking to his parents. Whilst they picked up the clue given by 'C', neither was able to decipher the message.

A friend of Mr Insoll was more succesful. He wrote home, asking for a tin of Magnapole cream. There was no such brand on the market. On the other hand, there was a Magnapole compass. It duly arrived in a tin of cream, snug beneath a false bottom. As Mr Insoll said, 'You've got to have someone at the other end who knows what you're talking about.'

J. L. Hardy's efforts to obtain freedom were, in the words of a companion, 'marked by a daring verging on recklessness'. They were also marked by a strange idiosyncracy. Once beyond the wire, he used to 'put on a very bad limp, half close one eye and open the other in a glassy stare'.

It would, he felt (in at least one case, incorrectly) make him less conspicuous.

Getting out of a camp was only part – some might have said, the lesser part – of the problem. A measure of freedom had been attained, but every movement had to be made carefully, every path explored cautiously, for fear of discovery. Total freedom came only on the far side of a neutral frontier, Switzerland, Holland or Denmark.

Hardy was in a camp at Halle at the time. At six o'clock one evening, when heavy rain had driven the sentries into their boxes, he climbed down from a roof, using a rope made from scraps of leather. He negotiated the outer barriers and – with his limp, his glassy eye, and wearing a Norfolk jacket – walked to the station, where he bought a 4th (*sic*) class ticket to Berlin. Unfortunately, he boarded the wrong train, and found himself travelling to Leipzig. Eventually, after returning to Halle, he reached Bremen. But, by then, it was well into the night and bitterly cold. 'Trains,' he wrote, 'trains were good. You couldn't freeze to death in a train.' He moved on – this time, to a village named Delmenhorst. It was here, thawing out his aching limbs in front of the waiting-room fire, that he was recaptured.

It had been a strange odyssey. For part of the time his fellow travellers had been offering him their sympathy because, for want of any better idea, he had explained away his lack of identity papers by telling an inquisitive policeman that he was making haste to attend his father's funeral.

On another occasion, he had acted the part of a drunken German labourer. Indeed, if his knowledge of German railways had matched his gift for impersonations, he might have got away.

Railways were dangerous. Ticket inspectors had to be convinced, and so did itinerant policemen who roamed the corridors. As another POW put it, 'half the German population seemed to want to examine the papers of the other half'.

One officer, caught between the accusing eyes of a railway guard and a German sentry, made a bolt for it through the carriage window during a halt on the journey. Once down on the ground, he fancied a cigarette. His preparations for escape had been meticulous up to a point. He had, however, forgotten to take any matches with him. With a coolness amounting almost to arrogance, he helped himself to a light from an oil lamp on the rear of the last carriage. Then he trudged away into the night.

Most escaped prisoners preferred to take fewer chances. They journeyed by night, and hid up during the daytime, avoiding towns, villages, and main roads. Invariably, they underestimated the time that it would take them to reach sanctuary. Consequently, they soon ran out of food, and had to assuage their hunger with such far from appetising items as raw potatoes dug up from the fields of unsuspecting farmers.

These men (or most of them) suffered abominably. Since many of the escapes took place in winter, the weather was a constant enemy. Indeed, the majority of failures were accounted for by sheer hunger, fatigue and cold.

Some never got beyond the wire: they were betrayed from within. The attitude of escapers was to trust nobody who was not absolutely essential to the attempt. There were, of course, times when this was impossible. Nor were their less-restless companions wholeheartedly in favour of these adventures. Whenever a POW managed to outwit one or the other of the Neimeyer twins, the whole camp was punished afterwards. There was even one Senior British Officer who threatened to court-martial any escaper on his return to the UK (in contrast to the SBO of Holtzminden, who was among those who reached freedom from the tunnel mouth, and who afterwards sent the kommandant an affectionate telegram from Holland).

Whether an anti-escaper would betray an escaper to the Germans seems very doubtful. At one camp, an officer from Poland was thought to be an informer, largely because his offer to obtain contraband goods on the black market had been turned down. At a barracks in which Norman Insoll was interned, 'there were the escape people arranging things, and there happened to be a French captain, whom we thought was a spy. He was very privileged and had a little room to himself. One evening, about five of us went into his quarters and covered him from head to foot with jam. He screamed, "Secours! Secours!", and we never saw him again after that. He, obviously, was in the German camp.'

Beyond the wire, nobody was safe. One escaper (J. L. Hardy), who reached the Baltic, might well have made passage to Scandinavia aboard a neutral ship, if it had not been for an inquisitive landlady. When he asked her whether he might lodge at her house for the night, she became suspicious. While his attention was diverted, she slipped out and summoned an NCO and two soldiers. They took him away to a nearby guardroom, where they removed his boots and invited him to bed down upon a mattress in a corner. The trio sat in chairs facing him with their rifles cocked.

Hardy fell asleep. When he awoke, seven hours later, he noticed that the time was five minutes to five. He also noticed that the German NCO and the two privates had followed his example, and were fast asleep.

With so slippery a character, this was a fatal mistake. He grabbed his boots, tip-toed out of the room, and ran down the road until he found cover in a field.

The NCO was so worried by the loss of his captive, that he put the muzzle of his rifle into his mouth and shot himself. When, later, the truant was recaptured again, he spent a week in a civil prison and was then returned to Magdeburg – whence he had escaped. Briefly, there was talk of trying him for the murder of the luckless under-officer, but the two privates explained what had happened, and the matter was dropped.

In Germany, the camps were heavily guarded and surrounded by formidable obstacles. At Yozgad, amid the mountains of Anatolia, no such precautions were necessary. The camp was 120 miles from the railhead and 130 miles from the nearest port on the Black Sea.

Between this prison camp for captives of the Turks and these extremities of civilisation there were mountains, desert and brigands who were reputed to be more fearsome than the Turks themselves. As E. H. Jones, author of *The Road to Endor*, observed, 'The chances of final escape were about the same as those of a snowball surviving in the South Sea Islands.'

Nevertheless, to discourage any such wicked thoughts, the Turkish commandant, Major Kiazim Bey, frequently reminded the prisoners that, if one got away, all the rest would be punished. The SBO preferred to take no chances. The POWs, he insisted, must give their parole, otherwise, he would inform Kiazim Bey.

It may seem to have been a questionable attitude but this officer probably knew what he was doing. Of all the prisoners captured in the Turkish theatre of operations, two-thirds had vanished without trace by the time of the Armistice. If a Turk threatened reprisals, caution was advisable.

Despite all this, the thoughts of E. H. Jones were apt to stray beyond the confines of Yozgad, and beyond the peaks of the more distant mountains. The problem was to remove himself without bringing down the commandant's wrath upon those who remained behind, and to survive the perilous journey to freedom.

To go was impossible: to be sent was another matter. Might it be feasible, by some trickery, to enlist the help of the Turkish camp authorities? The very thought seemed enough to daunt the most ingenious imagination, but then chance dealt Mr Jones the ace of trumps.

In their efforts to overcome the tedium of life in this most austere and remote place, the officers applied themselves to study. They explored mathematics and philosophy: some tried to master the Turkish language. One day, a small group decided to experiment with spiritualism. One of them constructed a ouija-board. Jones wrote:

> Two at a time we would close our eyes, place our forefingers lightly on an inverted tumbler in the centre of the board, ask a question, and wait for the tumbler to move to the letters and spell out the answer. We found that the tumbler would move without our consciously pushing it; it even touched letters. But the letters it touched never spelt anything – they were meaningless nonsense.

This went on for two weeks, with the roving tumbler producing nothing but gibberish. By this time, Mr Jones had discovered that, using a little sleight of hand, it was possible to cheat. Not only could his agile fingers direct the journeys from letter to letter in such a way that a coherent message emerged, he also invented contacts on the Other Side. Among them were spirit creatures of his imagination named 'Sally', 'Dorothy', 'Silas P. Warner' and several others.

It had begun as a joke. Nevertheless, Jones decided that he would not reveal his deception. He challenged the others to investigate his remarkable abilities. Various tests, some of them 'very difficult', were set up. The agile-fingered Mr Jones passed them all. Indeed, his performance was so convincing, that nearly half the camp's population became converted to spiritualism.

Before very long, accounts of this strange phenomenon reached the ears of the Turkish authorities. The interpreter – a young man affectionately known as 'Pimple' – fell into the habit of consulting Silas P. Warner (or was it Dorothy?) about his love affairs. From time to time during the seances, Jones had relayed scraps of fictitious news about the war. Somewhat to his surprise, the commandant suddenly issued instructions that these items were not to be recounted in letters home.

Why this concern? When 'Pimple' was consulted, he explained that Kiazim Bey was himself a convinced spiritualist.

The game – for such it was – had begun in February. By September, almost everybody in the camp, captors and captives alike, were involved to some degree. 'Pimple', his love life now presumably in better order, wished to know whether the spirits could locate buried treasure. The spirits obligingly answered that they could.

A new figure came, so to speak, on the air – the spirit of a dead Armenian of great wealth, who had been killed in a recent massacre. He had, he explained, been one of three brothers. The elder whom he referred to as 'B', had also died; but the third ('C') was still alive. His home was many miles away on the coast. Before the killing had begun, they had buried their riches to prevent them from falling into Turkish hands. To discover the whereabouts of what amounted to a considerable sum of gold, it would be necessary to consult all three.

At this point, an escape plan began to form in Jones's mind. The idea was too large, and too complicated, for him to carry out on his own. He needed an accomplice, and for this purpose he chose an Australian pilot named Hill.

Matters had now reached a point at which the spirits, diligently questioned by Jones and his ouija-board, were more or less running the camp. The commandant's belief in them was absolute. Like the 'Pimple', he, too, was now eager to lay his hands on the buried treasure. Communications with 'B' should surely not be too difficult, but what about 'C'? Was there not some such facility as thought-transference? Was it not called telepathy?

Jones agreed that this was so. Unfortunately, he pointed out, the mountains surrounding the camp blocked communications (rather, one must suppose, on the principle of VHF radio in more recent years). To question 'C', it would be necessary to travel to the coast. He and Hill would have to make the trip – escorted, naturally, by the 'Pimple' and by a squad of guards.

Once clear of the mountains, the escort would be drugged (Jones had hollowed out the handle of a shaving brush, and inserted 'enough morphia to put a Turkish battalion to sleep'). The two officers would then steal a boat and, given good luck, sail to Cyprus and freedom.

They planted various clues in the vicinity of the camp, a few gold coins, an old revolver and so on. Each was eagerly dug up and handed over to the rapacious commandant. The journey to the coast seemed certain; but, at almost the last moment, information of the planned escape leaked out, and a fellow prisoner informed Kiazim Bey. In fairness to the man, this was not intended as an act of betrayal. He was afraid that, once 'C' had been approached, Jones and Hill might be shot in the back 'while attempting to escape'. The pretext for such executions was almost as old as the hills that surrounded Yozgad.

Kiazim Bey became alarmed, though he never doubted the authenticity of the seances. There could no longer be any question of travelling to the coast. Might it, perhaps, be sufficient to visit Constantinople? Could this remarkable mind-reading act be carried out there?

The spirits replied that it would probably work. There were no topographical barriers between the city and 'C's' residence. The reception might be quite good.

But the problem was not yet solved. Even an officer of Kiazim Bey's standing could not, upon a whim, remove two imprisoned officers from his custody and send them to Constantinople. There must be a reason for such action. What could it be? He could not think of anything. Perhaps the spirits, so helpful in the past, might make a suggestion?

Promptly, they submitted an idea. Why not, they ventured, report that Jones and Hill had gone mad?

Assisted by the camp's medical officer, Dr O'Farrell, the two men now practised the art of posing as lunatics. Their performances were so convincing, that two Turkish doctors who were called in had no qualms about certifying them. Jones, they observed, was 'a furious, who was suffering from a derangement in his brains'. Hill was described as a 'melancholic'.

This was enough. It was agreed that they should be escorted to Constantinople, whence they would be repatriated as lunatics. The act, of course, had to be kept up until they were free. When they broke the journey for a night at a small town on the way, they decided to add to their respective dossiers by feigning an attempt at suicide. 'We pretended to hang ourselves,' Mr Jones recalls. 'This part of the scheme was too well acted. Owing to a mistake of the "Pimple's" we were both just about unconscious when we were cut down.'

At Constantinople, they spent six months in an asylum, waiting to be exchanged. Through this period, they maintained the deception. At last, the arrangements necessary for an exchange were completed, and they were sent home. Two weeks later, the Armistice was signed. It was, perhaps, much ado about not very much. But, in the remoteness of Yozgad, even 'the spirits' could not realise that the war was approaching its end. And at least, as Mr Jones wrote, 'we had the satisfaction of having done our best'.

Germany was surrounded by possible havens for escaped prisoners of war, provided they could reach them. In Britain, it was very much more difficult. As one German officer (Oberleutnant Heinz Justus) pointed out, the relatively poor record of success was 'due to your splendid isolation'.

Bad luck was another factor. Justus himself was particularly unfortunate. Using a wig that had been sent to him from Germany camouflaged as tobacco, and some women's clothes smuggled inside a quilt, he devised two characters to assist his escape from a camp near Masham in north Yorkshire. One of the regular visitors from the outside world was a gentleman named Mr Budd, who managed the canteen. Mr Budd set off for home every evening at 8 pm. With the help of a false moustache, a pair of spectacles and some home-made civilian clothes, Justus saw no difficulty in impersonating the Englishman. If he walked out a few minutes before Mr Budd, he might well pass the sentries unremarked. But, as he reminded himself, the real Mr Budd would soon follow him, and it would not be long before the ruse was detected.

Consequently, as soon as he was out of sight of the camp, he proposed to strip off disguise number one – and to assume the identity of a woman with blonde hair, a large hat and a silk coat.

Everything went wonderfully well. When he passed some soldiers on the road, they bade him a polite 'good evening' (which was a relief; he had been half afraid that they might attempt to pick him/her up). Using English money, which he had smuggled out of the camp in a package normally used for Gillette razor blades, he proposed to buy a railway ticket to London.

Unfortunately, before he reached the station, another soldier approached him. A prisoner of war had escaped, he said. By a strange coincidence, he had been carrying a bag not unlike the lady's. Had, perhaps, she seen anyone who looked suspicious?

To appear as a woman is not difficult; to speak as one is much harder. Justus attempted a falsetto, but his talents as a female impersonator were limited. A squeak quickly descended into a croak; another soldier, who had arrived on the scene, asked whether he might examine the bag's contents, and that was that. Oberleutnant Justus's brief outing earned him thirty-five days in Chelmsford prison.

He made his next attempt when being transferred from a camp at Maidenhead ('the best camp I'd been in as regards personal comfort, but ... a very depressing place for an escaper') to an establishment near Wakefield. He had hoped to evade his escort amid the crowds at either Paddington or King's Cross stations, but the guards were too alert. Eventually, however, he made a break for it as the train was slowly moving away from a station near Doncaster. Now wearing a somewhat rough-and-ready civilian disguise, he walked to Doncaster, took a train to London, and then set off for Cardiff, where he hoped to make an escape to Spain aboard a Spanish ship.

On this occasion, it really seemed as if he might get away with it. He reached Cardiff without let or hindrance, located the docks, and took a room in a small hotel under the name of Allan Hinckley, an American opera singer. During the journey, he had visited two theatres to pass the time – a musical comedy at Doncaster (the title was *You are Spotted*, 'which was indeed rather appropriate from the point of view of an escaped prisoner') and, in London, a spy drama entitled *The Hidden Hand*. It was fiercely anti-German, but he found it 'a very, very thrilling play indeed'.

If Justus had not been out of luck, he would probably have found his Spanish ship and, with it, freedom. But, in this sordid little Cardiff hotel, the unkindest cut of all came about. He went down with 'flu.

The bug was a bad one. Far from improving, his condition became worse. Eventually, he became so ill, that he was obliged to go to the local police station and give himself up.

After medical treatment, he was sentenced to fifty-six days at Chelmsford prison. It was a poor substitute for convalescence.

Dyffryn Aled Camp in North Wales near Denbigh was mostly occupied by captured U-boat officers. It was unusually well guarded: six sentries were employed instead of the usual two, and there were four searchlights around the perimeter and double the number of daily roll-calls held at other camps. Among those interned there, at the end of 1914, was Korvettenkapitan Hermann Tholens, formerly second-in-command of the German cruiser *Mainz*, which had been sunk in the Heligoland bight twenty-four days after the declaration of war.

That Christmas, a number of German orderlies who had lived in England before the war, were exchanged for the same number of British POWs in Germany. There was no reason, Tholens decided, why one of them should not act as a courier. The letter, which he composed with uncommon care, was addressed to the commander-in-chief of the German Navy's submarine branch. It suggested that it might be possible to break out of the camp and to reach a point on the coast of North Wales. If this were accomplished, would the Admiral care to send a U-boat to ferry him back to Germany?

All the letters were written in code, addressed to Tholens by 'friends' and discussing whether or not the wedding of a mysterious lady referred to as Mrs 'X' would take place on 14 August 1915. Eventually, Mrs X seemed to make up her mind, and Tholens was glad to hear that the nuptials would definitely take place. This meant that Germany's supreme submariner had agreed to his plan, and that a U-boat would surface off the coast at an appointed time on that very date.

With surprising ease, Tholens, a friend named Hennig, and a third officer who is not identified, climbed through a window (one of the bars had been previously removed), removed the lock on the main gate and walked away. By 7.30 on the following morning, they had reached Llandudno, where they took breakfast at what he described as 'a nice little restaurant near the sea'.

The head of the submarine service had carried out his part of the deal. Indeed, he had detailed two boats – the U-38 and the U-27 – for the operation. By the evening of 14 August, U-38 was 30yd out at sea, off the Great Ormes Head. The weather was calm: Tholens and his companions had no reason to doubt that the venture would succeed. Using a flashlight, they signalled that they were ready to embark. There was no answer. In desperation, they lit a fire. Again, there was no reply.

Presently, as is the way with British weather, the wind got up until a gale was blowing. This made any attempt to put off from the shore impossible – even supposing that, out there somewhere in the murk, there *was* a submarine. Neither of his two friends spoke English. Consequently, Tholens left them to their own devices (which meant, giving themselves up), and walked to Llandudno station. His plan was now to catch a train to London, where he would smuggle himself on board a Dutch or a Scandinavian ship. But, he wrote, 'at the station ... a policeman stopped me. He said I looked very like a certain Lieutenant-Commander Tholens who had escaped from Dyffryn Aled three days before. I could only answer "Right you are".'

What had gone wrong? The U-boat had been a mere 500yd away, when the three men made their signals. She had, however, been brought nearer the shore than Tholens had expected, and the captain was slightly ahead of schedule. When the three German officers were trying so desperately to communicate, she was screened from them by a projecting ledge of rock. Unable to see the torchlight, the commanding officer assumed that they had failed to get out of the camp. He waited for a while and then, when the wind increased, he departed.

Gunther Pluschow, a naval pilot, was more fortunate. In February 1915, he was brought to the prison camp at Donington Hall in Derbyshire. 'Day and night I planned, brooded, deliberated how I could escape from this miserable imprisonment', he wrote. 'I had to act with the greatest calm and caution if I hoped to succeed.'

The method employed by Pluschow and his fellow escaper, Oberleutnant Treffitz, was nothing if not direct. In the dark, and taking advantage of a rain storm, they actually climbed over the elaborate arrangement of barbed wire so carefully designed to keep them inside. They were, admittedly, badly scratched and Pluschow lost the seat of his trousers. Nevertheless, their departure was not noticed. Walking through the night, and using the Pole Star for guidance, they reached Derby, where they spruced themselves up and put on their civilian disguises in a cottage garden. At the station, they found that a train was due to depart for London in fifteen minutes. They bought third-class tickets, changed trains at Leicester to obscure their tracks, and reached St Pancras Station that afternoon.

At some point, they separated. Treffitz was recaptured but Pluschow had better luck. Travelling on the upper deck of a London bus, he overheard a couple in the seat behind him remark that, every day at 7 pm, a Dutch ship left Tilbury for Holland. This, Pluschow decided, must be his objective.

The next few days were not easy. A ship sailed at seven – just as his unwitting informants had said. The difficulty lay in getting out to the buoy where she was moored, and climbing up the hawser. Several attempts failed – largely because he had not taken the tide into consideration, nor the fact that, at low water, the river front at Tilbury and Gravesend becomes a mass of soft, squelching mud. Each night, he returned to London, looking more and more dishevelled, but arousing nobody's interest. Indeed, the only time he came near to being detected was when he checked in a grubby mackintosh at the cloakroom in Blackfriars Station. Before filling in the receipt, the clerk asked for his name. Pluschow was not prepared for this. For a moment, he forgot his false identity and exclaimed, 'Meinen ...' But he need not have worried. The man hastily scribbled 'Mr Mine' and handed him the ticket.

Eventually, having grappled unsuccessfully with the Gravesend side of the river, he turned his attention to Tilbury. He managed to steal a dinghy and, late one afternoon, clambered aboard the SS *Princess Juliana*.

Nobody saw him but, still cautious, he hid in one of the lifeboats until, several hours later, the ship docked at Flushing. For his successful adventure, the Kaiser rewarded him with the Iron Cross, first class.

The war came to an end, and most people went home. British prisoners of war in Germany were repatriated on the not unreasonable system that those who had been longest in captivity should be the first to go. Mr H. Jeffrey of the King's Royal Rifle Corps had (see previous chapter) been working in a tannery. 'We were the last to go home,' he said, 'as we were the last to be captured. We were sent back to the camp at Parchim. As we left the tannery, the girls who worked there came down to the station to see us off. We got on all right with them – we used to give them chocolate.'

At the beginning of 1919, Mr Jeffrey was still at Parchim. 'There was,' he remembers, 'this terrible 'flu epidemic. About 1,000 of the blokes died in a fortnight – some of the poor devils had been prisoners for four years. I remember we buried thirty in one day in a mass grave. I was lucky. I had a bit of a cold, but nothing worse.'

Eventually, he travelled by ship from Stettin to Copenhagen, and thence to Leith.

Much has been written about the fate of Russian prisoners who were sent back to the USSR at the end of World War II. Those who returned to their homeland after World War I fared no better.

The Germans had treated them with a brutality and a contempt such as they would never have vented upon the British. In the spring of 1919, there were many of these unfortunate men still in various parts of Germany. They were in a deplorable condition; sick, hungry, filthy and paralysed by a tremendous apathy. They badly needed help. Germany did not have enough food for her own people, let alone for these left-overs from a lost war. Nor could they be repatriated in the manner of British, French and other members of the Allied forces – with a revolution ended and a civil war blazing across the land, Russia was too politically unstable.

Eventually, the British Red Cross and the Order of St John agreed to supply 'foodstuffs to their support to a value exceeding £½ million sterling. The plight of these men, unable to return to their own country, was met by the establishment, with the consent of His Majesty's Government, of an organisation of British officers, mostly themselves ex-prisoners of war, for the temporary control of the Russian camps in Hanover, and the administration of their supplies' (Report issued by the British Red Cross and the Order of St John).

Among these officers was a pilot, who had recently resigned from the RAF, named J. Stuart Castle. On 23 March 1919, equipped with suitable documents and a Red Cross brassard, he set off from London. Some days later, he arrived at a camp on Muggenburger Moor, which was still policed by German guards. Mr Castle wrote:

> My first impression was one of filth and utter despair. Ragged men in all stages of sickness and that appalling lazaret full of skeleton-like beings dying, if not already dead, of tuberculosis ... Together with malnutrition, these men had to endure the knowledge of their helplessness and, in some ways worse, of the helplessness of their families now caught up in the Russian civil war. All they wanted to do – if the urge to do anything at all had survived – was to lie in bed.

Work was the only solution: the answer to the filth and the remedy for the apathy. Mr Castle organised them into teams, arranged competitions for which he provided prizes, and generally brought order to this slatternly hell. Later, he performed similar feats at Minden and Celle.

But this could only be a provisional solution to the problem of the Russian prisoners. Eventually, they would have to leave Germany to try to resume life as ordinary citizens. Many of the officers were sent to Newmarket in England. From there, they were offered a choice of destinations – among them China, Hong Kong, France, Turkey and back to Germany. Mr Castle wrote:

Before the final dispersal, we had already heard reports of ex-prisoners being executed on return to Russia. Apparently, the Bolsheviks were in a frenzy of suspicion about those who had spent time abroad, and these ex-prisoners were considered 'politically unreliable'. Soon I received a letter from the inter-allied Commission, instructing me to warn them of the dangers facing them if they returned to Russia. Carrying out this instruction, I particularly remember the response of some officers of the Guards Regiments of St Petersburg and Moscow. 'But we are Russians!' they insisted. 'We are going back to our own country, our own people. How could such things happen?' I could only repeat the warning. Many went back. What happened to them was learnt from a few survivors who passed the news to Russian émigré circles in the Netherlands: they were herded into the square of a small town and machine guns were turned on them.

It may be a cliché to say that history repeats itself but, like most clichés, there is much truth in it. Other countries welcome home repatriated prisoners of war in a manner that might be worthy of a hero. The Russians are different. They shoot them.

8

BARBED WIRE ACROSS EUROPE

Perhaps, the most prescient of all newspaper cartoons published in Britain during the years between World Wars I and II was a drawing by Bill Dyson of the *Daily Herald*. It depicted the statesmen leaving the conference chamber at Versailles. Behind a pillar, a naked tot bore a label marked 'Class of 1920'. The caption was, 'Funny thing – I thought I heard a child cry.'

The years between 1918 and 1939 were, indeed, no more than a long truce. The argument was not concluded: the Germans (certainly under Hitler's tutelage) did not really believe that they had lost. They had been compelled to pay an abominable price for an ill-defined mistake. Eventually, they would try again.

Such may be an over-simplification, but Dyson was right. The class of 1920 was, in fact, one of several that paid for the politicians' mistakes. The armourers, in well-cut suits and snug behind executive desks, now thrived again: the troops marched, and the guns fired. Europe, that insane continent which had seen so many wars, was involved in another holocaust.

Among the first soldiers taken prisoner by the Germans were members of the 8th Battalion, The Sherwood Foresters. The unit – a not yet fully trained part of the Territorial Army – had been given the task of halting a division of crack German Alpine troops that was thrusting its way northwards up the centre of Norway. Predictably, it failed. The battalion was virtually wiped out, and many of its members were captured.

Hitler, no doubt anxious to see examples of the enemy, ordered a selection of weapons and personnel to be brought to Berlin. Second-Lieutenant W. K. Laing (a public-school master, who spoke German), a sergeant named Harrison and Private Lorton of the 5th Battalion, The Leicestershire Regiment, were detailed to satisfy the Nazi leader's curiosity.

On arrival in the German capital, the three men were driven to the Chancellery in a taxi. A colonel escorted them to the Führer's private garden.

It was, Mr Laing recalled,

A German captive taken by the Commandos at Dieppe. Alleged ill-treatment of these prisoners resulted in British POWs at Stalag VIIIB being manacled as a reprisal (*Imperial War Museum*)

One of the compounds in Stalag VIIIB (*From the collection of Don Bruce*)

On Armistice Day, 1918, the flag flew at half-mast at prison camps in Germany (*Literary Executor of the late J Stuart Castle*)

about the size of a fairly large Oxford quadrangle. There was no lawn, only longish grass in the Continental style, trees, shrubs, flower-beds, an occasional bronze animal and fountains. One of the buildings had an arcade; another a large white bow-window, at ground level, with a door. At the door were two footmen in white coats.

A lorry arrived, containing British equipment taken or found by the Germans in Norway. This was laid out in the arcade ... Finally, there was movement at the bow-window and I was amazed to see Hitler (or his double) appear. I just couldn't believe it and wondered for a moment what I should do. Eventually I saluted. He acknowledged my salute by raising his arm level with his shoulder. He had with him a large retinue. In it was Colonel-General Keitel. [Keitel, soon to be promoted to Field Marshal, was Hitler's chief military adviser.]

He went straight up to the arcade and we were taken up as well. The major, who had brought us from Norway, had to lecture on our uniforms and equipment. In Norway he had been full of self-confidence and appeared a very capable officer. Now he was like a nervous schoolboy ...

Every time it was claimed that German equipment was better than British, Hitler would give us a pitying look as if to say: 'Why did you ever try to go to war with us?' The thing which interested him was the anti-tank rifle. He picked up the clip of rounds and crunched them in his hands. He said very little beyond 'yes' and 'no'. The only time he ever approached a smile was when the German major suggested opening a tin of bully beef.

Keitel never said a word.

When Hitler was about to leave, he was told that the officer spoke German. He asked two questions: '*Waren Sie in Berlin Vorher?*' (Were you in Berlin before?) When I said 'no', he asked: '*Wo waren sie in Deutschland?*' (Where were you in Germany?) I replied that I had been in Heidelberg several times. He then muttered something I could not catch and went away, looking hostile.

This, presumably satisfied him. He never visited a POW camp – nor did he ever inspect a concentration camp.

Four years before Hitler came to power, in 1929, delegates from a number of nations – including the USA, Britain, Germany and Italy – gathered round the conference table at Geneva. Their purpose was to consider the agreement concerning prisoners of war signed in 1907 at The Hague, and to decide whether any amendments were necessary. The result was the so-called Geneva Convention, which was to have considerable effect upon the lives of POWs in World War II.

Among the items was Article 9, which gave chaplains and doctors the status of 'protected personnel'. Technically, they were not prisoners of war at all, and were to be sent home as soon as possible. By agreement, however, a number would remain behind to look after the needs of less-fortunate captives. They were to be allowed certain privileges – such as the right to send more letters – and greater freedom of movement.

Officers could not be compelled to work. NCOs were required only to supervise the toil of their subordinates, though they could volunteer for jobs if they wished. POWs could not be forced to undertake assignments that had any 'direct connection with the conduct of the war'. Their hours of employment should not exceed those of civilians in the same area, and they were entitled to one day's rest a week, preferably a Sunday.

The rations issued by the detaining power were to be the equivalent of those consumed by its depot troops. Adequate clothing was to be supplied: the representative of a protecting power (Switzerland for the British) was to visit all POW camps regularly to hear any complaints about ill-treatment. The International Red Cross undertook a similar responsibility. During the course of the war, 180 Red Cross delegates toured the camps: ten of them died in the course of their duties.

Germany accepted the terms of the convention in spirit, though by no means according to the letter. A booklet entitled *Prisoner of War*, published by the War Organisation of the British Red Cross Society and the Order of St John of Jerusalem in 1941, pointed out that, so far as food was concerned, 'sometimes the issue falls below this standard [that of German depot troops], so if it were not supplemented from outside, British prisoners would be in a poor way'.

And, from a handbook for relatives and friends of POWs printed by the War Office:

> You may say that experience has taught us to be sceptical of the value of paper treaties [ie the Geneva Convention]. It is true that the German Government have committed serious breaches of the Convention. Of these, the most grievous is their failure to provide men with adequate food and clothing. Fortunately, however, these deficiencies are largely being made good through the excellent parcel service provided by the War Organisation of the British Red Cross Society and Order of Saint John.

During the course of the war, the International Committee of the Red Cross transported 33 million parcels to POWs in Germany. They came from Britain, America, Canada, even from the British community in the Argentine. In theory, a POW was entitled to one a week, though this was by no means certain. In Italy, the system sometimes broke down from administrative chaos; in Germany, when an excuse was needed, the Allied bombing offensive was usually blamed. On one occasion, the real explanation was more discreditable. A batch had been stolen by German soldiers, who were selling their contents to civilians in the town of Lübeck.

According to the Geneva Convention, whatever other punishments might be inflicted on a POW, the withdrawal of Red Cross parcels must not be among them. This rule was sometimes broken as reprisal for an alleged act of inhumanity by the Allies. On such occasions, the German authorities did not bother to make any excuse.

So far as clothing was concerned, the obligations were ignored completely, and the Red Cross again assumed the role of provider. Working conditions varied considerably. One soldier captured in Italy, was compelled to assist in preparing the fortifications of Monte Cassino. When he complained that this was against the rules of the Convention, he was told that they only became effective once he had been sent to a proper camp. Another POW related how, on some working parties, the men were forced to work fourteen to fifteen hours a day, seven days a week. When they protested to the guard, 'he taps his rifle and says "Here is my Geneva Convention".'

Conditions varied enormously. Mr Edward Lee, who was captured in France while serving with the Royal West Kent Regiment, recalls:

> We used to take turns peeling potatoes for the camp, and one day, when I was doing it, the sergeant in charge came in and asked 'Is there a gardener in the place?' I was a gardener in civvy street, but we always said we wouldn't volunteer for anything, so I kept quiet. Eventually, one of our chaps said, 'Go on – tell him' – so I did. He took me to a German chap who'd lived in America before the war, and was now running a market garden. I was there more or less until we had to move because the Russians were coming.

Between them, Mr Lee and his companions managed quite well. A POW who worked in a bakery used to hump sacks of flour back to the camp; Mr Lee used to take back apples, potatoes and eggs. Nobody seemed to mind. Indeed, agricultural work of any kind was preferred by the prisoners. There was more freedom; the guards, on the whole, were more friendly; and the work kept away boredom and depression – which were the twin enemies of those, such as officers, who were never allowed to stray beyond the camp except on an occasional walk.

On the other hand, many of the captives in Silesia were forced to labour in the coal mines. Mr Don Bruce, an RAF navigator who spent two years in Stalag VIIIB, was a sergeant and, therefore, not required to work. He recalls:

> I wouldn't really have wanted to because all the jobs were heavy – such as coal mining – and several people were killed. They used to lose legs in mining accidents. The only way to get out of it was to undergo a medical exam and be regraded. They used to swallow balls of silver paper, because they showed up in X-rays of the stomach. If they were asked for a stool, they used to put red ink on it, so that it would look as if they had dysentery. They used to do all these gags to try to get what they called a 'light work grading' away from the mines.

Between a defeated soldier and a prison camp, there was a gulf that had to be crossed, a readiness on the part of the victor to give quarter to his victims. Hitler's notorious *Kommandobefehl* (Commando Order), issued in October 1942, instructed that raiders, whether from the sea or from the sky, should be executed after interrogation. Towards the end of the war, he decreed that Allied airmen who baled out over the Third Reich must be put to death.

The fate of ordinary soldiers depended upon the unit that captured them. Members of the Wehrmacht (German Army) were, on the whole, tolerably humane. To fall captive to the SS (*Schutzstaffel*) made the prospect of survival less certain.

For example, on 26 May 1940, 100 men of the Royal Norfolk Regiment were cut off near the village of Paradis in northern France. When they had run out of ammunition, their commanding officer surrendered to the 1st Battalion, 2nd SS Totenkof Regiment. Their personal possessions were taken from them, and they were marched into a nearby field. There, under the supervision of their captors' company commander, Fritz Knochlein, two machine-guns were turned upon them. Two men (Privates Pooley and O'Callagan), though severely wounded, managed to escape. The remainder died.

Similarly, on 17 December 1944, at the height of the German Ardennes offensive, 129 American troops were slaughtered in cold blood by members of the SS. Their column had been enfiladed by German tanks and armoured cars, and they were compelled to take cover in a ditch. Eventually, when that, too, came under heavy fire, they surrendered. They were marched a short way up the road and, like the Norfolks, assembled in a field. According to the official American report, 'A German soldier, either an officer or a non-commissioned officer in one of [the] vehicles stood up, drew his revolver, took deliberate aim and fired into the group. One of the Americans fell. This was repeated and another American soldier fell to the ground.

At about the same time, from two of the vehicles on the road, machine-gun fire was opened on the group of American prisoners in the field. All or most of them dropped to the ground and stayed there whilst the firing continued for two or three minutes. Most of the soldiers were hit by the fire. The German vehicles then moved off towards the south and were followed by more ... As they came opposite the field in which the American soldiers were lying, they also fired with small arms from the moving vehicles at the prostrate bodies in the field ... some German soldiers, evidently from the party who were on guard at the crossroads, then walked to the group of wounded American soldiers who were still lying in the field ... and shot with pistol or rifle, or clubbed with a rifle butt or another heavy object any American who still showed any sign of life.

In the autumn of 1944, thirty-two members of the 1st SAS (Special Air Service) Regiment were rounded up after a parachute drop into northern France. Two days later, they were executed. The Red Cross was informed that they had been 'killed in action'. There were many similar atrocities. In November 1944, the OKW (*Oberkommando der Wehrmacht*) issued the 'Bullet Decree' (*Kugelerlass*), which stipulated that all recaptured Soviet POWs, all Soviet officer prisoners who refused to work, any POW who had committed an offence for which the kommandant of his camp had insufficient disciplinary powers, and any captive in a special category (eg Commandos) – all these were to be handed over to the Gestapo for 'special treatment'. In other words, they were to be dispatched to a concentration camp and shot dead in the backs of their necks.

The majority of prisoners captured from the Western Allies, however, were allowed to survive. They were grouped according to type. *Oflag* signified a camp for army officers; and *Stalag*, for other ranks (though *Stalag Luft* III at Sagan was occupied almost exclusively by British and American air-crew officers – most of the other ranks engaged on flying duties being sent to Stalag VIIIB). *Marlags* were for naval personnel; *Milags* were for members of the Merchant Navy and *Ilags* were for civilian internees (not to be confused with concentration camps, which are beyond the scope of this book). The number of a camp (eg Oflag VIIB at Eichstatt) was derived from the military district in which it was situated.

No doubt the most celebrated of POW camps in Germany was Colditz (Oflag IVC) – partly, no doubt due to the popular TV series, but also because it housed the more glamorous members of the POW fraternity. The majority of its inhabitants were famous (or notorious, depending on your point of view) escapers, but there was also a select minority know as the *Prominente*. These were relatives of British VIPs who had been unfortunate enough to be captured. They were kept apart on the assumption that, one day, they might serve a useful purpose as hostages.

Colditz Castle dated back to 1014, when it had been a hunting-lodge for the kings of Saxony. Over the years, innumerable additions and modifications had been made to the buildings. In 1800, its role as a residence for the nobility came to an end. Since then, it had been employed as a civil prison, a lunatic asylum (to which, according to Reinhold Eggers, latterly its security officer, it bore some resemblance in its function as a POW camp), a concentration camp, a work camp for Hitler Youth, and, in 1939, a POW camp for Polish officers.

Under Article 48 of the Geneva Convention, it was in order to create what was known as a *Sonderlager* – a repository for difficult captives, in which more searches for escape projects were carried out, roll-calls were held more frequently, and generally stricter surveillance obtained. Colditz was just such a place. For exercise purposes, there was a 40sq yd court-yard. During the rare occasions when nothing much was happening, the inmates were allowed into the park outside, for brief periods only, and accompanied by a substantial escort of guards.

Nowadays, Colditz Castle lies in East Germany. It is partly used as a hospital and partly as a home for the aged. Nevertheless, its past is recalled by a museum down in the village, where relics of the escaper's art are on show. Its aspect remains gaunt and sinister – a better setting, perhaps, for a tale by the brothers Grimm than for a haven of peace, in which the deserving elderly can pass the winter of their years.

To the uninformed eye, the castle looks impenetrable, and so it may be. The point is, as Herr Eggers and his colleagues discovered, those Saxon princes had been concerned to keep people *out* of it. They had been less preoccupied with the notion that it might be a good idea to keep the inhabitants *in*. Nor, it seems, was there any limit to the ingenuity of the captives. One of the more talented eccentrics actually built a glider in an upstairs room, as a last, desperate, vehicle to freedom in the event of an emergency. According to Herr Eggers, 300 would-be escapers were caught in the act; 130 actually got out of the place, but were recaptured; and thirty (six Dutch, fourteen French, nine British and one Pole) were successful.

Reinhold Eggers, who was a schoolmaster in civilian life, regarded his flock rather as he may have approached 'a class of naughty boys'. But it is possible to read affection as well as rebuke into his writings. The penalty for minor infractions of the rules was five days in the cells. 'Later on,' he wrote in *Colditz, the German Story*, 'when the camp got crowded, people actually asked to go in the cells to "get away from it all". I told them we really could not arrange rest cures for them, there was a war on.' At Colditz, as in other camps, one certain way in which to achieve the not altogether disagreeable solitude of a few days in the cooler, was to refer to the Germans as 'Huns' in letters home. It was rather like a parking offence; the penalty was fixed and no trial was necessary.

A prisoner-of-war camp enforced a monastic existence upon young men who had no wish to devote themselves to a life of austerity and contem-plation. They were restless, often bored, sometimes depressed, and they wanted to go home. Attempting to escape was a means of absorbing energy with the tantalising possibility that it might succeed.

But such endeavours were not confined to the younger members of the POW community. Before the Badoglio armistice of 1943, there had been many attempts to break out from camps in Italy, of which only three were successful. Two of them were from PG12 – in peacetime, a residence known as the Villa Vincigliata.

The occupants of this building were nearly all senior officers. At 9.30 pm on 29 March 1943, two generals, an air vice-marshal and three brigadiers crawled out through a tunnel. The generals decided to walk to Switzerland: the others preferred to take their chances on the railway. At 10.30 on the following evening, two of the brigadiers (both New Zealanders) reached Como. Soon afterwards, they crawled through the barbed wire into Switzerland, at a point near Chiasso. The others were recaptured.

Colditz was the star repository for 'naughty boys'. Some other camps were borderline cases. When the Italians capitulated under Marshal Badoglio, the more restless POWs hastily removed themselves and set off, with varying degrees of success, to find the Allied lines. The majority did as they were told, and remained behind the wire – presently, to be removed to Germany in cattle trucks. When the tally of early arrivals was taken, it was discovered that several of these unwilling passengers had quietly stolen away during the journey. One method of making an exit had been to saw a hole through the wooden floor of the truck.

As a result of this, the procedure was tightened up. Members of the Waffen SS (the military arm of Himmler's élite corps of thugs) replaced the more amiable members of the Wehrmacht (German Army). The doors of the trucks were securely locked; no food or water was provided; and anyone caught attempting to escape was either shot or brutally manhandled.

One of the destinations was Stalag VIIA at Moosburg, a few miles from Munich. This, reputed to be the oldest of the German prison camps, was a vast cosmopolitan community. In one compound, you could observe the Yugoslav captives next door practising folk dancing; you could bargain across another stretch of wire with commercially minded Americans, who seemed to have an enviable talent for acquiring eggs; or you could receive visits from agile Russians, who regarded barbed wire as no more than a minor obstacle. One Russian, an oriental with a large patient face, was employed on re-wiring a compound. As he worked away, it was obvious to everyone (except, surprisingly, the German guards), that he was scrupulously removing the barbs as he went along.

Another transit camp for arrivals from Italy was Stalag VIIIB at Lamsdorf. From here and from Moosburg, a mixture of South African, British and New Zealand POWs was taken across Germany to Strasbourg where, for a while, they rested. Their residence was an underground fort. Its name depended upon which power had control of it. The French called it Fort Napoleon; and the Germans, Fort Bismarck.

Fort Bismarck was, for most people, a very depressing place. It lacked that first essential of tolerable prison–camp life, Red Cross parcels. The premises were damp; there was a severe shortage of fuel for the stoves; and the outside world was screened off by the wall on the far side of a moat (which did not have any water in it).

That summer had been unusually fine even by Italian standards. The sky was always blue. A POW could sit contentedly in the sun, occasionally enjoying a mug of wine. The wine came in two varieties, Marsala, which was drinkable, and 'vino' which, by any standards other than that of POW life, was not. However, under the circumstances, it was considered passable – even after one supply had removed the bottom from the zinc basin in which it had been stored. It was also capable of rendering purple more or less any piece of cloth that was immersed in it for long enough. In this capacity, would-be escapers found it useful.

In Italy, it had been possible to come to terms with captivity: at Fort Bismarck, it was very much harder. Some of the inhabitants discovered for the first time in their lives the morning gloom of the depressive; a feeling of not wanting to wake up, of not wishing to endure the day that lay ahead, of suddenly realising that there was nothing to enjoy.

Rather like Colditz, Fort Bismarck, with its huge moat, its steep walls and the tangle of wire around the perimeter, looked as if it were the ultimate in escape-proof lodgings. And, also like Colditz, it was not. There was one weak spot in its array of obstacles. It meant, admittedly, climbing an almost perpendicular wall and scrambling through the hazards on the far side, but it was not out of the question. Indeed, on one night, it was possible to discern a queue of prisoners in the moat, each waiting to make his exit.

Precisely how many escaped is not recorded. But, what with this, the departures on the train journeys from Italy, and the fact that, before very long, a great deal of the fort's woodwork had been removed to provide fuel for the hungry stoves, the inhabitants of Fort Bismarck had become a lot less than popular with the detaining power. When, a week or two later, they were moved on to a more permanent place of captivity (Oflag VA at Weinsberg), they had acquired a not wholly deserved reputation as desperadoes.

Weinsberg is a rather pretty little place, and there is no gainsaying that the view from the camp was pleasant. On the far side of the village, there was a hill with the ruins of an old castle on top. Round about there are fields and woodlands. In the booklet *Prisoner of War*, the author assured his readers that 'An airman's life in the Dulagluft [a transit camp for airmen near Frankfurt, where they were interrogated before dispatch to permanent camps] in the mountains has advantages; the men are provided with four good meals a day, can walk in the country, and go out to meals at inns.' Such remarks – written, presumably, by somebody who, in peacetime, composed blurbs for travel brochures – were no doubt reassuring. They may even have inspired such questions as that posed by one wife to her husband, 'Do you want your golf clubs sending on, if I can arrange it?' In fact, there was not a word of truth in it.

Under such circumstances, one can imagine that Oflag VA would have been a far from unpleasant location for an inland holiday resort. Unfortunately, attractive scenery is not enough to make a POW camp pleasant. The Gauleiter of the neighbouring town of Heilbronn was, presumably, a hard-line Nazi. At all events, he opposed all requests that an area outside the camp should be made available for recreation purposes. As a result, apart from an occasional walk on parole (which, again, the Gauleiter tried to forbid), the prisoners' only means of exercise was to amble up and down a pathetically small compound.

The camp had previously been occupied by French officers. It was a collection of wooden huts, each divided up into rooms that might have accommodated four people in reasonable comfort, but which were frequently crammed with twelve officers sleeping on two-tier wooden bunks. For the first couple of weeks, there were no Red Cross parcels, hardly any fuel for the camp kitchen, only one blanket per man, and no water for the showers.

Since the new arrivals were judged to be unruly, microphones were concealed in the rooms – and in the earth around the perimeter (to betray any tunnelling attempts). But this was the least of the strictures. Much worse was the rule that all POWs were to be locked in their huts after evening roll-call – at first at 5.15 pm and, later, at 4.30 pm.

On two occasions the SBO (Senior British Officer – in this case, a lieutenant-colonel in the South African Army) appealed to the protecting power. The representative from the Swiss Embassy agreed that the censorship of mail was carried out in a 'rather narrow-minded fashion'. He also agreed that the camp was overcrowded, and that facilities for recreation and exercise were 'almost non-existent'. After the first inspection, in October 1943, 100 officers were removed to another camp. It was supposed to relieve the pressure on space but, in fact, this accounted for less than one-tenth of the camp's population, and none but an unusually discerning eye would have noticed any difference.

In January 1944, the Swiss diplomat returned. This time, he reported that there were only two alternatives. Either all the officers should be moved to another camp or else the kommandant must be replaced by an officer with more understanding 'and a stronger sense of responsibility'.

The kommandant was replaced. There was a slight improvement in the conditions, though the overcrowding remained, and so did the rule about being locked indoors after the evening roll-call. The one exception was a night towards the end of the war, when bombers of the RAF blasted the heart out of Heilbronn. During the air raid, the inmates were allowed out into trenches that had been dug at one end of the compound.

Prisoners of war in Germany during World War II could be divided into roughly two categories, servicemen from the Western Allies' forces and Russians. The fate of captured Russians was only marginally better than that of concentration-camp victims. By contrast, and unlike their compatriots in Japanese hands, the treatment of POWs from NW Europe, Britain and America was tolerable, if austere. Writing many years later, when Americans in the custody of North Vietnam had experienced what must surely be the ultimate in suffering and humiliation, Rear Admiral James B. Stockdale of the United States Navy observed, 'The conditions under which American prisoners of war existed have changed radically since World War II. It is no longer a matter of going to a reasonably pleasant "Hogan's Heroes" prison camp, and sweating out the end of the war.'

Much, of course, depended upon the temperament of the individual. One officer who came to terms with the situation, and adapted himself to a life far removed from his normal existence, was an RAF officer named Stewart Stubbs.

Mr Stubbs was a solicitor in civilian life. He was shot down over Hanover on 8 October 1943, while flying as bomb-aimer in a Lancaster. Whilst there is obviously no such creature as a typical POW, he can, perhaps, serve as an example of one who 'sweated out the end of the war'.

At Dulag Luft near Frankfurt, he was interrogated. The technique, he remembers, was:

> rather cunning really – mainly along friendly lines. They sort of said, 'ah yes – if you let us have details of this, that or the other, we can get it through quickly, and your people at home will want to know you're safe. Just let us know the squadron number ...' All that sort of business. Eventually, the intelligence officer said, 'Thank you, Mr Stubbs', and I was about to leave the room. Suddenly, he called me back. 'Oh', he said, 'we need to check the name of your wife. Wasn't she a Miss....' And he mentioned her maiden name. The one mistake he made was to call her 'Joan' instead of Jean. That really rattled me; you know, I really wondered what I had left in my pockets that I ought not to have done.

Mr Stubb's pockets had contained nothing that should not have been in them. The episode suggests that some industrious branch of German

Intelligence had been going through the British Newspapers, cutting out any item to do with RAF officers. Mr Stubbs had been married six months previously, and the event had been announced in *The Times*. It might not have been of earth-shattering importance, but presumably this zealous newspaper clipper considered it worthy of a place in his files.

From Dulag, he was sent to Stalag Luft III at Sagan, where he settled down to a captive's life. 'People who just sat back and said "This is a bloody awful life" went round the bend', he said. 'But there was a lot to do, if one accepted that you were more or less in a small village community cut off from everywhere. I taught French – I suppose that was my main sort of activity.'

It was, indeed, amazing the number of talents that POWs displayed. For metal-workers, and there were many of them, the first essential was cans, which were amply available from Red Cross parcels. The classic was the Klim tin, a feature of Canadian parcels, which contained a superior sort of dried milk. In Italy, there was a craze for building small stoves from them: in one camp experts vied with one another to beat the record for the least time taken to boil a specified amount of water. In Germany, one officer prisoner manufactured a clock from empty cans. It kept very good time. The products of Messrs Klim were used to construct ventilating systems for tunnels, and they were invaluable for more humdrum purposes. Mr Stubbs recalls:

We were rather lucky in our room, because we had a chap who had been a craftwork teacher. His tin-bashing was excellent. He made coffee pots, tea pots, a coffee percolator, and all that sort of thing. He did a lot of soldering. Technically, it was illegal; but there was a lot of solder in a corned beef tin. He sweated it out, using a blow lamp made from a 1oz tobacco tin with a bit of pyjama cord as a wick and German margarine as the oil. The margarine also served as the flux.

In Italy, the mechanically minded built stoves which were used out of doors; and in Germany, the inhabitants of at least one camp produced somewhat rudimentary versions of immersion heaters. Basically, they amounted to metal plates (another Klim tin product), each nailed to a strip of wood with a terminal on top. Two – one positive and one negative – were required per container. A length of flex connected them with the electric light.

They were banned by the German authorities, not because they were dangerous, which they probably were, but because they consumed too much electricity.

Each camp had its own theatre. The tea chests in which Red Cross parcels were packed provided timber. Props were manufactured from all manner of odds and ends, though *papier mâché* was made from old newspapers and provided the raw material for a number of items. Costumes were either tailored by the prisoners (an activity viewed with some suspicion by the Germans, for it could equally well be applied to the making of escape outfits), or loaned by the Red Cross, which also provided the musical instruments for camp orchestras, scripts for the plays and so on. Each camp had its own theatre. In the Empire Theatre at Oflag VA, due to the lock-up rules, the shows had, perforce, to be matinées. Elsewhere, performances took place in the evenings.

Among the star performers were Rupert Davis, Roy Dotrice, Peter Butterworth (Sagan), Denholm Elliott (Stalag VIIIB: Mr Elliott has gone on record as comparing POW life to that of a public school – to the latter's disadvantage) and John Paul (Weinsberg). By February 1944, Oflag VIIB had become so well equipped with musical instruments, sheet music and sufficiently talented inhabitants, that the occupants were able to stage a 'Musical Festival' lasting two weeks. There were thirty-three performances – including a symphony concert, a light orchestral recital and a dance-band concert – with 120 singers and musicians taking part, and an audience of 6,660.

Each man filled up his time according to his taste. Some studied (by the end of October 1941, 2,975 requests had been received by the Red Cross for study courses, and 2,069 were preparing themselves for exams). Stalag Luft VI – where, at one period, more than 1,000 airmen were studying such subjects as the arts, science, medicine and law – became known as 'The Barbed Wire University'. Fifty-four lecturers were responsible for the tuition. Books were provided at all camps, though they were strictly censored to make sure that they contained no opinions running contrary to Nazi doctrine. Many people played cards, and there was a considerable demand for chess sets. These were difficult to procure: most of them were manufactured in central European countries that had been overrun by the Nazis (German prisoners in Russia also had a liking for chess: they spent long hours carving the pieces from wood gathered in the surrounding forests).

The Geneva Convention made no reference to captured animals and certainly not to birds. Nevertheless, a kestrel named Cressida shared her owner's life in captivity, and managed very well. She was the property of a private soldier named Gerald Summers. Some while after being captured in North Africa, Mr Summers changed places with an officer, who needed greater freedom of movement for an attempt to escape. It was no doubt a wise move. Having survived a battle, and endured an ill-fated attempt by Mr Summers to reach freedom in Italy, Cressida was now resigned to however many years remained to be spent in custody. The more settled life of an Oflag may have been to her advantage. Certainly, when she was repatriated she was in better physical condition than her human companions. Falcons are, after all, more adept than orthodox POWs at procuring food.

In another Army camp, there was a cherry tree. It was forbidden to pick the fruit, though one officer was able to enlist the help of a local bird. The feathered friend perched on a bough and picked a cherry. The officer chased it; and the bird squawked and dropped the precious morsel. The bird returned to the tree for another attempt, and the procedure was repeated.

Each camp had the POW equivalent of a house magazine, which was devoted to local gossip, reviews of shows in the theatre and satirical items. The real news was culled from the German newspapers, which were not to be relied upon for their accuracy in anything pertaining to the war, and from the radio.

Mr Stubbs recalls that, on being taken prisoner, he was briefly confined at a Luftwaffe station, where the personnel 'were not hostile; fairly neutral. They told us we'd really been rather stupid – the good old thing about "for you the war is over", and that sort of thing. But I think they attempted to talk us into believing that really the Germans weren't too bad after all, and that: "If you beat us, you'll be having to beat Communism next" ' – which was not entirely wide of the mark. Nevertheless, there was little or no attempt to brain-wash prisoners – if one discounts the transmission of 'Lord Haw-Haw's' broadcasts over the camp tannoy systems. 'Lord Haw-Haw', thus nicknamed on account of his accent, was a fascist named William Joyce, who was hanged for treason after the war.

Not surprisingly, however, the German censors were careful to confiscate anything that might be regarded as adverse propaganda. It is, then, remarkable how many camps had illicit radio sets and how, in some instances, the authorities, knowing that they were there, made no attempt to remove them.

Shortly before the end of the war, one camp security officer asked the SBO for the latest news, as broadcast by the BBC. He had, he explained, known of the radio set's existence for some time. 'We could overhear you discussing the reports,' he said, 'and we were grateful. It was the only way in which we could find out what was happening.'

Since anyone taking up residence in a POW camp was searched with reasonable thoroughness, there were obvious difficulties about importing a wireless along with the other baggage, which often amounted to no more than a couple of battered Red Cross parcel boxes packed with personal belongings. Nevertheless, a doctor from the 51st Highland Division brought a set into Oflag IXA at Rotenburg with comparatively little difficulty. It was concealed in a suitcase, which he hid behind the radiator in a lobby. When the questing fingers of the man on duty had completed their exploration of his other possessions – and, possibly, his person – he returned to the outer room, picked up the case, and carried it into the camp.

Later, when he was moved to another Oflag, he concealed it inside a medicine ball.

Elsewhere, components were bought from the more venal members of detaining soldiery (in return for such things as cigarettes or soap), or else smuggled in one or two at a time. There was no lack of talent to assemble them, and British radio parts had the edge on their German equivalents. They were smaller.

No doubt transmitters were also manufactured but there is no evidence to suggest that they were ever used. Among the more unusual members of the prison-camp population in Germany was a civilian scientist named Howard Cundell. Disguised as a flight-lieutenant, Mr Cundell was making a trip in an RAF aircraft to try out some new equipment, when the aeroplane was shot down over Brittany. After two weeks at large, he was captured.

Happily, his uniform convinced his captors that he was just another aviator who had wandered into sky above occupied territory. His real identity was never discovered, which was just as well. Had the German intelligence authorities realised that here was an above-average scoop, his interrogation would have been long and uncomfortable.

In some instances, it was easy to find out what the BBC had to say. Mr Lee recalls that one of his companions was employed by a smithy. 'There was a radio in his shop', he said. 'During the one day a week when we didn't work, we'd made a little tunnel under the wire at the back of the camp's toilets. This chap had made a key to the blacksmith's shop, and we used to get out of camp on Saturday nights, go down there, and listen to the news from England. They never found us out.'

Among the departments of the War Office to concern itself with prisoners of war was MI9, a collection of inventive individuals headed by Brigadier Norman Crockatt. MI9 was concerned with escape and evasion. Ideally, of course, a member of the fighting forces, no matter how desperate his plight, would not be captured. To assist him in this respect, all manner of ingenious little devices were produced. There were collar studs that concealed compasses, silk scarves which were really maps, and so on. Air-crew members were issued with escape packs containing a compass, a fishing line, such items of nourishment as malted milk tablets, and even benzedrine to revive them when their energy (and, one must suppose, their determination) began to flag.

MI9 devised a code which prisoners could use in their letters home and thus, if indirectly, correspond with the department. Among its uses was that of conveying information that might be useful to Allied intelligence. POWs in camps situated near railway lines were able to report the movements of troop trains: near the camp at Sagan there was an airfield where the Me 262 was under test. This was the first of the jet fighters, faster and more lethal than the RAF Meteor, and capable of large-scale production. If Hitler had been more enthusiastic about it, it might have enabled the Luftwaffe to regain control of the sky. Instead, although 1,433 had been manufactured by the end of the war in Europe, only one hundred were used on operations.

The letter from Stalag Luft III which reported the existence of this revolutionary aeroplane was unable to provide any details. Nevertheless, it revealed that a new generation of aircraft was being produced in Germany.

Letters took time to travel between Germany and Britain. MI9 required some rather quicker means of communicating with its captive clientele, and radio provided it. The messages were transmitted in code at set times and on specified wavelengths. One of the more popular features of the Forces Programme (the ancestor of Radio 2) were short talks by the so-called Radio Padre (actually Dr R. Selby Wright, who later became Moderator of the Church of Scotland). There were, it was estimated, 7 million listeners to the broadcasts, among them a number of POWs.

When Dr Wright began his remarks with the words 'Good evening, Forces', it meant that, somewhere in the text, a message was concealed. The minister never knew what it was but, when it had been taken down in shorthand and de-coded, it made sense to the prisoners.

In the event of an extreme emergency – such as an order from Hitler that all POWs must be put to death – all the BBC channels were to be used and, since there would be very little time in which to decipher the warning, it would be broadcast in clear. Happily, the need for it never arose, nor did the Germans ever succeed in cracking the code used for less-desperate matters.

Escaping was a matter of temperament. The British and French were said to have a greater aptitude for such exploits than the Germans and Russians, who were more inclined to do as they were told. It was, said the War Office, the duty of every POW to attempt to get away. There were no doubt many good reasons for this. A restive captive population required more guards than a more supine community and, consequently, it tied up troops that would have been better employed fighting.

Of the escapers who managed to reach home, some afterwards distinguished themselves; others were less able to adjust to their old lives as fighting men. In 1942, a survey made by Army psychiatrists among personnel who had either escaped or been repatriated, showed that many found it difficult to rehabilitate themselves. Those who returned to duty, for example, suffered a high rate of breakdowns. Even the discipline of regular soldiers, with previous records of good service, revealed cracks. They displayed a need for sympathetic treatment, and 'an understanding of their special requirements'.

A study of prison-camp inmates might have divided them into three groups: the compulsive escapers, who either got away or else ended up in *Sonderlagers* such as Colditz; those who toyed with the idea, but did little more than assist other people's efforts; and those who decided not to make any attempt at all.

One or two other ranks and enlisted men managed to get away, though, as in World War I, escaping tended to be regarded as a game for officers. For example, Mr Lee was able to make his regular weekly journeys to the radio set in the blacksmith's shop, and yet he and his friends always returned to camp.

'We had thought of escaping,' he said, 'but you had to have so many documents. Officers and airmen were in a far better position to escape; they'd had more training with maps and compasses. And, also, you had to speak very fluent German. Some of our lot did try, but they were always brought back.' Mr Stubbs recalled that:

> I didn't really consider it partly because I thought that, as a live prisoner, I was using up their supplies, and had to be looked after by them. As a dead prisoner, I was no trouble to anyone. I felt that, unless you had a really good chance of getting home and doing something useful, you might tie up half-a-dozen or so people who were looking for you; but, apart from that, there was not much achievement in it. In any case, I'm a natural coward!

It would require a book to itself (and there have been several) to record the various exits, successful and unsuccessful, made by Allied POWs in Germany. Few of them reached home. According to one estimate, only one out of every thirty-five tunnelling attempts advanced the cause of their builders' freedom. But this was just one of many techniques used. Some tried to make their getaways concealed in baskets of laundry; some masqueraded as Germans; and some made a grab at the wire – and, not infrequently, also made a literally fatal mistake. Some even tried to escape by stealing aircraft.

British POWs in Germany shortly after the World War I Armistice (*Imperial War Museum*)

(*Left*) POWs in Japanese hands returning to camp with a consignment of rice (*From the collection of Harold Payne*); (*below*) POWs in Japanese hands were victims of disease, starvation and extreme brutality (*From the collection of Harold Payne*)

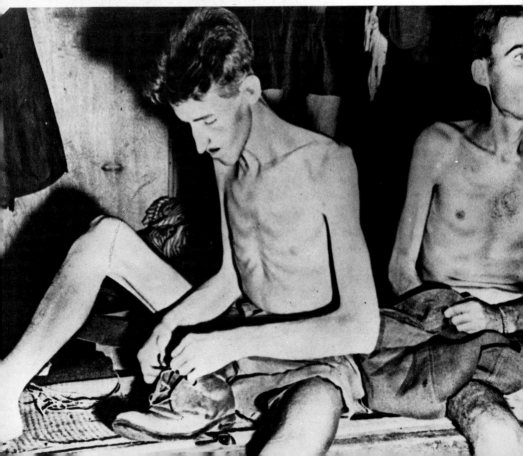

A Norwegian pilot succeeded during the 1940 invasion of his country, when he helped himself to a German floatplane. An American pilot, Lieutenant Kelly of the US Army Airforce, managed to insert himself in the cockpit of a Focke-Wulf 190, but he was baffled by the instrument panel and unable to start the engine. Lieutenant Ted Strever of the South African Air Force was more successful, but he appropriated the aircraft in flight.

Mr Strever was shot down over the Mediterranean in April 1942. He and his crew were picked up by an Italian destroyer, which took them to Greece. At Piraeus, they were transferred to a flying boat, en route for a POW camp in Italy. At some point on the journey, they managed to overpower the guard, hijack the machine and compel the pilot to land at Malta.

Other ranks employed in working parties occasionally changed places with officers, the deal being that the latter would escape (or try to) within a stipulated period. Mr Lee, who was interned for a while in one of the complexity of forts and camps that made up Stalag XX at Thorn in Poland, was put to work in the winter of 1940, clearing away snow from the nearby aerodrome. He recalled:

> There was an officers' camp nearby and some of our chaps used to go there to do the cleaning. Two of the officers made arrangements to swap with two of our men. They came back to our camp, and joined this working party on the aerodrome. They had the idea to get an aircraft going and fly home.
>
> Unfortunately, the plane they chose was cold, and wouldn't start. The Germans in the control tower saw them, and caught them. We were kept on parade all day – until seven o'clock that night. There were roll-calls and things like that. I don't know what happened to the officers, but they must have been punished.

The three classic break-outs are popularly known (from the titles of books and films that have re-enacted them) as *Albert RN*, *The Wooden Horse* and *The Great Escape*. The scene of the first was Marlag und Milag Nord near Hamburg (a camp for naval and merchant-service personnel). Lieutenant D. P. James decided that there were so many different uniforms to be seen on the streets of Germany, that no disguise was necessary. If he were wearing a tolerably smart British naval officer's rig, but carrying an imitation Bulgarian identity card, he would not necessarily be conspicuous.

His reasoning was probably correct. During a journey by train across Germany, a small party of British Army officers (one of them a Gordon Highlander wearing a kilt) was permitted by its guards to take cover in an air-raid shelter at Regensburg. Despite the fact that, among the other occupants, there was a high official of the Nazi party – probably the local Gauleiter, his uniform was worthy of such a position – they were unremarked. Indeed, when they tried to return to the train, they were caught up in a stream of German troops on the far side of the platform, and nearly ended up on the Russian front!

Lieutenant James proposed to leave his place of captivity when a party was marched to the showers, which were on the far side of the wire. To satisfy the statistics (it was obvious that, if the guard counted X number of officers leaving the compound, he would expect to find the same number returning), a dummy, not unlike a ventriloquist's doll, was built and finally assembled in the lavatory. It (though it was so lifelike, it is tempting to use the pronoun *he*) was named Albert.

The ruse worked. James made his escape: Albert deputised for him on the return trip. On the first try, he was recaptured at Stettin. But the secret of Albert was preserved for long enough for him to make a second attempt. On this occasion, he reached Stockholm after a passage in a Finnish vessel from Danzig.

As at Oflag VA, the ground around the perimeter of prison camps tended to be littered with microphones. The object of the *Wooden Horse* was to confuse them. The escape took place at Stalag Luft III. While gymnasts exercised themselves over a home-made vaulting horse, others were beavering away below ground making a tunnel. Three officers (Michael Codner, Oliver Philpot DFC, and Eric Williams, who was later to write the deservedly famous book about it) got away, and all of them eventually returned to England.

Stalag Luft III was also the scene of the Great Escape, which was at once a triumph and a tragedy. Master-minded by an RAF officer always referred to as 'Big X' (a pilot who had commanded the RAF's top-scoring squadron until, one day during the evacuation of the BEF in 1940, he was shot down over Dunkirk), there were originally three tunnels. One was code-named 'Tom', another 'Dick' and the third 'Harry'. Eventually only 'Harry' was used. It was proposed to dispatch 200 officers, whose names had been selected by ballot, through it.

Quite apart from the sheer daring of the scheme, the civil engineering involved was amazing. 'Harry' set a couple of world records: with a length of 350ft, it was the longest tunnel that had ever been dug by POWs, and, with a depth of 30ft to evade the sound detectors, it was also the deepest.

At 10.15 pm on 24 March 1944, after work that had occupied 500 men in one way or another for fifteen months, the exit was opened. Eighty RAF officers (including Big X) wriggled their way towards freedom. Only three of them reached home. The majority of those who were recaptured (again including Big X) were shot by the Gestapo. It was one of the appalling scandals of the war.

In the words of a former SS officer who was interrogated after the war, 'The shooting took place on the express orders of the former Führer Adolf Hitler.' Even Ernst Kaltenbrunner, the hard-drinking head of Reich security, is said to have referred to it as 'a dirty affair', and one of Keitel's aides, General Graevenitz, pointed out that 'Escape isn't a dishonourable offence'.

Nevertheless, fifty men were shot, without trial, on the lame excuse (as conveyed in a note to Switzerland) that so many escapers at large in the land represented 'a danger to public security in Germany'.

The dead men were cremated, and the urns containing their ashes were sent back to the camp, where the kommandant (soon to be relieved of his position) was given the unenviable task of informing the SBO. Afterwards, the occupants of Stalag Luft III wore black patches, each cut in the shape of a diamond, on their sleeves.

According to the Geneva Convention, there could be no mass punishments, and certainly no penalties involving the withdrawal of Red Cross parcels. Both rules were broken in August 1942, after the raid by Commandos and Canadian forces at Dieppe and that of a much smaller Commando operation on Sark. During the former, there were complaints about the ill-treatment of German prisoners; and in the latter, four German soldiers, who had been snatched from their beds in an hotel, were killed while attempting to break free.

The effects on POWs of these two raids were confined to Canadian personnel taken at Dieppe (many of whom were lodged at Stalag VIIIB) and to the RAF NCOs and Warrant Officers who were interned in this camp. The men were denied Red Cross parcels and exercise facilities, and their hands were bound. Don Bruce was among those involved. He said:

Apparently, they [the Dieppe raiders] tied up the prisoners to take them back – and then I don't know what happened: it all went wrong. They shot them, and they were found with their hands tied. As a reprisal, the Germans said 'Your Commandos do this sort of thing, so we're going to tie *you* up.' It started on 11 October 1942, when we had our hands bound from 8 am until 11 am and then from noon until 9 pm. After a bit, the German MO said that this was dangerous so far as our health was concerned; it was restricting the circulation. So then they brought in Gestapo handcuffs, but they put 18in of chain in between. It was a bit of a farce, because you could get a nail file and take them off. This went on for about six months, I think. You know the Germans: when they did anything unpleasant like that, they immediately stopped all Red Cross food.

Inevitably, the British and Canadian authorities retaliated by manacling German prisoners and, no less inevitably, the Germans counter-retaliated by trebling the number subjected to this form of ill-treatment in their camps. There had been a move to spread the ordeal to the inmates of Colditz. But it was obvious that the ingenious inhabitants would find it easy enough to remove the manacles and they might find the metal useful for an escape scheme. Consequently, the idea was dropped.

The German guards at the camps concerned were described as being, 'quite sympathetic and a little disgusted about it all'.

When the Russians were within striking distance of Germany, and as the other Allies crossed the Rhine in the west, prisoners of war were moved away from the advancing armies. This was not for their safety but because they represented the Third Reich's rapidly waning store of human capital. Some marched, and these journeys were both hard and dangerous.

On 14 April 1945, the officers and other ranks who had been interned in a former cavalry barracks at Eichstatt (Oflag VIIB) set off on the road for Stalag VIIA at Moosburg. When they were a few hundred yards from the camp, pilots of a squadron of Allied aircraft mistook them for the enemy. Seven of the POWs were killed and forty-six were wounded (four of them seriously). The column returned to Eichstatt and, afterwards, marched only by night.

POWs converging on Moosburg from Oflag VA were more fortunate. They travelled by train and, to avoid any case of mistaken identity by marauding aircraft, they were allowed to paint the letters POW and large Union Jacks on the tops of the cattle trucks. There were no incidents on the journey.

By VE-Day (8 May 1945) nearly all the British POWs in Germany were on their various ways home. According to the Army psychiatrists, 'Most of the returned prisoners will be suffering from minor mental abnormality.' They would, the doctors warned, 'find difficulties in resocialisation and reintegration in the community.' Since, initially, they would be swept along by the euphoria of freedom, the effects would not become evident for the first three months. After that, there might be problems.

Naturally much depended upon the individual. Mr Stubbs, thinking back into his past, recalled:

> I didn't find it too difficult to adapt to freedom. I suppose we were restless for a time, and it was difficult to settle down, but I think you soon got over that. I think the experience of being a POW did me a lot of good, for I believe that many things fell into place. I certainly was a far better solicitor after the

war than I was before it. I think it gave you a far better understanding of people. You began to accept the fact that they could make mistakes with the best motives in the world.

Even nowadays, Mr Bruce hates 'watching those prisoner of war things on the box. I don't think it is because they're farcical; I just get a certain feeling of helplessness such as we used to experience, and it all comes back to me.' As for Mr Lee, 'I had pneumonia twice when I was a prisoner. When I came out of the Army and settled down at home, I had it again, and it left me with a bit of asthma. No – I don't have any bitterness towards the Germans. There were one or two guards I didn't like, and I'd have liked to kill. But that's all.'

He was, perhaps, more tolerant than an NCO of Don Bruce's acquaintance, but then, he had less provocation. This young man was in charge of a working party. Nearby, Jews from the Auschwitz concentration camp were engaged in some task or other. At some point, the SS guard beat up one of the Jews. As Mr Bruce recalls, 'This NCO of ours was a boxer who came from Poplar. He was a really tough little nut, and he just couldn't stand it. He belted this chap straight on the chin, and he went out like a light. He was threatened afterwards, but he wasn't shot.' Mr Bruce's own views are that, 'I don't like the Germans, and I can't say I liked POW life one bit.' But, with memories of Auschwitz internees and the months of wearing manacles, he has good reason for resentment.

9

BRITAIN IS AN ISLAND

On 2 July 1940, Günther Prien, captain of the German submarine U-47, watched through his periscope as a two-funnelled liner steamed into close-up. Prien was one of the aces: he had already won fame throughout Germany for his sinking of the British battleship, HMS *Royal Oak*, as she lay at her moorings in Scapa Flow. Now he was close to some sort of record for destruction of British shipping. He gave the command to fire.

The ship, the Blue Star Line's *Arandora Star*, 15,000 tons gross, was struck by the torpedo at a point somewhere beneath her forward funnel. Wearily, she heeled over on to her side. Then she died quickly, sinking before there was time to launch more than one or two lifeboats.

Prien and his crew were jubilant. The dispatch of the *Arandora Star* had elevated U-47 to the top of the league. They might have been less pleased, if they had realised that the well-aimed torpedo had just killed over a thousand German and Italian civilian detainees. The prisoners were on their way to camps in Canada.

As everyone knew, conditions in Canada were better than they were in Britain. Food was plentiful, and there were no air raids. The trouble was that you had to get there. As the fate of the *Arandora Star* had shown, the journey was dangerous.

The disastrous campaigns in Norway and France during 1940 had brought a spate of British prisoners of war into German hands. German POWs took longer to reach the UK in any quantity though, later on, there were more than sufficient to keep the authorities busy. Strangely, perhaps, none of them managed to escape. Throughout the war, only one German POW made it back to the Fatherland. And he, Freiherr von Werra, somewhat improbably succeeded during a train journey in Canada. He had already tried it in England – and failed.

Usually, the reason given for this lack of success was the fact that Britain is surrounded by sea. Actually, this does not stand up to serious study. Provided he had forged documents and a sufficiently good command of English (such as anyone of reasonable intelligence could pick up within a year), a POW had only to break out of camp and reach a port such as Liverpool, where there were frequent steamship services to the Republic of Ireland. In many ways, the prospect was easier than that facing a captive Englishman in Germany.

A more probable explanation is the German love of law and order. It certainly should not imply any lack of spirit. German POWs in Russia, where conditions were atrocious, managed to adapt themselves to their circumstances. For want of writing paper, they used birch bark stripped from trees; and for want of cigarette papers, they tore off scraps of *Izvestia* or *Pravda*. They even managed to play football, using balls manufactured from the discarded tyres of old Russian lorries.

The instructions to soldiers guarding POW camps in Britain were that the captives should be treated 'fairly but firmly. No member of the staff will be permitted to adopt an aggresive or bullying attitude towards them'. The commandant of a camp was allowed to punish offenders with periods of detention not exceeding twenty-eight days, or by confinement to quarters for not more than fourteen days. Any crime that, under English law, would be tried by a criminal court, was a matter for court martial. According to the regulations, the court must be made up of no fewer than five members. The scale of penalties ranged from the death sentence to detention for anything up to (but not exceeding) two years.

Discipline at the camps was, in fact, exercised on two levels. The British guards, obviously, were the ultimate authority; but, within most of these establishments, the prisoners had their own codes of conduct. As one of them (Fritz Wentzel) put it, 'We all had to live together, and so each of us had the right to expect a certain degree of order and consideration from the others. If we could all do just as we liked, life would become intolerable. In a POW camp, the need for order is so great, that it even justifies a certain degree of compulsion. By that, I don't mean spineless submission.'

So far as food and clothing were concerned, the British seem to have more regard for the terms of the Geneva Convention than the German authorities. There was, for example, no need for Red Cross parcels. Strangely enough – or, perhaps, because their systems became adapted to a more frugal diet – the reactions of prisoners to food were in inverse ratio to the quantity of rations supplied.

The scale laid down initially was 3,300 calories a day – higher than that provided for British civilians, but lower than that of the armed forces. At the end of the war, due to the world food shortage, this had to be reduced to 2,800 for men employed on working parties (certainly a light diet for a labourer) and 2,000 for non-working personnel such as officers.

However, when, on return to Germany, the POWs were questioned by a Professor Mitscherlich at a reception camp in Munster, sixty-seven per cent declared that the food had been bad to begin with but that later on, it improved; forty-eight per cent said that, during their early days in captivity, they suffered continually from hunger; and seventy-six per cent told the professor that, at the end of their residence in Britain, they were never hungry.

Possibly these observations can be explained, at any rate, to some extent, by the fact that the POWs at most camps cultivated vegetable gardens, and some of them even raised domestic animals.

Upon coming into captivity, the prisoners were graded according to their beliefs. 'Black' indicated convinced Nazis, who might be expected to make trouble. 'Grey' was applied to men of more moderate views who, nonetheless, were apt to confuse National Socialism with patriotism; and 'white' suggested somebody who was unlikely to cause anyone undue concern and who might, indeed, be anti-Nazi. So far as possible, they were grouped – in compounds, if not in camps – according to their gradings.

Camp 18, at Featherstone Park, near Haltwhistle in Northumberland, for example, was reckoned to be a tough camp. Americans who visited it used to refer to it as 'Death Valley'. For much of the time, it was used exclusively for officers. The 'black' compound housed members of the Waffen SS, U-boat officers and paratroops. The inhabitants were quartered in Nissen huts. For exercise, they were taken on route marches in the area of Hadrian's Wall.

Initially, there was a lot of hatred in Camp 18. If, for instance, the British officer who supervised roll-call offered a cigarette to the Senior German Officer, the latter felt bound to refuse it. If he accepted, he would be branded by his subordinates as a semi-traitor.

A camp's nature was often determined by the attitude of the British commandant. The inmates of Camp 18 complained to the Red Cross, and a delegate was assigned to investigate. His report suggested that the POWs had a case that merited sympathetic treatment. The commandant was replaced by a lieutenant-colonel named Vickers.

Colonel Vickers was an officer who had risen from the ranks in World War I. He had also, as it happened, been a POW in German hands. As soon as he had moved in, he assembled the prisoners. 'Gentlemen,' he said, 'in the 1st World War, I was in a German prisoner of war camp, and I was treated as a gentleman. I will therefore treat you in the same way.' Provided they would give their word not to escape, he promised to look after them as well as circumstances allowed.

One of his first actions was to advise that soldiers from General Anders's Polish Army in exile were not necessary as reinforcements for the British guards. They were withdrawn and restrictions generally were eased. Morale at Camp 18 improved almost at once and 'Death Valley' lost its sinister reputation.

Camp 186 at Llanmartin near Newport in South Wales was also reserved for officers. Although it had a reputation for less severity than Camp 18, its need for such strictures may have been greater. A party of German officers escaped from the camp by means of a tunnel. They were, however, all recaptured.

The interrogation of a German POW in Britain depended upon the value of the information he was likely to yield. Early in the war, the Combined Services Detailed Interrogation centre was set up. Initially, it worked inside the Tower of London. Later, it moved to a camp at Cockfosters and, later still, to Beaconsfield in Buckinghamshire.

Physical force was never used, but the methods were, nonetheless, effective. Basically, three techniques were employed. The first, and arguably the best, was direct interrogation. If a prisoner showed any signs of being co-operative, he was offered inducements, such as better treatment, as a reward for information. It took between two and nine days to achieve results. In many cases, two officers were employed; one adopted a friendly approach ('we don't want any harm to come to you – have another cigarette?'), the other was very much harsher. The prisoner never quite knew where he stood, and this was apt to disorientate him. The Germans used a similar system.

The interrogators were well briefed. Part of the establishment was occupied by a library crammed with the results of industrious delving by intelligence officers. There were reports from agents, and decoded signals that had been picked up on the radio. The probability was that a good deal was known about the POW's unit and, quite possibly, about the man himself. There was also data on technical matters, which was sometimes used to suggest that the investigating officer knew more about the subject under discussion than, in fact, he did.

All the rooms were equipped with concealed microphones. POWs were kept apart until after their first interrogation, then they were carefully paired off. The idea, presumably, was that they believed the worst of the ordeal to be over, and that they could talk freely with each other. According to Volume 1 of *British Intelligence in the Second World War* (HMSO), 'It proved to be of considerable value, not only for the new intelligence it produced but also in suggesting new lines for further interrogations.' The snag was that 'it allowed of no stage management'.

To overcome this shortcoming, a system of stool-pigeons was devised. These men were carefully briefed about the characters they were supposed to represent and, also, about the prisoners themselves and the topics on which they were likely to be well informed.

Most of these men were recruited from the ranks of refugees who had fled Germany after Hitler came to power. At the end of 1940, four were employed. By the end of the war, forty-nine had been used. Latterly, certain POWs agreed to assist in the work. The strain was considerable – far greater than that endured by any actor playing a part – and there were some instances in which they could not be put to work. The danger of discovery would be too great.

Such methods yielded a mine of valuable information. German Luftwaffe officers captured in Norway rendered up precious gems of knowledge about their service's tactics; and submariners had details of the U-boat order of battle squeezed out of them. However, on one occasion at least, the intelligence was misleading. The U-boat crews were under the impression that there had been delays in the construction of their vessels; that, indeed, the strength of Admiral Dönitz's marauding 'wolfpacks' was less than, in fact, it was.

Later in the war, the famous ('infamous' to anyone who had been interrogated there) London Cage was set up in a large house in Kensington Palace Gardens. It had doubtless once been the home of a very wealthy man, for the street was known as 'Millionaires' Row'. But the traces of affluence had long disappeared. The paint was flaking from the walls, the place appeared seedy and dark. This was not entirely the result of neglect: the commandant, Lieutenant-Colonel A. P. Scotland, may have deliberately contrived it. It suggested a kind of hopelessness.

The methods of interrogation were similar to those employed by the Combined Services Interrogation Centre in its previous habitats. Colonel Scotland had served a long spell of solitary confinement in a prisoner of war camp run by the Germans in South West Africa during World War I. He was clearly aware of the depths to which a human being could fall, though he was humane after his fashion. The rule that no prisoner should be physically touched remained, and no 'truth drugs' were used.

Probably, the most feared of the interrogators was a major, who was known by his victims as 'the poison-dwarf'. According to one of his colleagues, 'He had great professional pride. He would rather break his heart and his larynx than fail to break his man.' Speaking of the staff of the London Cage in general, a German U-boat commander said, 'Their tone was very harsh and even brutal. I shouldn't have liked an extended cure at their hands.'

Among the achievements of the interrogators was a forewarning of Hitler's secret weapons, the V1 and V2 rockets. Two Afrika Korps generals, Thoma and Cruewell, were captured in March 1943, when Rommel's forces were finally squeezed to death. They met by appointment (Colonel Scotland's, not theirs) at the house in Kensington Palace Gardens. An eavesdropper put down his paperback book, adjusted his earphones, and settled down to listen.

Once they had exchanged the customary greetings, one of them was overheard to remark that he was surprised to find London in such good shape. He had expected it to be more or less rased to the ground. His companion asked him why. The general then went on to talk about an unmanned machine of fearful potential that he had seen under test at some highly secret firing range in Germany.

In November 1939, a mysterious document that became known as the 'Oslo Report' was delivered to the British Naval Attaché in Norway. Its authorship has never been discovered, but it contained a wealth of technical information that the Allied intelligence authorities would have done well to have taken more seriously. Among it was a reference to remote-controlled gliders, 'small aircraft of some 3m wing-span and 3m length which carry a large explosive charge'. They were, apparently, being tried out at Peenemünde on the shores of the Baltic.

Since they did not have engines (the idea was to launch them from aircraft flying at considerable heights), they were only the beginning of a research programme that ultimately produced the 'V' rockets. Nevertheless, the information might have been treated with less scepticism. It was only after the conversation between Generals Thoma and Cruewell, the MI6 applied itself to a more thorough investigation of the matter. As General Ismay noted in a memorandum to Winston Churchill, their talk indicated 'a foundation of fact even if the details are inaccurate'.

A liner named the *Gripsholm*, owned by the Swedish-America Line, spent much of the war plodding backwards and forwards across the North Sea, repatriating protected personnel and seriously ill or wounded POWs from Germany, and performing a similar task for German personnel in Britain. Among her passengers in May 1944, was another senior officer of the Afrika Korps, General Cramer, who had been interned in Camp 186 at Llanmartin. General Cramer had not been in the best of health, and it was decided to send him home. His first call on his journey back to Germany was at the London Cage. Here it was decided that he might unwittingly perform a small service on behalf of the Allies.

One of the preludes to D-Day, when Allied troops landed on the beaches of Normandy, was an operation named Fortitude. It was an exercise in deception, intended to convince Hitler and his subordinates that the invasion would take place across the Dover Strait, and that the soldiers would come ashore in the region of Calais. Cramer, it was decided, could support the carefully contrived evidence with a first-hand account of preparations.

He was due to join the *Gripsholm* at Southampton. Since the general had no knowledge of the English landscape, he was driven to the port along a devious route that wound through southern and a fraction of south-west England. As he looked out of the car's windows, he saw ample evidence of tanks, troops, guns and all the other ingredients that were being assembled for the invasion. He was impressed. When he asked his escort for details of the journey, the names of places in eastern and south-eastern England were mentioned. The word 'Calais' was also allowed to slip into the conversation from time to time.

Cramer saw no reason to doubt the authenticity of this highly inaccurate geography lesson. When he reached Berlin on 23 May, he made haste to report his experiences to the German Army's chief-of-staff. After the war, Goëring remembered that, 'One of our generals had been captured by the British and subsequently returned to us by exchange. Before his release, he was thoroughly indoctrinated by [the British] and shown the vast stores of *matériel* and equipment along the southern coast of England. He came back to us with all those impressions [and] ... a defeatist attitude.'

Since Hitler had already made up his mind that the invasion would be launched from ports in the south-east, General Cramer had no difficulty in being believed.

Now and then, the system back-fired. German prisoners of war whose attitude was thought to be co-operative, and who might talk freely without very much persuasion, were accommodated in greater comfort at a camp near Ascot racecourse. Some of them, it was thought, might even be coaxed into broadcasting to their fellow countrymen.

One of the visitors to Ascot was Peter Scott, who was writing the official history of Motor Torpedo Boat operations. Among the detainees was an E-boat (*Schnellboote*, a German equivalent of the MTB) officer named Charlie Mueller. Mueller was prepared to discuss the project from a German point of view. During the course of the conversation, British convoys up and down the east coast of England were mentioned. Scott expressed his surprise that large formations of E-boats, operating out of North Sea ports, had not attacked them. Mueller agreed that yes, indeed, it did appear to have been an oversight.

Shortly afterwards, Mueller was suddenly repatriated as part of an exchange of prisoners. The intelligence people were not told of it, nor that any such thing had ever been envisaged. On his return to Germany, he must have reported those talks at Ascot in some detail. At any rate, and it cannot have been a coincidence, attacks on merchant shipping by packs of E-boats were introduced by the German Admiralty.

British guards, on the whole, treated German POWs as their instructions required, 'firmly but fairly'. Within the camps, especially inside the 'black' compounds, the standards imposed by the prisoners themselves were sometimes far more brutal. Three months after the German super-battleship *Bismarck* had been sunk in May 1941, a submarine designated U-570 surfaced in the North Atlantic somewhere to the south of Iceland. By sheer coincidence, a Hudson bomber of the RAF's Coastal Command happened to be overhead. The Hudson dived and dropped a stick of bombs, and U-570's commanding officer, Kapitanleutnant Rahmlow, surrendered. The boat was eventually taken to Barrow-in-Furness, where, after modifications, she became HM Submarine *Graph*.

Rahmlow was separated from the rest of his crew, which was just as well for his health and safety. The others were interned in a camp at Grisedale, Westmorland.

According to Henry Faulk, who was concerned with the detention of German prisoners: 'There was never, at any time, a question on which [they] all agreed in the same way just because they were all POWs.' No two camps were alike, and the ages and family commitments of the captives affected their outlook. The older prisoners were more worried about what was happening at home, and, consequently, they suffered more. The younger men often despised them on the grounds that, being less depressed, they were therefore stronger characters than their melancholy elders.

At Grisedale, the POWs were tough and intolerant, and deeply infected with the Nazi doctrine. The Führer had insisted that naval vessels in danger of falling into enemy hands must be scuttled by their own men. The crew of U-570 had failed to do this.

Admittedly, Rahmlow's surrender had presented the Royal Navy with a free submarine; but the U-110, which was taken, so to speak, alive in May 1941, had been a much more serious loss. Despite the fact that she was commanded by Kapitanleutnant Fritz Lemp, one of U-boat Command's most famous submariners (he had torpedoed the liner *Athenia* shortly after the outbreak of war), the vessel had been allowed to fall into the Navy's hands after a depth-charge attack. On board, the radio equipment was intact, and so was the Enigma machine (complete with operating instructions) used to scramble and unscramble signals. Thereafter, the

Allies were able to decipher all W/T signals transmitted by the German navy, and by the *Abwehr* (German military intelligence).

But this was a matter of no importance to the prisoners at Grisedale who, in any case, probably did not know about the significance of U-110. Their only concern was that the crew of U-570 had disobeyed one of Hitler's orders and that somebody would have to be punished for it. Since Rahmlow was not available, there were three possible scapegoats: the officer of the watch at the time, the chief engineer, and the third officer, an Oberleutnant named Bergmann.

A prisoner of war *Ehrenrat* (Council of Honour) was convened; and the three men were put on trial. The first two of the accused were exonerated, Bergmann was convicted.

From that moment, the unfortunate Oberleutnant was ostracised by all members of the camp. Eventually, the strain was so great and he became so afraid of the eventual outcome, that he asked permission to commit suicide. This, he suggested, might redeem his honour.

Permission was refused. If he were to regain his self-respect, and that of his fellow prisoners, he must break out of the camp, walk to Barrow-in-Furness (which was not all that far away), and sink the submarine as she lay in dock.

Bergmann agreed. He managed to get through the wire. On the far side, however, he was challenged by a member of the Home Guard. Under more normal circumstances, he would probably have given himself up; but the thought of being taken back to Grisedale was too grim to be considered. He broke into a run. The Home Guard called to him again; and, when there was no reply, he fired. He had intended to hit Bergmann in the leg, but his aim was too high and the bullet went through his chest. The young submariner died immediately.

Camp 23 at Le Marchant Barracks, Devizes, Wiltshire, had originally been a reception centre. New arrivals into captivity were taken there, de-loused, given medical inspections by German doctors, and designated according to their political categories ('white', 'grey' and 'black'). Each was issued with a mauve battle-dress with diamond markings on it, and then dispatched to a permanent camp. Life at Devizes was nothing if not efficient. It was, somebody estimated, possible to process 2,000 POWs in one day.

By the winter of 1944, however, Camp 23 had a resident population, most of whom were unyielding Nazis who believed that, despite the many reverses, Germany would eventually win the war. An escape committee was formed and a mass break-out planned.

Had it worked, the scale of the operation would have been without precedent. This was no matter of a man sneaking away like a thief in the night. The inmates of Camp 23 intended to form a mobile column complete with transport; fight their way in the direction of Sheffield, where the prisoners in another camp would follow their example; and then thrust across the Midlands to East Anglia. At some point on the shore of the Wash, they planned to take over a radio station and make contact with the naval authorities at Bremen. Once this link had been established, they would ask for a fleet of small warships to proceed to the coast of Norfolk and pick them up.

H-hour for the break-out was to be on Christmas Day, when fewer guards than usual were likely to be on duty, and their attention might be more relaxed.

Each man was given a specific duty. Two were instructed to make a survey of the roads in the vicinity of the camp; another had to examine the wire in an attempt to find a weak spot. The locations and number of vehicles were established, and the positions of the food stores, the amount of ammunition and weapons available, and all manner of other details (down to the types of padlocks used) were carefully noted.

The timing was worked out meticulously, and the prisoners even managed to acquire a number of maps.

Among the other roles of Le Marchant Barracks was that of a centre for US intelligence officers, where they were trained in the art of interrogation. One of them, who spoke German fluently, was walking through the prison camp in mid-December, when he overheard a remark about the armoury. He reported it to the commandant, who immediately ordered a search. During the course of it, a number of hand weapons were discovered. Thirty of the POWs were promptly taken to the London Cage, where they were questioned individually by Colonel Scotland's talented inquisitors.

Camp 23 was promptly emptied of its dangerous occupants, most of whom were moved to Comrie in Perthshire. The camp there was specially designed for the accommodation of really tough Nazis. Among its assets was remoteness.

There the matter might have ended, had it not been for the POWs' passion for revenge. Two men were suspected of betraying the plot. One was the ring-leader, who broke down under interrogation and admitted that the American intelligence officer's theory of a break-out was correct. The other was a pleasant young man, liberal-minded and completely opposed to Nazism, named Wolfgang Rosterg.

Rosterg should never have been sent to Comrie: not only was he innocent of treachery, he was not even involved in the plan. Nevertheless, here he was in this wasp nest of grumbling Nazis, an innocent surrounded by devils.

He would have done well to have crept into a corner, hoping that nobody would notice him. Instead, he criticised the conduct of the German campaign in the Ardennes, and read extracts from English newspapers to illustrate his points.

This was too much. One night after lights out, he was taken from his bed and brought before an *Ehrenrat*. The trial lasted nearly all night. When it was over, he was taken to the washroom and hanged from one of the water pipes.

Five men were accused of his murder. They were taken to London for trial and later executed in Pentonville prison.

Lodge Moor near Sheffield had started its life as a training camp for British soldiers during World War I. As a POW camp, the conditions were thought to be bad and, like Comrie, it was reserved for hard-core Nazis. In March 1945, a sergeant-major named Emil Schmittendorf – a man of about thirty who had joined the Wehrmacht in 1934 – started work on a tunnel. It was a long job, and it was discovered before Schmittendorf was able to make use of it.

The sergeant-major was furious. Somebody, he felt certain, had betrayed him. The question was: who? An unpleasant young eighteen-year-old named Armin Keune, who was well known for his fanatical Nazi beliefs, offered his services as an investigator.

It seems doubtful whether Keune did any investigating at all. He simply picked on the two men in the camp who, in his opinion, were the most likely traitors. One was Gerhardt Rettig: the identity of the other has never been revealed. Their only crimes were that they were anti-Nazis and that they were not afraid to make their views known.

Rettig was warned that Keune was preparing a case against him. He protested that he had not informed the guards about the tunnel. Nevertheless, he took the precaution of asking one of the British soldiers to convey a note to the commandant. An interview followed, and both men were assured that they would be moved to another camp as soon as possible.

Soon afterwards, the Lagerführer (the senior German warrant-officer) told Rettig and his friend to get their things ready for departure. They packed their kitbags, and sat down on their beds. There were forty men in the hut; and each knew the reason for their transfer.

At 5.30 pm, the prisoners paraded for roll-call but there was still no sign of an escort to take Rettig and his friend away. Rettig was walking back to the hut afterwards, when he noticed that his fellow POWs were standing around in groups, ominously silent. Suddenly Keune darted towards him.

When he was about 20ft away, the others, still bunched in tight little groups, began to advance slowly towards him. Rettig ran towards the hut, but there was no escape.

First of all, he was beaten until he was unconscious. Then somebody threw water over him, which revived him. But Keune was determined to bring matters to a conclusion, and he had already worked out where it should take place: among the camp dustbins.

The scene of violence moved to this squalid corner: the beating was resumed. But now the noise attracted the attention of the guards, and a squad of soldiers doubled into the compound. Rettig's friend, who had been overlooked by the thugs, took sanctuary among them and the mob was dispersed. What was left of Gerhardt Rettig was rushed to hospital, but it was too late. He died a few hours afterwards.

Sergeant-major Schmittendorf and Armin Keune were tried for murder and they, too, were hanged in Pentonville. Schmittendorf had been worried about his wife and children who were in Berlin. Keune had been dragged into a Nazi youth camp more or less from his cradle and his mind pumped continuously with Nazi propaganda. But this was no excuse. He and Schmittendorf had arranged what amounted to a lynching: their victim certainly had not deserved to die.

The only way out of Britain by sea was to take ship to the Republic of Ireland, which was by no means impossible, provided an escaper embarked on the correct vessel, and did not end up in Ulster. To an airman, however, the most likely means of departure seemed to be an aeroplane.

Hauptman Freiherr von Werra had been shot down during the Battle of Britain. He was not the type of man to bide his time in patience, cultivating the camp garden and waiting for the war to end. He was a loud-mouthed fellow, full of self-confidence and inclined to be boastful. No camp was secure enough to contain him, he told his fellow captives – a statement they may have doubted when his first attempt at a break-out failed. But von Werra was not deterred. At the end of 1940, he determined to have another go.

On this occasion, he was quartered at a camp near Swanwick in Derbyshire. About ten miles away, the mining town of Hucknall had an aerodrome on its outskirts or, rather, *two* aerodromes. On one side of the road, there was an RAF station, where aspiring pilots were coached in the art of flying. The machines used were Tiger Moths.

On the far side of the road, however, Rolls-Royce had an establishment for testing its engines. In the winter of 1941, strange noises could be heard in the area – prolonged shrieks which, to the local population, meant nothing. In fact, they were the sounds of a jet engine on trial. The aircraft here were, undoubtedly, more advanced than those at the disposal of the student fliers.

Von Werra extracted himself from the camp at Swanwick and walked to Hucknall. He strolled on to the Rolls-Royce property. When somebody asked him what his business was, he explained that he was a Dutch aviator named Captain van Lott, and that he was stationed at Dyce Aerodrome, Aberdeen. He needed to get back to his base quickly, and he would be grateful for the loan of a Hurricane.

If Hauptmann von Werra had imagined that it was possible to walk on to an aerodrome, and to help oneself to a fighter without anyone taking any great notice, he was to be disappointed. The duty officer promised that he would telephone Dyce to check the story. In the meanwhile, perhaps he wouldn't mind waiting.

Naturally he minded waiting – not least because, as soon as the 'phone call was made, his cover would be blown and he'd be back in Swanwick within the hour.

He walked over to a Hurricane parked on the runway and beckoned to a mechanic. He told the same story, adding that he had full approval of the duty officer. The mechanic could see no difficulties. But, he wanted to know, had von Werra signed the visitors' book? Indeed, all manner of signatures seemed to be necessary. Von Werra explained that he was in a hurry; perhaps, the man would bring the necessary pieces of paper to him?

The mechanic agreed. As he walked off towards the offices, the Luftwaffe officer climbed into the Hurricane's cockpit. This should have been the moment he had so eagerly anticipated. Unfortunately, he had not been able to make sufficient study of the workings of a Hurricane fighter. One did not simply press a button, causing the engine to come alive in the manner of a car. To get the thing started required the assistance of a mechanic – the very man who was now on his way to the office.

Hauptmann von Werra became aware of this simple truth as he looked at the controls and applied himself to understanding the instruments. Before very long, a figure appeared beside him. It was not the mechanic but the duty officer, who was now holding a revolver and pointing it in the general direction of von Werra's head. He had telephoned Dyce: no officer by the name of van Lott was known to the people up there. The man was certainly an imposter.

Back he went to Swanwick. It was now clear to the authorities that a prisoner of such restless temperament; a man with such scorn for barbed-wire barriers, and of such ingenuity, would be better confined on the far side of the Atlantic, in Canada. He was duly taken across the ocean, though there seems to have been a shortcoming in the matter of communications. Nobody had yet informed the Canadian POW authorities that here was somebody who required special attention, a POW who was about as slippery as a cake of soap in a bath.

It was mid-winter, and the St Lawrence was frozen. At some point on the train journey between the port of disembarkation and the camp, he managed to elude the guard, jump from the carriage, cross the ice that covered the river, and make his way into the United States, which were not yet at war with Germany.

The US authorities arrested him, and he was put into prison, presumably for entering the country illegally. But von Werra knew his rights. He demanded to see the German consul, who secured his release. Indeed, this official did more than this: he enabled him to return to Germany, where he received a rapturous welcome.

As the only German POW to make his escape during World War II, von Werra became a legend and, like most legends, it becomes difficult to separate fact from fiction. The one certain thing is that he did not survive the war. He is said to have been seen at Colditz (though Eggers does not refer to him in his book), where he may have advised the kommandant on how to improve his security arrangements. One account of his life suggests that he was eventually killed on the Russian front, though a more likely version is that he crashed when flying over the North Sea in October 1941.

In November 1941, two Luftwaffe officers, Lieutenants Wappler and Schnabel, managed to become airborne, which was an achievement in itself. They broke out of a camp near Penrith (possibly Grisedale), made their way to an aerodrome and climbed aboard one of the two-seater training machines. Nobody seems to have suspected anything unusual. When they took off, the personnel in flight control assumed that they were merely putting in a little homework – practising circuits and landings.

But Wappler and Schnabel did nothing of the kind. Without wasting any time, they set course in the general direction of Germany. They might have done better to ensure that the aircraft had sufficient fuel on board to make such a trip possible. As they approached Great Yarmouth, the needle on the gauge pointed to zero, and the engine began to make unhealthy coughing noises. They landed at a nearby RAF station.

Like von Werra, they explained that they were Dutch officers serving in Britain. The RAF staff were sympathetic. They gave the two German pilots a good meal and provided them with quarters for the night. Next morning, they promised, the aircraft would be refuelled and they could return to their base.

When they retired to bed, the two Germans must have suspected that, to all intents and purposes, their exploit was over. You cannot help yourself to an aeroplane without somebody eventually wondering what has become of it. They are, after all, expensive. During the night, an alert was broadcast to all RAF stations, asking personnel to keep their eyes open for a stolen trainer. The men at Great Yarmouth were able to make the necessary deductions. Wappler and Schnabel were returned to the place from whence they had come.

These stories about German POWs in Britain have, perhaps, been on the sensational side, which may be unfair. After all, the destruction of presumed traitors was not entirely confined to them. In a German Stalag, a French Canadian was thought to have informed the camp authorities of an escape project. Not long afterwards, his body was discovered. Although nothing was proven, and nobody was punished for the act, there appears to be no doubt that he was murdered.

After the invasion of Normandy, prisoners began, almost literally, to pour into Allied hands. There was even one soldier, whose age was apparently seventy-eight. He had, he told his captors, been unable to serve in World War I. He had been dismissed as too old.

In the early part of 1944, a circular was received from the German high command, recommending all POWs to devote their leisure to the study of non-military matters. This seems strange: D-Day had not yet taken place, and there is nothing to suggest that any member of the Nazi hierarchy had yet resigned himself to losing the war. Was it that the poor escape record made it seem unlikely that any of the prisoners would again be in a position to assist Germany's military effort? Or was it issued under the assumption that Germany might yet *win* the war, and that civilians' skills would be needed for the colonisation of Europe under the new order? History is vague on this point.

Certainly the attempt on Hitler's life by senior German officers on 20 July 1944, seems to have stiffened morale in some British POW camps. As Fritz Wentzel, a commander in the German Navy, wrote, 'We were nearly all opposed to the officers' revolt and we regarded it almost as an intervention of Providence that Hitler had not been killed.'

When, at last, Hitler killed himself and the war came to an end, there was more than his ashes buried beneath the ruins of the Chancellery in Berlin. A dream had died, too, and, in the minds of many former Nazi believers, there was a void. Some, such as Wentzel, studied religion. It was not, the commander asserted, that he had suddenly espoused the cause of

Christianity – substituting the most sacred for the most profane – but that he wished to discover the Truth (his capital letter). He was, perhaps, bewildered, just as a great many of his companions were.

Procedure at the POW camps continued much as before. Twenty-five thousand German other ranks were billeted with farmers, and they, no doubt, had the best deal of all. There were large gangs of labourers (about 500 in each) employed under the supervision of the Pioneer Corps – though, towards the end of the war, fewer small working parties were sent out. This was partly due to the shortage of petrol, which made transportation a problem, and also to lack of guards.

So far as the prisoners were concerned, this was not a misfortune: they disliked being moved about.

Most of the POWs were accommodated in Nissen huts situated in compounds surrounded by tall double fences of barbed wire. Later, when prisoners from other countries began to converge on Britain, the newcomers had to be put in tents. Throughout the cold winter of 1945–6, many suffered severely from these inadequate arrangements. Not unreasonably, there were protests to the Red Cross delegates. These gentlemen frowned on the situation, but they had to agree that there was little alternative. There had been 200,000 German POWs in Britain, 43 per cent of the European total. Now, from Canada and the USA, a great many more were on the way. These men had been well treated, and there had been few attempts to escape. They were, according to an observer, 'the best off' – though a German taken in Italy and presently brought to Britain, was given credit for being 'king of the local black market'. His dealings were said to have made him a millionaire, the precursor, perhaps, of German economic revival.

Prisoners from Belgium were, without doubt, the worst off. They had been stripped of everything and were, according to Wentzel, 'half starved'. Indeed, when columns of these unfortunates passed by a compound, the POWs inside used to throw them loaves of bread over the wire.

In Holland, POWs were put to work on clearing mines from the beaches, an inexact science that cost 210 of them their lives, and caused 460 to be injured (200 of whom were eventually repatriated as disabled). In France, some tried to escape and make their way home. Others headed for Luxembourg where, despite having endured the rigours of Nazi occupation, the people were extraordinarily kind to them. Anyone in French hands who was not prepared to wait patiently for repatriation was invited to enlist in the Foreign Legion.

At POW camps throughout Britain, the routine continued. Fritz Wentzel recalled:

We attended roll-call twice a day though the counting of noses had lost all interest. No one was ever missing. There was nowhere for us to escape to. Back to Germany? The Allies were there, too. They would have recaptured us – and with the assistance of the German authorities, too – and brought us back to spend more time than ever in the camp.

Repatriation in Britain began in 1946 and was completed in 1948. But these were the fortunate ones. For the enormous number of German prisoners in Russian hands, the journey home took very much longer.

In the first week of February 1945, Winston Churchill, Franklin D. Roosevelt and Joseph Stalin met in the Crimean town of Yalta. Among the items on the agenda were prisoners of war. Stalin insisted that all Russian prisoners, no matter what their preferences might be, must be sent back to the USSR. Bearing in mind the number of British and American POWs likely to be 'liberated' by the Red Army, and who might be treated as hostages, Churchill and Roosevelt felt compelled to agree.

This grim game of human barter was to produce death and terror on an appalling scale. There were, for example, 50,000 Cossacks in Germany, many of whom had fled from the Stalin régime. There were the followers of General Vlasov, a senior Red Army officer who had distinguished himself in the defence of Moscow and Leningrad during 1941, and who had been captured on 12 June 1942. Once in German hands, the general had reconsidered his ideas and had come to the conclusion that 'If Bolshevism survives, then the Russian people will die out, will cease to exist'. To avoid this, he had helped to form the 'Russian Liberation Army', which was anything from 500,000 to 1 million strong.

Some Russian POWs were coerced by sheer ill-treatment into serving with the German forces, many of them on the Atlantic Wall. When the Allies invaded, a great many walked innocently into captivity, hoping that this meant liberation from the nightmares of brutality and privation they had undergone.

All Russians in these categories were deemed to be traitors, and return to the USSR unquestionably meant that they would be executed. Some even attempted to take their own lives, rather than perish at the hands of their fellow countrymen. Nor could those who had been taken away from Russia and used as civilian labourers expect anything but death. According to Stalin's dark logic, they had been contaminated by contact with the West.

Even the Red Army soldier who had existed as a POW under atrocious conditions and yet who, despite this, had held out against German threats and blandishment, could expect little mercy. Stalin had ruled that none of his troops might surrender. To be taken prisoner implied such an action, and the least penalty was ten years in a forced labour camp.

The magnitude of the slaughter that resulted from the Yalta agreement was immense. Within two months of the war ending, 1,393,902 of the estimated 2 million Soviet citizens in western Germany had been handed over to the Red Army. Nor does there appear to have been a great deal of sympathy for them among the Western powers. At a press conference on 8 June 1945, General Omar Bradley countered suggestions that Russians in American camps were being ill-treated by saying, 'We do have some Russians, but I don't believe Russia would complain on anything we did to them. We captured 100,000 to 150,000 fighting on the side of the Germans. I don't believe these people have much future.'

He was right: they had none. When, for example, the liner *Almanzora* docked at Odessa with a consignment of Russian prisoners from England, a Soviet liaison officer told his British opposite number that they would probably be sent to 'educational labour camps'. It seems doubtful whether they got beyond the quay. Even as they were being disembarked, the sound of machine-gun fire could be heard coming from behind a nearby shed.

Solzhenitsyn described this sell-out to Stalin as 'the war's last secret'. It was also one of its greatest scandals – second only, it might be argued, to the extermination of Jews in German concentration camps.

As *The Times* commented, 'Whatever was done in 1945 and 1946, it is repugnant to liberal and Christian sentiment to force a man to return to a country against his will.' Several years later, in the House of Commons, Anthony Eden (later Lord Avon), the Foreign Secretary who had assisted in the arrangement with Stalin, appears to have had second thoughts about his own part in the affair. Speaking in 1952, he told MPs, 'I will not dwell on the practical difficulties of forcibly repatriating more than 62,000 men, many of whom could be expected to commit suicide on the way. It would, I think, clearly be repugnant to the sense of values of the free world to send these men home by force.'

But, by then, all the British and American POWs in Russian hands had returned home. It was, perhaps, easier to repent. He may also have been better aware of Stalin's methods. On 13 April 1943, Berlin Radio had announced the discovery in the Katyn Forest near Smolensk of a mass grave, containing the remains of 10,000 Polish officers. It seemed to be such good propaganda material, that the Nazis even went to the trouble of taking Polish POWs to view the site. The Russians vigorously denied any responsibility; and, when the Polish Government in exile appealed to the Red Cross, Stalin and his henchmen broke off diplomatic relations.

At the time of the announcement and for several years afterwards, the Katyn massacre was attributed to the Germans – as just one more item in a huge collection of barbarities. In fact, it has since become clear that all these officers were in Russian captivity, and that each was expertly shot through the back of his head by a member of the NKVD (the predecessors of the KGB). Ten thousand was an exaggeration: the actual figure was 4,500. But this does not lessen the magnitude of the crime. It might have been better if the representatives of the Western Powers had been aware of the real authors of this fearful crime when they met at Yalta. Or might it have increased even more their fears for the safety of captive Britons and Americans? The proposition can be debated endlessly – and probably should be.

10

THE DARK SIDE
OF THE RISING SUN

If you had been in Germany during 1938, you would have been able to buy a picture postcard showing a group of emaciated individuals posed amid appalling conditions. Issued by Dr Goebbels, it purported to show Boer prisoners in a British 'concentration camp'. The word *concentration camp*, the Propaganda Minister insisted, had been minted by the English in the South African War.

Anyone with a sufficiently long memory, or a discerning eye, might have questioned the accuracy of the caption. The scene bore no likeness to the South African landscape. Nor was this its first appearance. On its original publication, several years earlier, the photograph had been described as 'genuine Russian concentration camp scenes' – which was correct.

The Boer War concentration camps (which were a scandal in themselves) differed from the Nazi version in at least one particular. Although they were designed for the internment of people, they were not meant to be punitive. Death on an unacceptable scale occurred in both but the Boers perished as a result of administrative incompetence, whilst prisoners in such places as Belsen and Dachau were the victims of a terrifying malice.

Apart from the fact that German concentration camps were largely intended for civilians, Japanese prisoner of war camps had much in common with them. Some apologists have asserted that they were not, as in the Third Reich, intended for extermination. They were not, admittedly, purpose-built for such a role – though there is evidence to suggest that this possibility was not overlooked by the Nippon authorities during the latter days of the war.

Regarded from an ethical point of view, there is, perhaps, a gap between these two versions of hell. The Germans were acting in a manner contrary to Western behaviour: the camps and the conduct of those responsible for them were acts of perversion. The Japanese, on the other hand, were at least being true to their own culture. They beat up prisoners and, on many occasions, executed them. But they also thrashed their own men and, when it seemed appropriate, sentenced them to death. The POWs were overcrowded in their camps but so were the Japanese soldiers in their own quarters. The difference was that the latter preferred such conditions.

In his story *A Bar of Shadow*, Laurens van der Post (himself a captive of the Japs for some time) caused one of the characters to observe that 'the just parallel was not an animal one, and not even the most tight and fanatical horde, but an insect one: collectively they [the Japanese] were a sort of super-society of bees with the Emperor as a male queen-bee at the centre.'

Before the fall of Singapore on 15 February 1942, Winston Churchill insisted that 'There must ... be no thought of saving the troops or sparing the population. The battle must be fought to the bitter end at all costs ... Commanders and senior officers should die with their troops. The honour of the British Empire and the British Army is at stake.'

When the enemy had captured the island's water supplies, and the ammunition was almost used up, Lieutenant-General Arthur Percival, GOC Malaya, ignored the order, and 130,000 men were surrendered to 30,000 Japanese. General Percival's conduct was questioned at the time, and immediately after the war. Nevertheless, it could be excused as realistic, the action of a man who had been placed in an impossibly difficult situation. It was something that his opponents were never able to understand. To a Japanese general, it would have been unthinkable.

The life of a Japanese soldier was of no value if he was unable to render useful service to the Emperor. There were only two occasions on which he achieved any glory, when he was victorious and when he died. Mr Harold Payne, who was taken prisoner at Singapore when serving as a second-lieutenant with the 137th Army Field Regiment of the Royal Artillery, remembers Japanese casualties returning from the fighting at Imphal. He said:

> If you were wounded, you were disgraced. You were no good to the Emperor; you were useless. The poor devils had to make their own way back, roughly bandaged and using bamboo poles as crutches. They were not given any food or anything: I've seen POWs actually sharing their food with them.
>
> But if you were killed, you were the cat's whiskers. Your ashes came down in a nice little white box. You had died for the Emperor and you were a hero. The white box was taken back to mum and dad, and had to go on the mantleshelf. You were a good chap.

In view of this, Mr Payne observed, 'you can imagine what they thought of prisoners of war'.

The Japanese were certainly much possessed by death: it has even been said that they were in love with it. Six weeks after the fall of Hong Kong on Christmas Day, 1941, a British medical orderly at one of the hospitals committed suicide. The Senior British Officer, a colonel in the RAMC, wished the funeral to be as quiet as possible. The Japanese commandant, on the other hand, objected. As a soldier, he insisted, the man was entitled to the same honours as an officer of any rank. The colonel, possibly, saw the matter as a tragedy and as a disgrace: his opposite number no doubt looked upon it with approval. The surrender had been the disgrace; but the act of self-immolation was entirely honourable under such circumstances.

Any Japanese soldier who was taken prisoner was regarded as an outcast. When, the war over, he returned, there would be no welcome for him. His family and, possibly, his village, would refuse to take him back into its midst. It was not surprising that, until the later days of the war, few of them were captured.

Enough of the Japanese attitude was understood before the bombing of Pearl Harbor on 7 December 1941. There were, indeed, doubts about whether the enemy would take any prisoners at all. Mr Payne recalls that, after Singapore's surrender, his first action, if it can be so described, was to catch up with the sleep that had been impossible for so many days. On waking, however, 'it was a terrible feeling, because we'd always been told that the Japanese didn't take POWs. But when there were so many of us, this was our salvation: they couldn't bump us all off.'

Similarly, Mr W. J. Hodson, who was serving with the RAF at Bandung when Java capitulated, realised the importance of being taken in sufficiently large numbers. From the air-force base, he travelled to a tea plantation where, for the next few days, he and his companions camped out on the verandah of a large bungalow. 'If the Japanese found people in small numbers,' he said, 'the most likely thing they'd do was to shoot or bayonet them. But if there was a large number of people, they were rather confused about what to do, and there was a good chance that you'd be taken prisoner.'

Very sensibly, then, parties of the tea plantation's lodgers made daily excursions into the jungle – finding here a party of two or three men, there a group of twenty, and none of them knowing where to go.

The Japanese, presumably, had a reasonably good idea of what was going on. Every day, a spotter plane circled the estate. The pilot would have seen that the natives were still peacefully picking tea, but the population in the area of the bungalow was steadily growing. When about 300 people had been gathered together, they judged it safe to approach the Japanese authorities. A group of senior officers, wing-commanders and group captains, handled the negotiations. Not long afterwards, the fugitives were taken to the market place in a nearby village. It was about the size of a small field, covered with cinders and surrounded by barbed wire. The only source of water was one tap, which grudgingly yielded its burden, drip by drip. They remained here for ten days.

But Mr Hodson and his companions were fortunate. When Hong Kong surrendered on Christmas Day, 1941, fifty British officers suffered their feet to be tied, and were then put to death with bayonet thrusts. Out at Stanley, the nurses of Saint Stephen's emergency hospital had asked the local brigadier to admit them to the supposed safety of his fortress. The brigadier said that no such precautions were necessary: they were perfectly safe in the hospital. But he had a very much less than perfect grasp of the situation, even to the extent of not realising that the colony had surrendered. His own men, mostly Canadians, were still fighting on Boxing Day morning.

As for the safety of the hospital, this was a myth. When two medical officers pointed to the well-displayed red cross, and tried to prevent Jap soldiers from breaking in, they were quickly killed – and so was a Captain Hickey of the Royal Canadian Army Service Corps, who tried to help them. Patients were stabbed to death as they lay in their beds; the nursing sisters and four of the VADs were raped; and three VADs were bayoneted to death.

In the Philippines, the fighting stopped for a few days in February 1942, when 10,000 Japanese went sick with malaria. But this was no more than a reprieve. On 11 March, General Douglas MacArthur (the C-in-C) prudently removed himself to a safer place. On 9 April, General Jonathan Wainwright, who was now in charge of the American and Philippine forces, surrendered. Six days later, 70,000 of them were made to march 60 miles to a place of captivity. Only 54,000 survived the infamous 'Bataan Death March'. Some died of illness; some were clubbed to death; and some were run over by Japanese drivers, apparently out of interest to see what a flattened corpse looked like.

Even large numbers, it seemed, were not always a guarantee of survival.

In view of these immoderate brutalities, and the philosophy that inspired them, it may seem surprising that the Japanese had shown any interest whatever in the Geneva Convention of 1929. In fact, Nippon delegates had attended, though their government never ratified the terms. Nevertheless, in February 1942, a message reached Westminster by way of the so-called protecting power (Argentina – a power that, despite the best intentions, was powerless to protect) that the convention would be honoured so far as the British, Canadian, Australian, New Zealand and Indian prisoners were concerned.

Three months later, an opportunity occurred to dispatch a supply of Red Cross parcels. An exchange of diplomats had been arranged to take place at Lourenco Marqués in Portuguese East Africa (now Mozambique). There seemed to be no reason why food and medical supplies should not be sent back to Japan in the returning ships. It was a fiasco. The quantities were pitifully small, and there is no evidence to suggest they ever reached those who needed them.

As time was to show, there was a great deal of difference between the pious protestations of the Nippon government and their translation into some sort of action. There was endless debate, negotiations that seldom produced any ideas – and, when they did, still achieved nothing. For example, the International Red Cross was allowed to station delegates in Tokyo, Hong Kong and Shanghai, for the purpose of visiting prison camps. The man in Hong Kong had a somewhat limited view of the situation, for he, himself, was promptly put behind barbed wire at Stanley. For at least two years, the British and American governments were under the impression that there were only forty-two camps. In fact, there were well over 100 but it was not until October 1944 that this became clear.

It was, however, apparent that 240,000 food parcels would be needed each month if anything were to be done for the plight of men (and, in some cases, women, too) who, in the words of one doctor, were 'being slowly starved to death'.

Russia, which did not declare war on Japan until 6 August 1945, agreed to act as an intermediary. The idea was that supplies should be carried in Soviet ships from Portland, Oregon, to Vladivostok and thence taken to Japan in Japanese vessels. Since Stalin had forbidden his troops to surrender under any circumstances, and since the Japanese code regarded any such action as the ultimate in dishonour, not even the most optimistic observer could have expected much in the way of results. Nor was there. Few of the Allied personnel in Jap hands had so much as the sight of a Red Cross parcel until after the dropping of atom bombs on Hiroshima and Nagasaki. As for mail and medical supplies, the route was so complex (from Tokyo to Korea to Muckden, by the Trans-Siberian Railway to Moscow, from Moscow to Istanbul, and thence to England by way of Trieste, Geneva and Lisbon), that it took the better part of one year for a letter to make the journey. In the case of Mr Payne, two-and-a-half years elapsed from the time of his capture at Singapore to the moment his parents learned that he was still alive.

Most of the information about captives in Japanese hands came from the few who were repatriated, from the even fewer who escaped, and from one or two other sources (including the Swiss Embassy in Tokyo).

One day in January 1944, a celebrated Chinese Christian evangelist named Marcus Cheng presented himself at the British Embassy at Chunking. Pastor Cheng had much to tell. He had been in Singapore at the time of the fall. Five thousand Australian prisoners, he said, had been quartered in a large market known as the Great World Bazaar (anything would suffice: Mr Hodson spent some time in the centre of Surabaja, quartered in what had previously been a funfair). Regardless of rank, they were compelled to undertake such lowly duties as keeping the streets clean.

Later, travelling north, he had glimpsed a prisoner of war camp from a slow-moving train. 'It consists,' he said, 'of huts about 10 or 12sq ft with a few feet between each. I saw many prisoners clearly. They were skin and bone, unshaven and with long, matted hair. They were half-naked and looked longingly at the train.'

This was one of seven POW camps he had seen in Malaya. 'The fare provided for the prisoners,' he said, 'is below existence level. It is only a starvation diet, consisting of a small quantity of rice together with a handful of bean sprouts or some other vegetable per diem.'

But the most disturbing item of information concerned the building of a railway from Siam into Burma. The route lay through thick jungle – 'land', said Mr Cheng, 'in which no human being had probably set foot for thousands of years'. Four out of every six Chinese employed on the project died, usually from malaria occurring on top of malnutrition (the diet, he explained, was rice, a little salt and a few vegetables). Since the European members of this cosmopolitan labour force had been sent up first to clear the jungle, and since they were regarded by the Japanese as the lowest of all forms of life employed on the project, their death toll might be expected to be even higher (in fact, 15,000 died). 'The dead,' he said, 'were buried at once – like dogs.'

More information about the notorious 'Death Railway' came to light in September of that year. By this time, the project had been completed, and many of those who had survived it were taken to Japan. One of the ships employed for this purpose, the *Rakuyo Maru*, was torpedoed by American submarines. Of the 1,500 Australian and British prisoners on board, only 151 survived. They were sixty British other ranks, eighty-seven Australian ORs, three Australian naval ratings and one Australian airman.

After spending several days adrift on fragments of wreckage and rafts, they were rescued by the US submarines *Pampanito* and *Sealion*. Four of the survivors died on board and were buried at sea. The remainder recovered – largely, it seems, as a result of the care and attention lavished on them by the submariners. As one of the POWs said, 'the American crews were like a whole gang of nurses.'

The stories they told when they arrived at Pearl Harbor after a brief stay at Saipan, where ten were detained in hospital, were so horrifying, that the British Government had some doubts about releasing details to the press. Not only might they upset the relatives of POWs still in captivity, they might also jeopardise the fate of the estimated 140,000 prisoners in Japanese custody. As one official noted in a memorandum, 'The War Office already knew of the appalling conditions in which our POWs worked on the Burma-Siam railway, and this summary does not break much fresh ground, but it shows that the treatment of our POWs exceeds the worst that had been thought.'

According to one calculation, a native labourer died for every sleeper laid: the rate for Europeans was one death for every seventh sleeper. One of the worst spots was the grimly named 'Bridge 600', so-called because its construction had resulted in 600 deaths. They were mostly among coolie labourers who had been brought up from Malaya, and who had succumbed to an outbreak of cholera.

Ironically, the greater part of the 153km length of track was built from plans prepared by British surveyors before the outbreak of war. When the Australians arrived to begin work on the Burma end, the Japanese commandant left them in no doubt about the ordeal that lay ahead. The project, he said, had to be completed in nine months – that was the Emperor's wish. All the white men employed were to be 'considered as consumable material as they were worthless, and if none of them remained after the railway was completed, then well and good'. No medical supplies were to be provided by the Japanese: the only materials available to the two Australian and three British doctors were $\frac{1}{2}$lb cotton wool and six bandages for every 1,500 men.

After spending some time in the former civilian prison at Changi on Singapore Island, Mr Payne and his fellow prisoners were told that 'we were going to a much better camp. We were going to be taken to a proper holiday camp, where we'd receive very good treatment, etc, etc.' By this time he had reason to be sceptical of Japanese promises.

By some curious oversight on the part of those who had planned Changi Jail, there was no sanitation on the premises – with the result that anyone who wished to relieve himself had to go outside the camp. The guards were a collection of Sikhs who had been persuaded by the Indian Nationalist leader, Chandra Bose, that the Japanese offered a prospect of liberation from the British Raj. (Subhas Chandra Bose had escaped from India to Berlin via Afghanistan in 1941. In 1943, he turned up in Tokyo.) They were, in the words of Mr Payne, 'Horrible. They were really most objectionable individuals.'

The diet had been rice (of a very poor quality) and fish manure ('quite good'). All officers, no matter what their rank had been, were reduced to second-lieutenant. They were required to maintain some sort of discipline within the camp, and to oversee working parties. In Singapore, Mr Payne had been employed on a scheme to remove the top from a mountain. Once the site had been cleared, and a great deal of earth carried down in small baskets, a memorial to the Japanese war dead was built upon it.

The journey to the supposed 'holiday camp', was made in railway wagons normally used for the transport of rubber. After four days, the train arrived at a railhead somewhere in Siam; and there, recalled Mr Payne:

> We built our first POW camp. At this stage one was beginning to feel different. We were beginning to discover all those tropical problems such as sores and ringworm, and various things like that. We did our best to keep ourselves as clean as possible, though soap was scarce. One also had to get used to living so closely with other people. This was not a bad thing. As proven in the latter years, man is no good without man. This togetherness is something I just could not have done without. A person by himself is useless.

On the railway, Mr Payne was in charge of a squad of 800 men. Koreans (who were even more villainous than their Japanese masters) were in charge of the British and Commonwealth officers, and Japanese soldiers were in charge of Koreans. There was, as he puts it:

> an order of bashing. If something went wrong, a Japanese officer would hit an NCO, the NCO hit the private, the private hit a Korean, and the Korean hit the British officers for not controlling their troops. And that's where it finished. We had to say to the chaps, 'You can't do that'; but I accept wholeheartedly that the Japanese code of living is absolutely different from ours.

It was not always quite so simple as this. Upon occasion, a Japanese NCO would beat up an Allied soldier for no better reason than that the unfortunate man had obeyed an order previously given to him by a Japanese officer. Self-opinionated sergeants were liable to disagree with their superiors, and prisoners bore the brunt of their readily aroused rage. But that was the way of the Japs. As Mr Payne said, 'If something went wrong, it didn't take much to get them very excited. It really would have been better, if they'd left us to get on and do it in our own sweet way. They were so very bad tempered.'

Beatings-up took all manner of forms. There are ex-POWs whose eardrums are still fractured from swipes across the side of the head. Men were knocked about with fists, kicked by boots, hit with blunt instruments – and, sometimes, with sharp instruments.

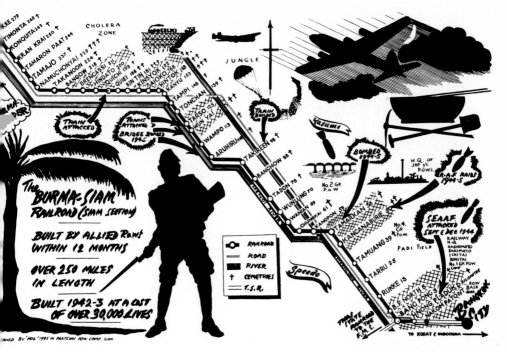

A map of the notorious death railway drawn by a POW at a camp in Siam (*From the collection of Harold Payne*)

These Japanese guards were among many condemned by war crime tribunals after VJ day. A few minutes after this photograph was taken, they were hanged (*From the collection of Harold Payne*)

A group of GIs photographed by an Hungarian journalist at a camp near the North Korean capital of Pyongyang. During the Korean War, brain-washing was added to the other torments of POWs (*Popperfoto*)

Kohe Island in South Korea was the scene of many disturbances by its Communist occupants. On this occasion, they set fire to the buildings, and order had to be restored by US paratroops using tear gas and concussion grenades (*Popperfoto*)

From Mr Payne:

> I greatly admire this particular Japanese. Somebody was caught doing something he shouldn't, and I was stood up to take the blame. This Jap took a swipe at me with his bayonet. I was standing to attention, and I could see the looks on our troops' faces. I thought, 'Here goes my arm!' However, as soon as the blade got anywhere near me, he turned it on to its flat side. It gave me a nasty bruise. I think, at the last moment, he got cold feet. I said 'Thank you very much' to him afterwards, and shook him by the hand. He didn't like that.

The drill on these occasions was to get up as quickly as possible. It was, Mr Payne recalls, fatal to 'lose face. That was the one thing. If you stood up to them, they were quite likely, later on, to come and give you a cigarette.' And, from Mr Hodson:

> Sometimes a beating would be a very mild affair; you'd rather laugh about it afterwards. At other times, for the most trivial thing, you'd have a most terrible beating – sufficient for a fellow to die.
>
> But the Nips had a very peculiar attitude. They'd beat a chap up very severely, and then they'd come along afterwards and give him some food – a plate of rice or some fruit. I hate the Japanese. They're a bad lot, but they have one characteristic we can learn from them. They didn't appear to bear any malice at all. Once they'd done their beating up, that was the end of it.

With so little room allocated to each man in the prison camps beside the emerging railway, it is hard to imagine that a POW was able to visit anyone beyond his immediate neighbours. However, when the Japanese permitted it (as on the occasion of the Emperor's birthday), the prisoners held sing-songs. 'But,' said Mr Payne, 'if we gathered together in too many meetings, they got the idea that we were inciting a mutiny – they were a very suspicious-natured people. However, we used to have little talks and discussions. People would describe their jobs; teachers used to teach French, and accountants used to teach us how to keep books.'

On some evenings, Mr Payne used to 'sit outside in the cool, and look up at the stars and moon. I used to think that it was the same moon that was shining on my mum and dad. Now we talk about pictures by satellite. I did that years ago, because it *is* the same moon wherever you are. I never, in all my captivity, I *never* thought that I wouldn't come home.'

Small things assumed an importance out of all proportion to their material worth. 'As long as you have something to set your life on,' Mr Payne said, 'it doesn't matter whether it's Him up there, or whether it's Buddha. The thing that I treasured – goodness knows what'd have happened if that had gone – was a small jar, the kind of thing that contains Marmite. In a way, I suppose, it was a kind of talisman. With that jar, I could keep my one razor blade sharp – and keep *myself* sharp.'

The doctors may have been very restricted in their supplies, but they did their best. Now and then, they were fortunate, for the Japanese troops seemed to have no medical services in the vicinity. Consequently, they visited the British MOs. If one of them needed to have a tooth extracted, the medical officer would protest that he had no cocaine. The Jap soldier procured some. The doctor filled the hypodermic syringe with water, removed the tooth, and added the drug to his small cache of medicines. Similarly, when the Japanese soldiery caught (as they not infrequently did) VD from the local Siamese girls, they would seek a cure, and there would be another excuse to increase the store of remedies. One evening, on returning to camp, Mr Payne and his working party discovered that American bombers had flown over and dropped bombs. 'One hundred and fifty of my mates were killed on the spot,' he said. 'Next day, the Japs said: "Why should we look after you when your own people come and bomb you?"'

There was probably a very good reason for the raid, and for its tragic consequences. Since POWs were deemed expendable, it was part of Japanese policy to site the camps close to ammunition dumps.

Harold Payne, like any other officer, realised that 'our duty was to escape'. He was also realist enough to recognise the impossible.

> Anyone who attempted it was a fool. You didn't have barbed wire; you could just push the bamboo poles aside and walk through. But you'd be surrounded by jungle; you didn't know the terrain, and there was always the problem of disease. On top of all this, with Asiatic races, one of the difficult things is knowing who's who. You could hardly recognise a Japanese from a Siamese; and, anyway, it's surprising what people'll do for money. The few that were recaptured were executed by the secret police [the *Kempeitai*].

When Mr Hodson arrived at an aerodrome near Djakarta, he found that 'there was a big argument going on in the camp. Apparently, a number of fellows had managed to get an abandoned American fighter together, and they believed it'd go. Then they had ideas of trying to cram in two or three people and flying off to Australia. Of course, there was an argument about who should be the two or three; and then there was the fear that there would be reprisals on the remainder of us.' Fortunately, the aircraft never took off.

Later, at an aerodrome near Malang, Mr Hodson and his friend, a Scot named Bill Wallace, planned an escape of their own. They carefully stored away a can of bully beef and two guilders in currency. Several other people, apparently, had similar ideas, including a group of four pilots who, in early May 1942, broke out of the camp.

The auspices could hardly have been better. Two of the escapers had been planters, a third was an Eurasian warrant-officer from Malaya. Between them, they had 700 guilders, which was a small fortune, and no language problems.

Possibly, they were betrayed by a Javanese. At all events, they were recaptured and brought back to the camp. 'Suddenly,' Mr Hodson said, 'the Nips stopped all working parties, and took us back into the compound. We were all lined up, and these four fellows were brought out in front of us and tied up. The Nips said that they'd escaped; that they had caught them, and that they'd be punished. Then, in front of us all, they gave each of them a fearful beating.'

But this was not the end of the matter. Next day, they were all paraded on the aerodrome.

> They'd got machine-guns positioned all around us, and we stood there for a while. Eventually, we saw a party coming away from the camp. There were our four fellows, there were Nips carrying shovels and others carrying wreaths. They lined the four chaps up in front of us; shot them; dug holes; buried them; and told us that, in future, for every man who tried to escape, they'd shoot one hundred men.

Three days later, the prisoners noticed two Japanese headstones about fifty yards away from the escapers' graves. They marked the resting places of the Japanese guards who had been on duty in the part of the camp where the airmen had gone over the wire. They, too, had been executed.

German kommandants might threaten reprisals for escapes, but it by no means followed that they would be carried out. With the Japanese, there was no doubt. When, for example, a British POW escaped from the town jail in Rangoon, twenty prisoners were executed. For all manner of reasons, of which fear of the consequences was only one, the number of attempts to get away were few. Not the least of the Nippon allies in this respect was the human body. What with a starvation diet, a catalogue of diseases ranging from malaria to beri-beri, from pellagra to sores and ulcers, there were not many with sufficient stamina.

In any case, life beyond the wire (or bamboo: it varied) was hard. Not long after Hong Kong had fallen, a member of the Winnipeg Grenadiers was discovered by the medical officer of a Japanese unit quartered in La Salle College. The man had been on the run for eleven days without food or water. At some point in his wanderings, he had broken his leg. Eventually, it had to be amputated.

Escapers were not the only people to suffer the death penalty – nor were the hostages (for such they were) who remained behind. The Japanese were sensitive. When Mr Hodson went out on working parties from the one-time funfair at Surabaja, he and his fellow POWs used to see Dutch women in the streets. Taking great care, the ladies gave them what could, with reasonable imagination, be interpreted as the 'V' sign. On one occasion, a guard noticed the encouraging gesture, and the lady was arrested. A stake was erected in the centre of the large square: the offender was stripped naked, and tied to it. She remained there for two days. Then she was taken away. 'When anyone disappeared like that,' Mr Hodson said, 'we knew what it meant.'

It was better to conform. At one camp in which Mr Hodson was interned, the POWs had to stir themselves from the doubtful comfort of the concrete floor and parade at seven each morning. He recalled:

> It became light in about fifteen minutes. As the sun came up above the hills, we all had to bow down. We weren't looking towards Nippon, because that would have been in the north-east, but never mind. We were supposed to be looking towards the Emperor, and the Japs went through quite a pantomime. You had to stand there for perhaps a couple of minutes, and the guards chanted something. Eventually, you'd hear one of our chaps saying 'God save the King', and someone else'd say 'Roll on the boats'. I had two thoughts about it. One was, 'For God's sake don't let the Nips hear you say anything.' But the fact that the chap next to you said 'God save the King', made you realize that you should say something. So you said, 'Roll on the boats', and then somebody else said 'Get stuffed!' Eventually you'd have about three thousand people all murmuring.
>
> One day, they wanted half-a-dozen people to go to one end of the camp first thing in the morning. I was one of them. We were working away while, about three hundred yards away, the main body was going through this performance. We could hear the Nips chanting their bit; then, all at once, there was a rumble like very, very distant thunder. That was the fellows saying 'Roll on the boats', 'God save the King', and so on.

In the Surbaja camp, the Japanese commandant (who must, one suspects, have been a mathematics teacher in civilian life) conceived the idea that all the prisoners should be able to count up to 100 in Japanese; and that, at roll-call, each should call out his number in the line-up. This may sound tolerably simple, but there were tricks attached to it. Sometimes they would be required to number backwards, and there were other permutations. Anyone who made a mistake was compelled to run round the square, a distance of about five hundred yards.

'When you'd spent all day working in the heat, you were almost on your knees,' he said. 'You were more or less incapable of running, but you had to go right round this square. Then you'd rejoin the ranks and do it all over again. Sometimes they'd keep us there until it was dark. We eventually learned to become quite expert.'

Working parties, despite the hardship, were a necessity of survival. Mr Hodson said:

> When our food was cut down, the first thing we thought was that we had to look after ourselves, and use as little energy as possible. If there was a working party, and enough people volunteered for it, you kept away from it. You didn't work unless you had to.
>
> But after a while, we realized that this was entirely wrong. The worst thing you could do was to save energy and do nothing. There were still people who didn't want to do anything; but, by and large, if you took this attitude, you just died off. The main thing, really, was your mental attitude, and you were a thousand times better off if you could work.

Sometimes the tasks were easy, sometimes 'absolutely beyond description'. Not the least of the advantages was that there were occasionally opportunities to acquire extra food. 'You might,' said Mr Hodson, 'unload a ship, or work in a plantation, or dig air-raid shelters. You could build bamboo huts, dig holes, fill in holes, cut jungle down to make roads – you might do *anything*. But you were always keeping an eye open for food. A good POW was also a good scrounger – there was no doubt about that.'

In April 1942, a squadron of United States B-25 bombers led by Commander (later Lieutenant-General) James Harold Doolittle took off from aircraft carriers, bombed Tokyo, and landed on airfields in China. The mission was thought to be virtually impossible; and, indeed, some of the aeroplanes were shot down. The crews were executed by the secret police, doubtless, as Voltaire remarked of another occasion, 'to encourage the others'. But the others were not deterred: the air-forces of the United States (Army and Navy) and the RAF attacked Japanese positions and some aeroplanes were destroyed. In many instances, the pilots were either shot or beheaded.

By the summer of 1944, the fate of airmen who literally fell into Japanese hands seemed certain. On 16 July of that year, newspapers in Allied countries shocked their readers with reports of a broadcast that had been transmitted by the Nippon authorities in Singapore. The announcer referred to a raid on Kyushu (the southernmost island in the Japanese complex), carried out in the previous month by a force of B-29 Superfortresses. The crews of those that were shot down had been put to death.

This, it seemed, was a precedent. 'Any Allied airmen who falls or bails out over Japan,' the broadcaster said, 'will be executed. This is an order of the day.'

In America and in Britain, voices were understandably raised in indignation. Opinions were divided about what to do. The Royal Air Force would have preferred the least possible publicity, though the matter was bound to come out. Somebody would write to an MP (and somebody did, almost immediately); the question would be brought up in Parliament; and the hounds of the press would be quick to pick up the story.

The American Government issued what, at first, was described as 'a protest' through the Swiss Embassy in Tokyo. Later, it was redefined as 'an inquiry'. Was this a threat, or was it really meant? Five days later, a spokesman for the Nippon Government called a press conference. There had, he said, been a misunderstanding. Wireless reception had been bad on the evening of the Singapore broadcast, and it was quite possible that the actual words had not come across clearly. The commentator had, he explained, said that 'Raiding B-29 bombers, by being shot down out of the skies of Japan, had thus come with a one-way ticket to hell.' This could scarcely be regarded as reassuring, though he protested that it did not follow that death sentences would be carried out. Indeed, the Japanese had no intention of executing captured airmen.

His remarks did not tally with an order dated 18 July 1944, that had been found on the body of a Japanese infantryman in Burma. It read:

Recent bombings in the Burma area have also become more intense. Targets of these attacks are not troops or military installations, but the unfortunate inhabitants and non-military installations. One can realize the barbarianism of these blind bombings. In view of existing conditions, all captured enemy air personnel will not be treated as prisoners of war. Instead, after having been searched for necessary information, they will be handed over to the gendarmerie [presumably the Kempetai]. All of them will be dealt with severely by the area army excepting those who can be put to some use. They will be separated from the other prisoners.

The order was signed Gatsuyama Koichiro, adjutant of the 138th Infantry Regiment, who added, as if by way of excuse, 'I have been ordered to issue the above.'

'Dealt with severely' had only one meaning in the double-speak of the time, and there was reason to wonder who was running the country: the government, who piously protested that the airmen, would not be killed – or the military, who were killing them. When another order was captured, stating that 'anything, including killing, may be done with prisoners below officers' rank', it was concluded that the matter was probably left to the front-line commander's discretion.

But this was of no comfort. In September, a POW who had escaped from New Guinea reported that, during his imprisonment on the island, no fewer than twenty Allied airmen had been beheaded in Hollandia and Wewak alone.

On Java, as Mr Hodson remembers, four Americans – the crew of an aircraft that had been shot down during a mine-laying assignment – were confined for several days in a small hut. One morning, he saw them being taken away. They were all filthy, with long beards. One of them was hobbling with the aid of a bamboo crutch. He never saw them again – though, two or three years later, he chanced upon a small news item in an evening paper. Their grave, it seemed, had been discovered. They had been shot.

But the unkindest cut of all was the fate of four Americans who were shot down over Burma one afternoon. That evening, their Japanese captors treated them to a magnificent dinner – and, next morning, they killed them. Apparently it appealed to the Nippon sense of humour.

Much of the information about the condition of Allied prisoners in Japanese hands was brought back by repatriated personnel. Such events were rare, though there were two exchanges – one in September 1943, and the other in October of that year. Those who came home were nearly all civilians, and the news they related was disturbing. Emily Hahn, a nurse who made the long journey from Hong Kong to her home in New York in the late autumn of 1943, had a tale to tell about a ship named the *Lisbon Maru*. The transport had been on passage between Hong Kong and Japan with a number of POWs on board, when she was torpedoed. According to Miss Hahn's account, 650 prisoners were drowned (in fact, the figure was more than 900). Some, she believed, had been recaptured: a few had used the occasion to escape.

The *Lisbon Maru* had left Hong Kong on 27 September 1942, with 1,800 POWs aboard and an escort of Japanese soldiers. The prisoners were crowded into three holds. They were not allowed to spend much time on deck, and there was insufficient water – though the food was surprisingly good and they were issued with cigarettes. When the ship was torpedoed, all the captives were ordered below. The Japanese abandoned ship when, after a brisk exchange of fire with the submarine, the vessel began to list. The only POWs to escape were those in number 2 hold who, on the instructions of the Senior British Officer, a colonel in the Royal Artillery, cut their way to freedom. Some were picked up by Japanese patrol boats, others by sampans owned by Chinese, who were fishing off one of the islands in the vicinity.

Miss Hahn was asked whether she knew the names of any of the *Lisbon Maru*'s officers. To leave a large number of prisoners enclosed in the holds of a cargo ship; and to make no effort to release them when the vessel was obviously about to sink – this was the most brutal of cruelties. When the war was over, those responsible must be called to account before a war-crimes tribunal.

But Miss Hahn knew the identity of only one Japanese officer who had sailed in the *Lisbon Maru*. His name was Arthur Niimori. Before the war, or so it was said, he had lived in America. In 1942, he was employed as interpreter at a camp for British officers in Argyll Street, one of the residential areas of Kowloon. Among Niimori's duties was that of examining parcels. He was assisted in this task by a colleague named Hasakawa, 'a very nasty bit of work', in Miss Hahn's opinion.

Niimori was, she said, 'supposed to be the worst of all the officers we women had to deal with. He was captious about what to accept in the way of food, and unreasonably sharp always, bullying the women until we hated him cordially.' Indeed, she said,

the one mitigating factor in the dreadful days after the sinking of the *Lisbon Maru* was that we believed that Niimori, too, had been lost. But after a month's absence, he showed up again in Argyll Street.

This, however, was a different Niimori – a man who had clearly been changed by his experience and, it must be said, for the better. He became sympathetic, helpful, even jovial, until before I left he was one of the most popular of the officers with whom we dealt ... I have often wondered whether the sinking of the *Lisbon Maru*, and the scenes he must have witnessed, didn't shock him into a reform. Or perhaps he saw the writing on the wall from that time on.

Hasakawa, who had remained at the camp, underwent no such redemption, but then Hasakawa was insane. Said Miss Hahn, 'It turned out after a long and bad period that he was going mad, whereas we always thought he was just drunk. His colleagues found him one day cleaning his teeth with a razor blade, and he was put into hospital or something. Anyway, thank heavens, he disappeared.'

Nobody in Japanese custody went on a journey for the good of his health, nor did he believe the promises that were often made. On one occasion, Mr Hodson recalled, 'A party came walking into the camp. The officer stood on an orange box to place himself above us, and an interpreter interpreted his speech. He said, "You're moving out tonight to another camp in another country. It'll be a good camp and there will be all facilities there – water for washing, and so on." Then he said, "Look into my eyes. I will look after you".'

Mr Hodson was not among those who went on this particular trip. It was just as well. Eighty-four per cent of them died.

He was eventually sent to an island in the Molucca group, where he was employed on unloading bombs from freighters. From time to time, there were signs of American air activity; though, with no news from the outside world, it was impossible to find out anything about the state of the war. All the POWs were in the worst of health, with beri-beri the most common of the complaints. 'You had one or two friends in a small group,' he remembers. 'You lived together and you tried to work together, so if there was anything worth taking, you shared it. If you were ill, the others would look after you.'

When the time came for these working parties to be taken back to Java, the full extent of the weakness wrought by disease and insufficient food became apparent. There were 350 POWs on the ship (an aged Dutch merchantman prone to engine trouble) – shortly to be joined by another 100, whose vessel had been sunk by an American aircraft. By the time they reached Java, 320 had died. Some perished from thirst, some from lack of food, some fell victim to dysentery, others went mad (which may mean that they died of pellagra – the first symptoms of which are cracking of the skin, the last, insanity). A soldier named Fisher was given the unpleasant task of throwing the dead bodies overboard. 'You'll never throw me overboard, Fisher,' they used to taunt; and Fisher, with grim humour, would reply, 'I'll have you'. More often than not, he was right.

By June 1944, Mr Hodson was back at Bandung. There was now talk of extermination marches. The idea was that the entire complement of a camp would set off on foot for no known destination. Whenever a POW was compelled to fall by the wayside, he would be shot. The dreadful journey would continue until there were no captives left. There had, if rumours were to be believed, already been at least one of these marches in New Guinea.

Some way to the north, on the border of Siam and Borneo, Mr Payne and his fellow officers had been marched up into the hills – at last segregated from the other ranks. Here, too, there was talk of a final solution, a mass extermination by the Japanese. But there was an almost equally disturbing idea put out by the British themselves. 'We had a radio,' Mr Payne said. 'We didn't know how to transport it, when we moved camp, for you could never tell when they'd have one of these spot checks. But then we decided that the Jap officer in charge of us should carry it in his pack. He insisted that some of us should act as his batmen, and we put the set in with his own belongings. He didn't know it was there.' Mr Payne insists that:

I'm only going by what I'm told; if it's true, whoever thought of it must have needed his brains tested. The idea apparently, was that our side was going to drop arms on our camp, and we were supposed to fight our way out. Quite apart from the fact that we were very weak, we'd been in the bag since 1942 and this was '45. A lot of things had happened in the British Army. For example, I'd never seen a jeep. If they'd dropped the arms, we probably wouldn't have known how to work them.

But no arms were dropped. One day, two American paratroopers came out of the jungle and announced that the war was over. Their opening remark was, 'Gee, you bastards stink!' – which was probably true; but, as a greeting, it might have been more happily expressed. The Japanese guards remained at their posts. The object, it now seemed, was to protect the prisoners against the Siamese until preparations had been made to take them home.

In Java, Mr Hodson had his first intimation that the war was over when he was out on a working party. They had been digging air-raid shelters; on the way to the site, they passed a large hoarding. It was usually decorated with paintings of Japanese aeroplanes bombing Americans, Japanese soldiers bayoneting Allied troops and so on. But, on this day, he noticed that the pictures had been removed by a lavish coating of white paint. He was hauling a cart at the time. Shortly afterwards, he accidentally knocked one of the guards off his bicycle. This would normally have been the occasion for a beating-up; but the guard, beyond grumbling, did nothing. This was so surprising, that he did it again, deliberately. The reaction was similar; no hand was raised in anger.

On the way back to camp, a procession of local inhabitants passed by, carrying banners with 'Freedom for Java' written on them. Since such demonstrations were banned by the Japanese, there could be only one conclusion.

But the Japanese were defiant until the last. Only a day or two previously, the Senior British Officer (a wing-commander) had been assaulted, and his jaw broken. In a nearby camp, where women and children were interned, a supply of Red Cross parcels had been received. The Japanese officer in charge did not allow their contents to be issued. Instead, he assembled the starving internees in the heat of the afternoon; placed some pieces of chocolate upon the ground; and watched their faces as stray dogs hurried on to the scene and ate the confection.

Nothing can excuse the brutality of Nazi concentration camps. The Japanese, who perpetrated similar atrocities in World War II, did not wish to be excused. They were, they might have protested, being true to their code: their actions were the result of a tradition spanning generations. Nevertheless, in one of his short stories, Laurens van der Post points out that the Nippon judges and executioners dared not look into the eyes of those who were doomed – for fear that, in such moments of human contact, they might have felt the stirrings of compassion.

Those who fell into Japanese hands during World War II suffered as few have suffered. Many were murdered, thousands died of sheer neglect. Some who came home never recovered from their experiences. Is it really necessary to explain – or to forgive?

Japanese, too, died in captivity, though on nothing like the same scale. When prisoners of war at Featherston, a small town to the east of Wellington in New Zealand, tried to break out *en masse* one day in the spring of 1943, forty-six were killed and sixty-six wounded. On 5 August 1944, POWs at Cowrah (to the west of Sydney, NSW) attempted a similar venture. Two hundred and thirty-one of them were fatally wounded and seventy-eight were injured. In this instance, four Australian guards were also killed. But, in both cases, the captives who survived were allowed to continue their lives. Had such incidents occurred in Japanese camps, there seems little doubt that all the internees would have been put to death afterwards. In his book *Prisoner of the British*, Professor Yuji Aida grumbles about his treatment after the war. When one considers that meted out to Allied POWs, one can only marvel at how lenient it seems to have been.

Nobody who was not a prisoner of Nippon during World War II can say whether there should be forgiveness. It does, however, seem to be a happy turn of fortune that, in the last two decades, the descendants of the samurai warriors have become preoccupied by the marvels of electronics and the manufacture of motor-cars. It may have upset a number of economic interests, but it is a great deal better than war.

I I

THE BATTLE FOR THE MIND

In 1910, the Japanese annexed Korea, that elongated piece of land that dangles like an ear-ring from the lobe of China. Thirty-five years afterwards (on 2 September 1945), when a haze of radio-active dust hung over Hiroshima and Nagasaki, and when the Japanese fortunes had been shattered by defeat, the Americans occupied the southern portion of the country. Four days later, Russian forces moved in from the north. Somebody drew a line along the 38th parallel: a boundary had been created – across it, the armies of capitalism and communism eyed each other warily.

The United Nations attempted to create a unified Korea, but the United Nations had already lost the apparent singleness of purpose that led to its wartime creation. Korea remained divided. Eventually, the United Nations (minus the communist bloc) gave its sponsorship to the Republic of Korea, and to its president, a politician of dubious integrity named Syngham Rhee. The USSR assisted in the formation of the People's Democratic Republic of Korea under Kim Il Sung. The dividing line between South and North Korea remained the 38th parallel.

If one is to believe contemporary reports, South Korea busied itself with the task of building up an industrial community: North Korea concerned itself with amassing arms with the intention of unifying the country – after its own fashion and to its own advantage.

The five years following World War II were a period of change and uncertainty. The guns might have ceased to fire, but the world still writhed in an agony of conflict. The wartime leader of China, Chiang Kai-shek, attempted to come to terms with his communist rival, Mao Tse-tung. He failed. In July 1949, after a succession of military reverses, he removed himself and his forces to Formosa. To the Western World, Formosa now became 'China' and China became 'Red China', a massive outcast that was denied admittance to the United Nations. Likewise, in the Western World, the artificial union between communism and capitalism, which had served to defeat Hitler, was on the edge of divorce. An Anglican clergyman remarked that it was 'better to be dead than Red'. Conservatives in Cheam, and other Tory strongholds, applauded. In America, they began to suspect that a Red lay concealed beneath every bed. Senator Joseph McCarthy awoke to the possibility that there might be political capital to be gained from such notions. In short, whilst the world remained in orbit round the sun, its far from perfect population, freed from the brief euphoria of peace, was back at its old game of learning how to hate.

One of the few places where there was any hope for people of more humanitarian inclinations was Geneva, where, in the August of 1949, delegates assembled for yet another convention. The idea was to tidy up the old agreements in the light of experiences gained in two world wars. Among those that eventually ratified the findings were the People's Republic of China (but not until December 1956) and North Korea (in August 1957). In other words, the Convention had nothing to offer prisoners of war in the trouble that lay immediately ahead.

At dawn on Sunday 25 June 1950, the forces of North Korea rolled forward. They crossed the 38th parallel and, three days later, captured the South Korean capital of Seoul. The invasion was condemned by all right-minded members of the United Nations. On 8 July, General Douglas MacArthur was appointed supremo of a United Nations army. He was pledged to remove the forces of Kim Il Sung from the soil of Syngham Rhee and his people. On 15 September 1950, MacArthur accomplished the apparently impossible (no doubt because the North Koreans believed that it *was* impossible), by landing an invasion force at Inchon. Eleven days later, Seoul was recaptured; and, less than one week after that, the men of the United Nations and their South Korean side-kicks were pushing northwards beyond the 38th parallel.

Kim Il Sung had no doubt overlooked the likelihood of United Nations' involvement when he laid his plans. To a casual observer, it might have appeared that his high ambitions were disintegrating along with his army. However, matters are seldom quite so simple as they seem. Not many miles away, the so-called Chinese People's Volunteer Army was limbering up. On 5 November 1950, reports of considerable troop movements on the Chinese-Korean border reached New York. Within three weeks, units of the CPVA were on the march, pushing back the UN forces that tried to block their way. On 28 December, they crossed the 38th parallel and, on New Year's Day 1951, Seoul was retaken.

There is reason to believe that many members of the Chinese forces were not really volunteers at all. They had been coerced into service by threats to their families, or else by the warning that, if they refused, they would be denied any opportunity to make a living in civilian life.

Such methods of recruitment do not promise the enthusiasm, the readiness, if need be, to die, so necessary to produce victories. However, anyone who believed that a simple way of escape lay in meekly surrendering was quickly disabused. Their opponents, the officers insisted, did not take prisoners. As one captive Chinese soldier said, 'I thought I would be killed, because I had been instructed for a long time that all prisoners are killed. In the People's Army, we were told that if we were captured by South Korean troops, we would be killed immediately, so that is what I expected.'

In one camp, a party of Chinese prisoners was detailed to dig holes for the disposal of waste. They went about their task industriously, though their faces were glum, and their thoughts seemed to be turned inward as if in meditation. Much to their guards' surprise, they suddenly burst out laughing when a truck pulled up and tipped its contents into one of the cavities. When asked for an explanation, one of them said that they had assumed they were digging their own graves before being shot.

Had it not been for the restraining hand of the United Nations, such might well have been their fate. As James Cameron points out in *Point of Departure*, Syngham Rhee's policemen were as unpleasant a bunch of ruffians as ever disgraced this planet. 'The South Korean police methods,' he wrote, 'continued to be the gossip of the rear-echelon HQs – the beatings-up, the crucifixions, the attachment of genitals to field telephones.' Such tortures were not being committed on the enemy but *on their own people*.

If the attitude of many Chinese soldiers was compounded of resignation, that of the United Nations' troops stopped some way short of enthusiastic. Those who had heard the stories told by POWs in Japanese hands during World War II, remembered that the Koreans were widely regarded as the most brutal of all the guards, surpassing, even, the excesses of Jap soldiers. Were such barbarians really worth the spilling of blood? In any case, many American servicemen (who made up the greater part of the UN force) knew so little about Korea, that they were uncertain of where it was.

Four days after the UN ground forces had engaged the enemy, and forty-eight hours after he had been captured, an American Army officer could be heard on Seoul Radio, delivering a 900 word talk. 'We did not know at all the cause of the war,' he said, 'and the real state of affairs, and we were compelled to fight against the people of Korea. It was really most generous of the Democratic People's Republic of Korea to forgive us and give kind consideration for our health, for food, clothing and habitation.'

The words had obviously been dictated by his captors, and the reference to North Korean generosity was rubbish. Nevertheless, many of those engaged in it did not know the cause of the war; and, had they done so, would probably have regarded it as a matter of small importance.

When journalists criticised the conduct of Syngham Rhee's policemen, UN officials were apt to point out that one must make allowances for local customs, and that one should not expect to find the attitudes of Palm Springs or Pinner in this bleak and not very pleasant land. The explanation may have satisfied some of them, but it would have been of small comfort to prisoners of war confined in camps north of the 38th parallel. As World War II had made abundantly clear, captivity at the hands of a Far Eastern power was something to be avoided at almost all costs.

In North Korea, the treatment was no more gentle. All the old familiar torments – such as malnutrition, inadequate accommodation, beatings up, and recurring attacks of beri-beri – were present, plus a newcomer to the list, *brainwashing*. It was, perhaps, significant that, in some cases, Chinese officials preferred to avoid the expression 'prisoners of war'. Instead, they called their captives, 'students'. But if a prison camp was to be converted into a university – running one course only, and that dedicated to overcoming the corrupting and decadent ideas of capitalism – they would have to realise that some of the pupils would show a greater aptitude than others. Some, indeed, would dissemble in the hope of winning rewards for good scholarship without, actually, taking the lessons to heart.

The North Koreans, at some point early on in the war, insisted that they would observe the rules of the 1949 Geneva Convention. The Chinese made no such promise. One camp commandant, who had doubtless been carefully coached for his task, described the proceedings at Geneva, and the work of the Red Cross, as 'Instruments of bourgeois idealism which it is impracticable to carry out'. They were, he said, devices 'used by imperialists and capitalists to cover their evil plans'. His own government, he explained, had a much better system. It was known as the 'Lenient Policy'.

Lenient Policy was another expression for 'brainwashing', and the first thing that any student of such matters should realise is that it was not lenient at all. Rather like Pavlov (the centenary of whose birth had, ironically, been celebrated in 1949) and his famous dog, it was based upon a system of rewards and punishments. It was not to be confused with 'heart-washing', which was a Buddhist custom entirely beyond reproach. Heart-washing meant that a man in his middle years might withdraw from the world, preferring a life of meditation to earthly cares and responsibilities. Brainwashing, on the other hand, was a not particularly subtle form of tampering with the mind, an attempt to remould political beliefs into whatever form those in control considered suitable.

Initially, it took its victims by surprise. Those who were captured by the North Koreans and Chinese had expected hardship and even brutality.

They had not, however, considered the proposition that they might have to fight for the safe custody of their own minds.

Admittedly, the Lenient Policy was a pale shadow of the brainwashing that went on in China itself. Nor did its practitioners expect to convert the mass of prisoners. A few would suffice; a nucleus, that is to say, who would argue the cause with their companions and, if there was reason to, inform on them.

The method took the form of tedious lectures, the filling-in of long questionnaires, and examinations in which the 'students' were required to comment on such matters as:

1 Give the reasons for the ever-deepening crisis of world capitalism.
2 Is peaceful co-existence between the different social systems possible?
3 Why does the Soviet Union head the World Peace Camp?
4 Who is the unjust aggressor in Korea?
5 Give Lenin's five contradictions within capitalism.
6 Say why the triumph of World Socialism is inevitable.

All the questions had to be attempted, and flippancy was not encouraged. When a United States officer criticised one of them as 'not worth the paper it is written on', he was removed to solitary confinement. He was accused not only of 'making a hostile remark' but also of 'slandering the Chinese paper-making industry'.

Even a less provocative incorrect answer was punished by twenty-one days in 'solitary'.

The authorities did their best to ensure that the POWs were isolated from Western influences. The *Daily Worker* (now the *Morning Star*) was the only English newspaper allowed inside the camps. Books by authors who might be considered unsympathetic to communism were banned though, with Dickens, Tolstoy, Victor Hugo, Upton Sinclair and Howard Fast, on the list of those that were considered suitable, the literary outlook was not entirely bleak. The singing of patriotic songs was forbidden. On the other hand, the regime clearly understood the value of a good tune. For example, *John Brown's Body* had been retitled *Solidarity* by some ingenious propagandist in Peking. The words, which the prisoners were required to sing frequently, now were:

> Solidarity for ever.
> Solidarity for ever.
> Solidarity for ever.
> The Party makes us strong.

American POWs paraded through the streets of Hanoi during the Vietnam War (*Popperfoto*)

An American POW is put on show for press photographers during the Vietnam War (*Popperfoto*)

Homecoming – in this case American prisoners from North Vietnam – is the best moment in a POW's life (*Popperfoto*)

Not surprisingly, the POWs preferred the original version. As the war progressed, compulsory singing was abandoned as useless, and the quality of broadcasts in English from Radio Peking, which were relayed over the loud-speaker systems, were improved. At first, there had been long and infinitely tedious political lectures. Later, however, there was less of this – sports news was included, and there were recitals of music by Tchaikovsky and Beethoven.

Visitors to the camps were restricted to those who were ready to praise the communist attitude – even if it meant that many of the POWs were ill, and that some were suffering extremes of ill-treatment. Among them was a reporter named Michael Sapiro, who was the *Daily Worker*'s man in Peking. Mr Sapiro promised that he would arrange for the prisoners to receive supplies of DDT, scissors, matches and cigarettes. He would also, he said, make it possible for them to be given shaves and haircuts. In fact, all that his influence produced was one tattered copy of *A Tale of Two Cities* and two copies of the *Shanghai News*.

If Mr Sapiro had expected an affectionate welcome, he was disappointed. A sergeant in the Royal Ulster Rifles, who was suffering from dysentery and beri-beri (he was later to die from one or the other complaint), chided him on being 'the poorest specimen of an Englishman I've ever seen, and if I could get my fingers round your scrawny neck, I'd wring it'. Sapiro's reply was, 'I'll have you shot'. He then proceeded to lecture a group of American POWs on their role as 'warmongering dogs'. The remarks were overheard by an English other rank who, though a member of the British Communist Party, was not impressed. The words 'disgusted' him.

The rewards for toeing the party line were better rations, medical attention and a degree of consideration. Without any doubt at all, the principal object of both the Chinese and the North Koreans was to obtain material that could be used for propaganda purposes. They were not disappointed. The Chinese were able to publish two booklets of candid confessions by American POWs who professed to having been converted. They contained such statements as 'We should never have poked our noses in here. We had our own Civil War in the States and would have resented any other country interfering. We are a peace-loving people, and we would defend our homes at any cost, but we resent being used for a cause such as this.' And:

> To the big firms, war means profits from aeroplanes, tanks, contracts for army clothing, guns, ammunition and other materials. To us soldiers, it means misery, desolation and loss of life, and to the folks at home it means the breaking up of the family, high taxes and hardship.

Four hundred prisoners of war appended their signatures to these observations, which entitled them to be classified as 'progressives'. Those who refused were dismissed as 'reactionaries' and suffered much more severe treatment.

Nevertheless, on 11 February 1951, 279 POWs (most of them American) signed a petition urging the war to be brought to an end. Like the 400 who endorsed the other document, it should not be assumed that all of the signatories were sincere. Some, certainly, succeeded in bluffing the authorities that they had undergone a change of heart.

But many stubbornly resisted all attempts to suborn them. One private soldier, who was wounded and captured on 24 April 1951, received no medical attention until 4 June 1953. A member of the Gloucestershire Regiment, who refused to impart certain information, was taken from his cell at 9 o'clock one morning, stripped to the waist, and beaten by two Chinese soldiers, using a club rather like a baseball bat, until 3 o'clock that afternoon. He was compelled to stand to attention throughout the ordeal.

An English soldier (Derek Kinne), who had carried his defiance to the point of making an unsuccessful attempt to escape, described his punishment thus:

> Just before dawn I was led into the next room where a stout beam ran in from the gable end of a house. Over this went a rope. They now placed handcuffs on my wrists behind my back, tied one end of the rope to these and pulled the other. Slowly my hands were forced up my back and, when these would go no further, they pulled me just clear of the floor.

Mr Kinne remained in this position for several hours. When he was released, he was unable to stand up. He was given a meal of tepid gruel, but: 'I was unable to hold the bowl as it was offered to me. The guard commander withdrew, leaving it on the floor. I crawled over, anxious to reach the moisture that lay inside. Heedless of my light beard, I pushed my face into the mush and lapped like an animal.'

As in most other wars, the North Korean forces had been ill-prepared to receive their captives. There were notorious death marches between the front line and the eventual prison camps, the first of which, at Pyotong, was not established until January 1951. The Chinese protested that the conditions were as good as those experienced by the local inhabitants and by their own troops. If this was so, they must have been very robust. Between January and August 1951, an estimated 1,600 United Nations troops died in captivity.

The Lenient Policy was lenient to the extent that nobody was liable to summary execution. If, on the other hand, a prisoner died as a result of treatment for refusing to become a 'progressive', that was his own concern. He was merely paying for his refusal to repent of his crimes; for being a 'war criminal'. As the commandant of the camp (Number 5) at Pyotong succinctly put it, 'We will keep you here ten, twenty, thirty or even forty years if necessary, until you learn the truth, and if you still won't learn it, we will bury you so deep you won't even stink.'

As an encouragement to learn the truth, so-called reactionaries underwent the severest possible punishments. Not only were they denied adequate food and medicine, they were sentenced to solitary confinement, which varied in its degree of awfulness. Some were required to stand to attention from 4.30 in the morning until 11 o'clock at night. Then, when they tried to sleep, they were continually roused by the guards – 'to make sure you're still here'. Even in mid-winter, they were allowed only their underclothing, nor did they receive any bedding or washing facilities. One POW in solitary was refused water for eleven days – 'to help,' he was told, 'with your self-reflections'.

But the worst ordeal in this horrible catalogue of confinement was that of the 'wooden boxes' used at Camp 1. Each measured only 5ft by 3ft by 2ft. Food, always bad, was stopped for several days at a time: water supplies seemed to depend upon the whims of the guard. A private in the Gloucestershire Regiment spent six months in one of these minute cages for some misdemeanour or other.

Beatings and torments similar to that suffered by Mr Kinne were commonplace. In mid-winter, men were hauled out into the snow, and compelled to stand at attention for long periods. One soldier was kept in this position for thirty hours, with a sentry on either side ready to jab him with a bayonet, in case he collapsed. An alternative that did not depend on the season was to make a captive kneel on two small, jagged, rocks. With his arms extended he was forced to hold a much larger rock over his head for several hours. Those who suffered this experience usually needed several days' recuperation before they were able to walk again.

Winter – which, in Korea, was extremely severe – was the constant ally of the communist torturers. They used it to particularly evil effect by marching POWs barefoot to the Yalu River in 20° of frost. The men were required to stand on the ice, while buckets of water were poured over their feet. The water froze immediately, and there they were – stuck fast and compelled to remain there for several hours. This, again, was supposed to be an opportunity to 'reflect on crimes'.

But the attitude of the enemy was not constant. Shortly after Mr Kinne became a POW, he found himself in an air-raid shelter with an English-speaking North Korean. The man waved his pistol at him, and brought out all the old jargon. He was, he said, 'a capitalist, imperial aggressor, a tool of Wall Street, a raper of Korean national aspiration', and similar phrases from the approved primer of invective.

When he had exhausted this theme, he stepped outside for a moment or two, presumably for a breath of fresh air. On his return, he was a completely different man. He produced photographs of his family, and asked Mr Kinne whether he had any pictures. What kind of a place was England? he wondered. If he went there, would he be welcomed? When the time came to depart, he offered Mr Kinne a lift into Seoul on the back of his motorcycle.

The Chinese protested that the 'Lenient Policy' was based on 'humanitarianism, equality and international law'. They also asserted that it was tolerant so far as religion was concerned. In the spring of 1951, the 1st Battalion of the Gloucestershire Regiment was virtually wiped out on the bank of the Imjim River, while holding up the communist advance on Seoul. Many of them were now behind enemy barbed wire, north of the parallel. As Christmas approached, the battalion's padre, the Rev S. J. Davies, MBE MA CF, prepared to celebrate Holy Communion. Lieutenant-Colonel Fred Carne, the unit's commanding officer, had shown himself to be a man of more than military talents. Using two large nails and a somewhat rudimentary hammer, he had carved a small Celtic cross out of stone. All that was now needed were bread and wine for the sacrament.

Surprisingly, the Chinese turned out to be co-operative. They provided both; indeed, they went further. The commandant, a Commander Ding, who was more commonly known as 'Snake-eyes', decided that Christmas might be treated as a festive occasion. The camp could be decorated, the POWs had permission to hold a concert, there would be a holiday from indoctrination lectures, and – very much to the point – a special meal of bread, potatoes and chicken would be served at 5 pm.

This was a most pleasant change. Did it mean that 'Snake-eyes' had undergone some strange revision of his ideas? Some while later, Mr Davies was disabused of any such notion. He was put into solitary confinement for giving talks on religion and the Bible, and for holding choir practice. The charge was that he had been conducting 'illegal religious activities and [had] a hostile attitude'.

Camp 2, where the population included 370 American and British officers, had once been a Korean school house. It was 10 miles away from Camp 5, where a large number of other ranks were imprisoned. There were thirty inhabitants in each room at Camp 2. The floor was covered with straw mats, on which the POWs slept shoulder-to-shoulder. The only source of warmth was a small wood-burning stove. In all conscience, it was uncomfortable enough, but Mr Davies was now confined to a cell 6ft long by 4ft wide, with clay and wattle walls, and rough dirt floor. His neighbour was a young American Air Force corporal, who had been there for several months. The NCO's crime, it seemed, was refusing to admit that the UN forces had used germ warfare.

Opposite, there was an American lieutenant, who lived in perpetual darkness.

The inhabitants of Camp 2 were frequently told about the good behaviour of the POWs in Camp 5, and how their zealous studies had earned them extra rations. This, clearly, was part of the technique. It may be that those in Camp 5 were told similar stories about Camp 2. In each, the majority (and in Camp 2, it was absolute) resisted the enticements of the Lenient Policy in its own way. Had it furthered the cause, the Chinese would not have been beyond pushing the POWs over the edge of sanity. As it happens, however, the prisoners drove at least one of their 'tutors' towards a nervous breakdown.

Wei was one of several brainwashers who were sent from Peking after receiving instruction in the technique. Each put in a few weeks attempting to teach the 'truth', and was then relieved by another. Wei was a tiresome individual, who made a habit of marching into the camp shortly before dawn, turning on all the lights, and expecting his 'students' to be ready for their lessons.

On one occasion, the POWs were up before Wei arrived. Scooping up their few possessions, they hastened out of the room and hid. When Wei entered, he found the place empty. He hurried away to report to his superiors. All the prisoners, it seemed, had escaped.

As soon as he was safely out of the way, the POWs returned from their hiding places. Some chatted in groups, other played games with home-made cards. The scene was entirely normal.

Brainwasher Wei, now accompanied by the commandant and several members of his staff, asked where they'd been. Somebody innocently asked, 'What do you mean?' Wei explained that the room had been empty a few minutes ago. '*Empty*,' he exclaimed, now becoming angry and no doubt aware that his senior officers were looking at him with that expression of sceptical inquiry which senior officers of all races affect so well.

One POW asked, not very helpfully, whether he had been having trouble with his eyes. Another sympathised with him about his job. The work must be a strain; no wonder he was going crazy. Perhaps he was right. Before the week was over, Wei had been replaced.

His successor was given similar treatment. On the first morning, he came into the room early and turned on the light. Some men were playing cards, others were studying propaganda leaflets, one or two were reading the *China Monthly Review*, and a few were sewing. This, apparently, had been going on in the dark. What on earth was he to make of it?

Prisoners were compelled to attend meetings in small groups, during which accounts of the United Nations' alleged 'germ warfare' atrocities were read aloud to them. Afterwards, the topic was discussed. Those who delivered a flat 'No' to the question 'Do you believe these reports?' were dismissed as 'reactionaries': those who wavered, were regarded as promising 'progressive' material.

The next step in this campaign was to produce evidence. There were photographs of sick farmers, smears of what was said to be bacteria and horribly distorted rats, pickled in alcohol. On one occasion, a Chinese officer brought in a container of what he claimed to be deadly insects.

An American soldier decided that the ruse had gone far enough. Reaching out, he snatched one of the bugs from the jar and ate it. The Chinese had to rush him to hospital (or that is what they said). His last words on leaving the room were that he felt no ill-effects at all.

In Camp 2, one week was elected to become 'Crazy Week'. It was by now clear that one of many things their captors were unable to understand was the Western sense of humour. Indeed, under the circumstances of the prisoners' confinement, they may have wondered how anyone could have a sense of humour at all.

To stage anything such as 'Crazy Week', the prisoners had to choose the occasion carefully. It had to be during a period when the Chinese were trying to project the image of sweet reason. In times of tension, the effects might have been disastrous. But when the word 'lenient' meant more or less what the dictionary says, nobody was likely to become too concerned. The worst that could happen was that somebody would say that the POWs' sanity had finally snapped.

A programme of considerable variety was arranged. On one day, the prisoners all rode imaginary bicycles. One of them stopped a guard and asked the way to the nearest post office. He wished, he said, to collect the mail.

On another day, each walked about the camp with an imaginary girl-friend on his arm. If one of the Chinese officials approached, he would stop and, very courteously, introduce his unseen companion. But the big event was when they, so to speak, turned a field into the deck of an aircraft carrier. POWs with their arms outstretched played the part of aeroplanes coming into land. One of them gave a very passable imitation of a helicopter. But he had a talent for such impersonations. On the 'bicycling' day, he had gone one better than the others, and ridden a 'motorcycle'.

Among the inhabitants of Camp 2, there was a British POW named 'Jungle' Aylward, who must have set some sort of record for enduring more than his fair share of hell. In World War II, he had been a prisoner of the Japanese; now he was in communist custody. To relieve the monotony of life, and to alarm one of the Peking 'tutors' (an officer who was known as 'Hedgehog' on account of his spiky little beard), they decided to burn Mr Aylward at the stake. It was well stage-managed, though there was a brief moment of anxiety when the fire seemed to be moving a little too near this latter-day Joan of Arc. 'Hedgehog', certainly, was impressed.

Why, he wished to know, was Aylward being burned? 'Because,' somebody said, 'we don't like him.' Why did they not like him? Because he was not likable. This essay in logic could have gone on for ever, and so 'Hedgehog' tried another angle. Did this sort of thing, he wondered, happen in England? Yes, he was assured: it was an English tribal custom.

His credulity on this point is hard to understand, for he had, apparently, received some of his education in New York, which should have introduced him to the habits of the West. But 'Hedgehog' was sincere to the point of naïvety. Sometimes he would exclaim excitedly that he, too, was far from perfect. 'I may have failed', he would say. 'If so, I am ready to criticise myself sincerely and conscientiously.' The POWs should do likewise – and forsake the apparently barbarous ways of their homeland.

Eventually, he ordered the long-suffering Mr Aylward to be released. Next day, an order was pinned up on the camp notice board. 'NCOs and men,' it said, 'are forbidden to burn their colleagues. This is an inhuman bourgeois practice that will not be tolerated.'

It occupied a place of honour beside two other compositions:

No man can be sick without getting permission.
When the commandant speaks, no man can joke and make strange noises.

Among the POWs themselves, a favourite piece of verse was a rewritten extract from *The Scarlet Pimpernel*. It was recited in two versions. One (as delivered by a sergeant in the Glosters) was:

> They seek him here, they seek him there,
> They seek the b***** everywhere.
> Will he be shot, or will he be hung
> That damned elusive Kim Il Sung.

The other was similar, except Mao Tse-tung was substituted for the president of North Korea.

South of the 38th parallel, the United Nations' authorities were also carrying out a campaign of persuasion among their prisoners, though nobody would have dreamed of describing it as 'brainwashing'. Entitled 'Rehabilitation Project for Prisoners of War', the methods were, in any case, more gentle. Mostly, it was a matter of listening to talks by educationalists, business men, diplomats and government officials, all of them explaining the advantages of the Western way of life.

When they were first captured, the communist troops presented just as sorry a picture as their capitalist counterparts. According to one witness, when they marched into the prison-camp complex at Pymgyong (on the coast to the north-east of Pusan), 'Thousands of prisoners of war were taken and in great hunger, for they had just been made POWs. A man could not look at them face to face, because they were miserable beasts, looking dull and withered.'

Nevertheless, the fight had by no means gone out of many of them, and not the least of the problems was to separate the ardent communists from those who had been forced into service. This was part of the plan, for the communists intended that a POW camp should not be a place removed from the scene of fighting, but a battleground in its own right. If there were confusion about who were likely to make trouble and who were not, it would make the guards' task more difficult.

There were many disturbances. Matters reached a head on 7 May 1952, when Brigadier-General Francis T. Dodd, the commanding officer of POW Camp 1, was taken prisoner by the prisoners during a tour of inspection of Compound 70 on Kojedo island. He was held for seventy-eight hours. The ring-leader was a character named Pak Sang Hyong, by all appearances a simple private soldier. In fact, he was the head of the captives, working under orders from General Num II of the North Korean People's Army.

Pak Sang Hyong was required by his master to stir up as much trouble as possible. The taking hostage of Brigadier-General Dodd was a masterstroke. Up at Panmunjong, a few miles south of the 38th parallel, communist and United Nations' negotiators were engaged in an apparently endless series of talks about ending the war. Among the major points of disagreement was the matter of prisoners of war. One of the questions was: should POWs in UN hands be sent back to communist countries against their will? There were, it appeared, 50,000 who did not wish to return.

The taking of Dodd seemed to be rich in propaganda potential. It indicated, surely, some degree of incompetence. To take a man prisoner on the battlefield was not remarkable. To carry out such an action within a prison camp; this *really* was an achievement. The wily Pak must have felt very satisfied with his performance.

Having abducted the unfortunate general, Pak's next move was to issue terms for his release. Dodd, he said, would be killed unless:

1 The UN high command admitted that bloodshed had taken place in UN prisoner of war camps, and promised that treatment would be more humane in the future.
2 The repatriation of prisoners would take place under conditions demanded by the communist delegates at Panmunjong.
3 There would be no more screening of prisoners – and no more searches.
4 That it would be in order for a representative group from the North Korean People's Army and the Chinese People's Volunteer Army to visit prisoners of war.

Dodd was prepared to admit that some prisoners had been killed by the guards. There had, he said, been so much rioting, that such casualties were inevitable. The question of repatriation was a matter for the peace conference: there was nothing that he could do about it. He denied that prisoners had been forcibly screened, and there was little he could do about visits from the communist armies.

Eventually, after an uncomfortable three-and-a-half days, Pak released him. Brigadier-General Dodd and a colleague, Brigadier-General Charles F. Colson, were sent back to the United States in disgrace. The brass hats believed Dodd should have refused to take part in any talks; but, rather, that General Colson should have secured his release by force. Whether Dodd would have survived a gun battle seems very doubtful indeed. Soldiers such as Pak and his fellow hard-liners were probably indifferent to their own fate and, certainly, to that of their hostage. They were simply servants of the machine.

Not the least of the problems confronting the UN negotiators at Panmunjong was confusion about the POW situation. In the early part of 1951, the communists claimed to have 65,000 UN prisoners in their custody. Later, however, they amended the figure to 11,500. The actual statistics are hard to unravel, partly because there is no record of the precise number of those who died in the eleven communist prison camps, and at the fiendish North Korean interrogation centre known as 'Pak's Death House' (after its commandant, another Pak).

So far as anyone can tell, the communists captured 92,500 men, of which 80,000 were South Koreans, about 10,000 were Americans and 2,500 were from other UN forces. On the other side, the UN forces took about 171,000 communist prisoners – 20,000 of them Chinese and the remainder, North Koreans.

It would no doubt have made the negotiations more simple, if the UN delegates had agreed that the 50,000 captives who opposed repatriation should be compelled to go home. But such capitulation would have been cruel. Eventually, 15,000 Chinese were sent to Formosa; and 8,000 North Koreans were allowed to settle in South Korea.

One estimate suggests that two-thirds of all the Americans taken prisoner either died or were killed in captivity. Since the urge to survive is a very strong one, it is, perhaps, surprising that more were not seduced by the 'Lenient Policy'. Some, certainly, were affected by it, and the authorities were not unreasonably concerned that, when the POWs came marching home, there might be a substantial number of communist 'moles' in their ranks. In fact, only about one-third seemed to have been affected by brainwashing; and, of these, most changed their ideas when they returned to normal home life. Only forty or so remained convinced communists, and only twenty-two (twenty-one Americans and one Royal Marine Commando from Britain) refused repatriation and preferred to remain behind.

A survey of the American defectors shows that fifteen of them were under twenty-one years of age; only three came from well-off homes; sixteen were withdrawn personalities – 'loners', that is to say; nineteen felt unloved or unwanted by their fathers or step-fathers; ten had either lost or been taken away from their mothers in early childhood; seventeen did not finish their courses at high school; twenty of them had, before the war, never heard of communist 'except as a dirty word'; and twenty of them had no idea of why they were fighting in North Korea. Only two were married men.

More surprising, perhaps, is the fact that two had won bronze stars for heroism in World War II.

This was the only occasion in American history on which any of that country's POWs had elected not to go home when the war was over – preferring, it seemed, the enemy's system of government to that of their own country.

Of the convinced communists who made the journey back to the States, fourteen were eventually court-martialled for alleged treachery. The most serious offender was a sergeant, who was said to have killed two of his seriously ill companions, by throwing them out of the hut to die in the snow. In the battle for the mind, it cannot be surprising if some men go mad.

12

THE NEW BARBARIANISM

The Korean War had done little to enhance the American reputation for enduring life in captivity. It was, admittedly, a conflict that lacked the glory of a crusade (How could a GI feel strongly about a country of which, until he arrived there, he had known little or, more likely, nothing?) It was, too, easy to criticise if you were not being starved and beaten, or if you were not dying for want of medical attention – and easier still if you were thousands of miles removed from this hellish place. The standards of Washington DC were, perhaps, higher than those of a wooden-hutted slum on the banks of the Yalu River.

Nevertheless, fighting men of no matter what nationality have seldom been required to understand the reason why. It should have been enough that they were fighting *communism*, and that some abstract quality known as 'honour' was involved. Seven hundred or so POWs had bought themselves slightly better conditions simply by signing their names. After all, who cared about being an imperialist lackey of warmongering Wall Street, if a confession to this effect brought one closer to the most simple of necessities for survival? Unfortunately, the fact that the wording may have seemed silly, did not lessen its value as propaganda for the enemy.

In 1949, the new Geneva Convention had restated what POWs had a right to expect from their captors. It now seemed necessary to itemise what the United States had a right to expect from its sons in captivity. It was, perhaps, all the more urgent since they might, again, become victims of treatment that would have made the Geneva pundits recoil in horror. The rules were issued by President Eisenhower as an executive order in August 1955. Referred to as the Code of Conduct, there were six articles. Thus:

1 I am an American fighting man. I serve in the forces which guard my country and our way of life. I am prepared to give my life in their defence.
2 I will never surrender of my own free will. If in command, I will never surrender my men while they still have the means to resist.
3 If I am captured, I will continue to resist by all means available. I will

make every effort to escape and aid others to escape. I will accept neither
parole nor special favours from the enemy.

4 If I become a prisoner of war, I will keep faith with my fellow prisoners.
I will give no information nor take part in any action which might be
harmful to my comrades. If I am senior, I will take command. If not, I will
obey the lawful orders of those appointed over me and will back them up
in every way.

5 When questioned, should I become a prisoner of war, I am bound to
give only name, rank, service number and date of birth. I will evade
answering further questions to the utmost of my ability. I will make no
oral or written statements disloyal to my country and its allies or harmful
to their cause.

6 I will never forget that I am an American fighting man, responsible for
my actions and dedicated to the principles which made my country free.
I will trust in my God and in the United States of America.

The code was not a legal document: it was an appeal, perhaps, to the
integrity of United States servicemen. According to Rear-Admiral Jeremiah
A. Denton Jnr, USN, 'There was no underestimating [its] effect, both on
our behaviour, or on the treatment we received in prison ... even under
the stress of a Vietnam prison camp.' Since Admiral Denton had been a
POW in the hands of the North Vietnamese, he was well able to judge.
Another admiral in captivity, Rear-Admiral James B. Stockdale, believed
that special training was necessary. Survival schools could teach resistance
to mental harassment. 'You have,' Stockdale wrote, 'to learn to take a bunch
of junk and accept it with a sense of humour.' So far as physical ill-
treatment was concerned, suitable training might be provided by various
sports: 'It is a very important experience; you have to practise hurting.
There is no question about it.'

In fact, it seems very doubtful whether anything to do with sport can
prepare men for the ultimate in barbarous treatment, the sheer and terrible
brutality that a suitably ruthless inquisitor can inflict upon his victim.

Conditions in North Korean prison camps had been bad enough. Those
in Vietnam took the horror story a shade further – not least because, in the
case of many American POWs, the ordeal went on for very much longer.
It was the most protracted war in which the United States had ever been
engaged; and, with some of the nation's men in captivity for seven years,
the most drawn-out saga of suffering.

The miracle of life in North Vietnamese prison camps is not the stoicism
with which the POWs stood up to their torments, but the fact that any
actually *survived* them.

Strangely enough, the North Vietnamese were among the signatories of the Geneva Convention. They avoided what many might have considered their obligations by stating that, since America had never declared war on their country, the captives were not, in fact, prisoners of war at all. They variously described them as 'criminals' and 'air pirates'. This permitted them to practise brutality on a scale that caused the Secretary of the US Navy, John H. Chafee, to write: 'In all the modern history of man's inhumanity to man, there is no example of crueller or more inhuman treatment than that being dealt to our prisoners of war and their families by the North Vietnamese.'

Mr Chafee was writing in the July 1971, *Proceedings of the US Naval Institute*. The United States and the South Vietnamese were, he claimed, scrupulously complying with the Convention (an assertion that, so far as the South Vietnamese were concerned, some might have regarded as debatable), whilst the enemy paid no attention to it whatsoever.

To illustrate his point, he described the case of a naval lieutenant who had been repatriated. 'He was held in solitary confinement,' said Mr Chafee, 'until he began talking to the rats. At one time he was forced to sit on a narrow stool without moving for four days until his legs became so bloated and he lost consciousness and fell off.' In twenty-two months as a POW he had lost 50lb in weight – existing on two meals a day, each of which amounted to no more than pumpkin soup, pig fat, and bread or rice.

He had chilling stories to tell of other POWs, who had been hanged from the ceilings of their cells, who had been dragged along the ground with broken legs, or had been denied food or sleep for long periods.

Although this officer's family had sent him 120 letters, he had received only two of them. 'When mail is permitted,' Mr Chafee wrote, 'it is capricious, irregular, heavily censored, and usually handled through extreme anti-war groups who forward it to the anxious families with propaganda tracts denouncing US policies.'

No inspection of the camps was permitted, though selected interviews under controlled conditions were sometimes allowed for propaganda purposes. Newspapermen were occasionally handed out photographs of American POWs being marched through the streets of Hanoi in front of jeering crowds. A few, carefully selected, journalists, were allowed to watch films of prisoners in the so-called 'Hanoi Hilton' – posed before a table laden with fruit and other items of food. As at least one discerning eye noticed, the reluctant actors in these motion pictures were never seen to be eating anything.

By contrast, Mr Chafee said, the International Red Cross was permitted to make frequent inspections of South Vietnamese camps.

One man who worked incessantly in attempts to improve the fortunes of American POWs in North Vietnam was a Dallas industrialist named Ross Perot. Whilst agreeing that representatives of the IRC had not been allowed into the prison camps of North Vietnam, Mr Perot was doubtful whether its representatives had made sufficient effort. Addressing a hearing before a subcommittee of the House of Representatives in 1970, he said that the International Red Cross's 'concept of aggressive action is a memo every six months. When a man is rotting, he deserves more than that. I urge you to use the full power of your position to get the IRC to move aggresively.'

Mr Perot, who had been one of the few Americans to visit North Vietnam, and one of the very few whose motives were entirely beyond reproach, did his best to explain the enemy's attitude to its captives. 'They place,' he said, 'the same value on these prisoners that I put on this pad of paper. If I have it, fine; if I don't have it, I can get another pad. They just cannot believe that a nation, most of whose population has been able to ignore that our men are being killed on the battlefield, can become aroused over, as they say, "just 1500 men".' The actual number of Americans interned in North Vietnam was 1,600, of which 760 were pilots.

Rear-Admiral Stockdale, who was seeing the situation from the wrong side of the barbed wire, believed that, to the enemy, American POWs represented a wealth of propaganda material. 'In Vietnam,' he said, 'the American prisoner of war did not suddenly find himself on the war's sidelines. Rather, he found himself on one of the major battlefronts – the propaganda battlefront ... Our captors told us they never expected to defeat us on the battlefield, but did believe they could defeat us on the propaganda front.'

'The enemy,' he elaborated, 'believed that, sooner or later, every one of us could be broken to his will ... Some of us might take more breaking than others, but all of us could be broken.'

Since many of the North Vietnamese leaders had spent some time as political prisoners, they had a certain expertise in such matters. They realised the strength that prisoners gain from within their own ranks and the value to their morale of good leadership. Anyone who showed any symptoms of this quality was singled out for particularly harsh treatment; but, even for the mass of prisoners, the policy for much of the time was to keep each isolated from another. Some men spent as many as four years in solitary confinement; one naval captain, Howard Rutledge, spent nearly five years; and Lieutenant Everett Alvarez Jnr, who was shot down in August 1964, held the record – with seven years in solitary. According to the rules of the Geneva Convention – and, come to that, of United States penal institutions – the maximum period that any prisoner should be required to suffer such conditions was thirty days.

From a flier's point of view, the transition from life on active service to that of a captive was abrupt and brutal. Lieutenant-Commander John M. McGrath took off from USS *Constellation* on 30 June 1967, in an A4-C Skyhawk. This, his 178th mission, was to be an 'armed reconnaissance' over North Vietnamese territory. He bombed a small pontoon bridge; and then suddenly, McGrath's world underwent a drastic transformation. The Skyhawk was hit by anti-aircraft fire. He ejected – whilst down on the ground, a small reception committee assembled to greet him. There were a few local farmers and one or two militiamen. The farmers were armed with what, when he could see them more clearly, he identified as 'rusty knives'.

They pushed him to the ground. One man pressed a knife against his throat, while the others applied themselves to remove his clothing. If they had understood more about Western flying attire, the task would have been easier, if no less rough. But these people did not seem to know anything about zip-fasteners; indeed, instead of unzipping, they took considerable trouble to cut the fasteners away.

Some minutes later, almost naked and with one shoulder dislocated, he was placed upon a bamboo stretcher and carried to a nearby village. An announcement by one of the militiamen, who was equipped with a battery-powered megaphone, brought the peasants out on to the street. Some of them beat McGrath with canes, others contented themselves with pinching him, and one or two enthusiasts amused themselves by twisting his leg. 'My knee would dislocate,' he wrote in *Prisoner of war; six years in Hanoi,* 'and the people seemed to get a kick out of seeing me scream in agony.'

Ten days passed until, at last, he reached Hanoi. On one occasion he was taken from a truck and forced into a narrow ditch. 'The soldiers who were guarding [a nearby bridge] took turns to see who could hit my face the hardest. After the contest, they tried to force dog dung through my teeth, bounced rocks off my chest, jabbed me with their gun barrels, and bounced the back of my head off the rocks that lay in the bottom of the ditch.

'I said my final prayer that night, because I was sure I would not reach Hanoi alive.' By the time he did reach the 'New Guy Village', a section of the 'Hanoi Hilton' reserved for the torture and interrogation of new arrivals, he had a badly dislocated shoulder, a fractured left arm, two fractured vertebrae and a fractured left knee. As if to round matters off, an interrogator dislocated his right shoulder and right elbow. 'I wished I could die! When the Vietnamese threatened to shoot me, I begged them to do it. Their answer was, "No – you are a criminal. You haven't suffered enough".'

Twenty days after arriving in captivity, a guard held him down and dry-shaved off his beard. Afterwards, he was allowed to shave and wash twice a week.

He was now quartered in a room measuring 7ft by 9ft. There was a peep-hole in the door through which, from time to time, a guard would look at him. On each occasion and, indeed, whenever he encountered a North Vietnamese, he was required to bow. Sometimes, according to his calculations, the peep-hole scrutiny was carried out 100 times a day. If, on any of these occasions, he failed to make his obeisance, he was thrown to the floor and kicked.

A high fever, boils and dysentery had now been added to his other ailments. After one month, he considered it an achievement to be able to sit up and urinate into a bucket.

The interrogation, or 'quizzing' as the prisoners called it, was probably the worst part. McGrath was required to admit that 'You are the blackest air pirate. You commit crimes of aggression against the peace-loving people of Vietnam. You have been duped by the capitalist warmongers of Wall Street. You have obstinate and bad attitude. Now the camp commandant allow you to write war crime confessions and condemn the imperialist warmonger United States. If you do not co-operate, you will be seriously punished.'

McGrath did not co-operate, and his ordeal continued.

The punishments varied. On one occasion, a guard noticed him on the floor of his cell, trying to look out through a vent. For this, he was compelled to kneel for thirty hours with a small rock under each knee. Many of the POWs were beaten with rubber hoses or straps: one nearly died after receiving 100 strokes a day for nine days. Another, who was caught attempting to escape, was tortured until his reason finally snapped and he went mad. The officer in the cell next to McGrath died of his ordeal – made worse, no doubt, by the fact that his room was smaller than most, and all the windows and air vents had either been bricked-up or plugged.

Each camp had its own style of punishment, and each torturer his preferred technique. So called 'torture-cuffs' were commonplace; they were handcuffs carefully fitted to ensure that they would cut into the flesh and impede the circulation. Some cells had stocks installed across the ends of the beds. The top half was wrought from rusty iron, making certain that the merest scratch would bring about an infection. If a POW's feet became too swollen for it to be fitted into place by normal methods, a guard applied his weight – usually by standing on it – to force it into position.

In *When Hell Was In Session*, Rear-Admiral Denton records that, after an eternity of torture, he eventually broke down and wrote, 'Dear Ho Chi Minh, I am sorry I bombed your country. Please forgive me.' There is no record of whether Ho Chi Minh was satisfied: he probably never saw the note. But Denton never forgave himself.

The so-called 'jungle camps' were mostly managed by the Vietcong, and conditions in them varied. A particularly unpleasant establishment was run by the leader, Pathet Lao. It was surrounded by a stockade manufactured from bamboo, and the accommodation amounted to a few primitive thatched huts. Among the amusements of the guards was that of tying a POW to a water buffalo and causing the beast to drag him through the bush. Others were trussed to trees and used for target practice. All the POWs in this camp suffered from malnutrition and intestinal parasites. Apart from the occasions when they were tortured, they were allowed out of their huts only to empty their toilet buckets. One of Pathet Lao's prisoners managed to escape. His weight on going into captivity had been 180lb. When he returned to freedom, it was no more than 80lb (5.71 stone).

At another jungle camp, conditions were rather better. The POWs received three meals a day; they were allowed to smoke; and, once a month, they received news of the world outside. It was, of course, carefully selected: they were told of the assassinations of President Kennedy and Dr Martin Luther King, and, later, of Nixon's election as President. Now and again, they were allowed to write letters, though it seems unlikely that they were ever collected from the camp. None of them, certainly, ever reached its destination.

It was possible, though very difficult, to escape from a jungle camp, and twenty-four POWs succeeded. Nobody ever managed to get away from a camp in Hanoi. There were three of these establishments in the city: 'the Plantation Garden', which had once been the home of the Hanoi's mayor, 'the Zoo' (formerly a film studio) and the 'Hanoi Hilton' – actually Hoa Lo Prison, a jail that had been purpose-built by the French.

Life at Hanoi Hilton was more formalised. The average cell measured 8ft by 8ft; there was a small, barred window looking out on to a wall crowned by fragments of broken bottles and an iron-reinforced door with the inevitable peep-hole. A bunk manufactured entirely from boards served as a bed; the only washing facility was a trough filled with cold water.

The day began at about 6 am, when the prisoners were awakened with a gong. In each cell, there was a loud-speaker through which, twice daily, propaganda broadcasts in English were relayed from Radio Hanoi. There were two meals a day, provided on wooden trays, and the POWs were allowed three cigarettes a day. Each prisoner was issued with two sets of pyjama-like clothing, two blankets, a tube of toothpaste and some soap. It was the only prison to which outsiders were ever admitted, and the only establishment from which POWs were repatriated.

Each man had his own methods of retaining his sanity. Rear-Admiral Stockdale later explained that 'most men need some kind of personal philosophy to endure what the Vietnam prisoners of war endured. For many it is religion; for many it is a patriotic cause; for some it is simply a question of doing their jobs even though the result – confinement as a POW – may not seem necessarily fair.'

As a reinforcement, there was, presumably, the Code of Conduct.

Commander R. J. Naughton, who spent six years as an unwilling guest of the North Vietnamese, points out that 'Something so innocuous as smoking a cigarette provides a feeling of security in that the act of smoking is a familiar experience, and, to one who has tried a Vietnamese cigarette, it is obvious that an ulterior motive is required to enjoy it.'

So far as the 'quizzes' were concerned, Commander Naughton believed that 'It was not necessary for the POW to yield control of himself to the interrogator, but merely to convey the impression of such.' For example, the interrogator might say, 'You know we can force you to answer, don't you?' If the prisoner replied 'Yes, you most likely can', the question or demand was often dropped. Similarly, many of these officials had preconceived ideas of what the answers relating to military matters, or else to covert POW activity, would be. If the prisoner could perceive what they were and if, as often happened, they were erroneous, it did no harm to earn approval by confirming the mistaken belief.

By and large, it seems, a POW's resistance to torture and propaganda depended to some extent on his education; that is to say, on values formulated during his early life. Ultimately, some strange combination of pride and obligation to his country/fellow POWs was capable of extending the limit of his endurance. Certainly, the leaders emerged, and the heroes best demonstrated their toughness, when there was an audience to witness it. Prisoners of war, like trade unionists, are at their most impressive when they are massed together. The Vietnamese, doubtless, acted sagely, if inhumanely, by keeping them separated.

But the human urge to communicate, to demonstrate that no man is an island and that no man wishes to be, is so strong that, even under these circumstances, it became possible to pass messages from cell to cell. The most common method was by tapping on the wall, using a code taught at Air Force survival school. Another technique was to talk *through* the wall. For this, a cup and a blanket were required. The blanket muffled the voice, and thereby ensured that none of the guards could hear; and the cup, with its base placed against the partition, somehow acted as an amplifier. It was, apparently, possibly to drive conversation through 3ft of concrete by this method.

Reading matter, apart from propaganda leaflets, was banned and so were paper and writing instruments. However, there had to be toilet paper – rough though it was – and it was possible to manufacture ink by an amalgam of cigarette ash and a small quantity of sugar. The cap of a toothpaste tube served as an inkwell, a sliver of split bamboo as a pen. Messages could be written and places were established as 'note drops'. Drains leading to sewers were favoured for this purpose: indeed, the more unpleasant the location, the better it was, for the guards were less likely to pry into such nauseous places and discover the correspondence.

So effective were the means of communication, that, at the camp near Son Tay, the POWs actually managed to convey a message to the pilots of American reconnaissance aircraft flying overhead. This resulted in the famous rescue attempt that took place on 20 November 1970. Unfortunately, by this time, the camp had been evacuated, and the 'Green Berets', who had been landed by helicopters, departed empty-handed.

Obviously, the Son Tay raid failed in its purpose, though John Chafee had other notions. 'Hopefully,' he said, 'you keep the enemy worrying night and day about the same thing happening again.' Another benefit may have been that it caused the Vietnamese to close down the outlying camps, bringing more and more POWs into Hanoi, until the solitary confinement system broke down under sheer weight of numbers. But, in any case, the North Vietnamese were now beginning to take account of world opinion and, indeed, of the possibility that, one day, the apparently endless talks in Paris might surprise everybody and bring about peace. 'Quizzes' ceased and likewise other attempts at indoctrination. It was, Commander Naughton observed, '. . . a tacit admission by the Vietnamese that control of another's body does not constitute control of his will'.

The outside world's first glimpse of men who had endured life in the 'Hanoi Hilton' occurred in 1969, when eight officers and one seaman were released as a token gesture. The Vietnam authorities stipulated that the names of those selected should not be announced until the last possible moment, thus producing the utmost anxiety among next of kin in America. They also insisted that the operation should not be carried out with the International Red Cross as an intermediary, but through the offices of a dissident American organisation that bitterly opposed the war. Eventually David Dellinger, the fifty-four-year-old chairman of the National Mobi-lisation Committee to End the War in Vietnam, was chosen as a go-between. Since Mr Dellinger's life was soon to become complicated by the necessity of answering an indictment on charges of conspiring to incite a riot in Chicago, he was unable to go to Hanoi. Instead, he was represented by one of his colleagues, James Johnson.

Within the 'Hanoi Hilton', the Code of Conduct was still alive and well. The spirit of it suggested that no POW should accept the offer of repatriation without the consent of the senior officer. Of the nine who eventually went home, only one of them, a naval rating named Doug Hegdahl, received this permission.

Doug Hegdahl had been interrogated by an official known as the 'Cat' (Most of the interrogators had nicknames: as, for example, 'Rabbit', 'Mickey Mouse', 'Soft Soap' and 'Pigeye'. 'Pigeye' was the master torturer and was otherwise known as 'Straps and Bars', for these were his favourite tools). The truth was that Mr Hegdahl had very little to tell even the most thorough investigator. He had been taking a photograph from the deck of his ship, when the blast from a broadside knocked him overboard. He swam ashore and was captured as soon as he stepped on to the beach.

However, he had tales to tell of the life at a preliminary training camp for recruits to the USN, and some lively accounts to relate of ping-pong matches aboard his ship. When the 'Cat' asked how long his vessel was, Hegdahl carefully halved the dimension. Apart from such matters, his knowledge of naval affairs was somewhat restricted. However, the 'Cat', who must have been uncommonly naïve, imagined that he had done well. When Hegdahl's number came up for repatriation, he warned him to make no adverse comment on POW life. If he did so, the inquisitor promised, he would make sure that his statement fell into United States' hands.

Obviously, Doug Hegdahl was not very worried by such blackmail, and his superiors in the 'Hanoi Hilton' saw no reason why he should not return home. The others were quite another matter. They were *officers*, and an officer's duty was to stay put.

At a stop-over in the Laotian town of Vientiane, they were allowed to talk to newspaper men. Although their spokesman, Lieutenant Robert F. Frishman, had been a captive for no more than twenty-one months (for obvious reasons, the North Vietnamese chose the more recent arrivals), he was described as 'pale and gaunt'. He was wearing dungarees and sandals.

If anyone had hoped for an outpouring of amazing revelations he was to be disappointed. Lieutenant Frishman was nothing if not circumspect in his answers. The interview (as reported in the *Air Force/Space Digest* – October, 1969) went like this:

Q How was the treatment you received?
A I received adequate food, clothing and housing.
Q Would you regard it as humane treatment?
A Sir, I believe I have answered that question.
Q Did they make any attempt to indoctrinate or brainwash you in any way?
A I have no comment.
Q Was their treatment better at all when they decided you were going to be released?
A As I say, my treatment has been adequate.
Q Are you concerned that other prisoners might be harmed by something you might say here?
A Yes. I in no way want to jeopardise any of the other people who have been ... (at this point, his supply of conversation ran out).

His pacifist escort, James Johnson, on the other hand, was more articulate. In a 500 word address, he told the reporters that, 'We know, as these pilots must know, that all over the world the United States has been branded as an outlaw nation.'

Lieutenant Frishman had privately told the authorities that, when taken prisoner, he had been wearing uniform and that, when he returned to the United States, he would prefer to be similarly attired. As garb for a homecoming, dungarees and sandals were not, perhaps, very impressive. To make this possible, the aircraft landed at Frankfurt before completing the journey to America. When, at last, the repatriates set foot on US soil, Louis R. Stockstill of the *Air Force/Space Digest* noted that, 'They were ashen in colour. Their eyes were deep hollow circles of darker grey, much like the exaggerated eyes of starving children. They smiled, but somehow their smiles seemed macabre; not forced but not exactly real; joyful surely, but with an underlying tautness; perhaps nearer to tears than laughter.'

The picture was not very encouraging. If a comparatively short spell in Vietnamese hands did this to you, the condition of the older hands must have been appalling.

Between 1970 and 1973, the rules were relaxed. Raids on the prisoners' rooms became less frequent, and the authorities were less fussy about bowing. The rule about no books was not, however, rescinded. For want of any other intellectual stimulus, people filled endless pieces of rough toilet paper with their thoughts and knowledge. 'A' might be writing down all the quotations he could remember from Shakespeare, whilst 'B' might be entertaining himself with abstruse mathematical calculations. Anything was acceptable, so long as it helped to kill time.

Time, that is the eternal enemy of every prisoner of war – the knowledge that, unlike a common criminal, his sentence is not defined and that there is no remission for good conduct. Commander Naughton wrote about the abrupt change from the snugness and security of an aircraft's cockpit to the exposed vulnerability of becoming a POW. 'The most dominant emotion,' he said, 'is of *bewildering fear* and the alien surroundings and *uncertainty* of one's ultimate fate ... Embodied in this sense of loss (friends, family) is the uncertainty of time. How long? Ever?'

It is possible to come to terms with the surroundings, even in a camp where prisoners of war can mingle with one another, to numb the sense of loss. But nothing can overcome the time factor, especially in conditions such as those that prevailed in North Vietnam, where all contact with the outside world was so rigorously excluded, and there was no knowing what the state of the world might be – and, within it, the state of the war.

The first requirement of many games that children play is that there shall be a cowboy and an Indian, a cop and a robber, someone who is popularly considered to be good ranged against someone who is, by tradition, evil. So it is when writing about a war. There has to be an enemy: the enemy has to be wicked, for without this the war would be wicked. It is only by castigating our foes, that we can endure our own sins.

An American in North Vietnamese hands during that terrible conflict suffered an ordeal which, at its best, was little better than death – and, at its worst, made death seem a very acceptable alternative. One cannot, indeed, consider such treatment without wondering what went wrong with humanity. Was man really made in God's image? It is difficult to believe.

But this, nevertheless, is only one side of the picture. Doubtless, at this very moment, some historian in Hanoi is writing about the war from an opposite viewpoint. He is, perhaps, recalling the photographs that even found their way into the Western Press, of Vietcong guerrillas confined in tiger cages at Saigon; or the picture of an irate South Vietnamese senior policeman shooting a captive Vietcong through the head. He is no doubt recalling the children burnt beyond belief by napalm bombs, or the fact that, during the war, the United States dropped more bombs on North Vietnam than the sum of those dropped in World War II. And, quite properly, he is probably preparing a chapter on the My Lai massacre, when all the inhabitants of a village – women and children, as well as men – were slain.

In his statement concerning the North Vietnamese and the Geneva Convention, Navy Secretary Chafee dealt methodically with its non-observation, point by carefully calculated point. At the same time, he managed to imply that the treatment of POWs by the United States and their South Vietnamese allies was beyond reproach. In war, neither side is inclined to report its own atrocities, though one cannot help wondering at the North Vietnamese logic which suggested that, by the ill-treatment of their captives, they hoped to win a propaganda victory.

At the beginning of this book, there was mention of the Hundred Years War, where the well-to-do captive could buy his freedom by payment of ransom money. It was, of course, very unfair, and had there been any socialists at the time, they would no doubt have fulminated against it. Why, after all, should freedom be the prerogative of the rich, whilst those without the necessary cash should be sold off as slaves?

Nevertheless (if one excludes the massacre of the French prisoners at Agincourt) there was nothing comparable to the barbarism of present-day warfare and of present-day captivity. Nowadays, you can presumably purchase clemency by the betrayal of your beliefs/country/fellow prisoners. In those days, it required no more than money. In some respects, it seems, the world has moved backwards.

But this is not the end of it. Without war, there would be no such people as prisoners of war. An American soldier in Korea was forced by his captors to admit that 'To us soldiers, [the war] means misery, desolation and loss of life, and to the folks at home it means the breaking up of the family, high taxes and hardship'. Despite the fact that these words may have cost some unhappy GI his self-respect, it would be difficult to gainsay the truth of them. Nevertheless, the agony persists. Far from learning how not to make war, mankind had discovered how to increase the destruction and loss of life, until the very planet itself is in danger. In fact, the real enemy is war itself; and all those who take part are its prisoners.

SELECT BIBLIOGRAPHY

Abell, Francis *Prisoners of War in Britain, 1756–1815* (1914)

Ackerly, J. R. *Escapers All* (1932)

Aida, Yuji *Prisoner of the British* (1966)

Alger, John G. *Napoleon's British Visitors and Captives, 1801–1815* (1904)

Allen, Ethan *A Narrative of Colonel Ethan Allen's Captivity* written by himself (and edited by J. Pell) (Corinth Books, 1930)

Aurenfeldt, Robert H. *Psychiatry in the British Army in the Second World War* (1958)

Barber, A. J. *Behind Barbed Wire* (1974)

Batchelder *Burgoyne and His Officers in Cambridge, 1777* (1926)

Bethell, Nicholas *The Last Secret* (Deutsch, 1977)

Billany, Dan, in collaboration with David Dowie *The Cage* (1949)

Boys, Edward *Narrative of a Captivity and Adventures in France and Flanders between the years (1803 and 1809)* (1931)

Bradbury, W. C. (ed.) *Mass Behaviour in Battle and Captivity* (University of Chicago Press, 1968)

Brown, Anthony Cave *Bodyguard of Lies* (W. H. Allen, 1976)

Cameron, James *Point of Departure* (Oriel Press, 1967)

Chatel, Hon J. H. 'POW Treatment principles versus propaganda', *United States Institute of Naval Proceedings* (July 1971)

China, Hsinhua News Agency *American POWs calling from Korea* (1951)

Clooch, C. N. *Returned Prisoners* (1864)

Cornelius, Elius *Journal of Dr. E. Cornelius, a Revolutionary Surgeon* (1953)

Coursier, Henri *The International Red Cross* (1963)

Davies, the Rev S. J. *In Spite of Dungeons* (1954)

Denton, Rear-Admiral J. A. *When Hell was in Session* (1976)

Dorris, Jonathan Truman *Pardon + Amnesty under Lincoln and Johnson* (1953)

Drummond, A. Deane *Return Ticket* (Collins, 1953)

Durnford, H. G. *The Tunnellers of Holzminden* (1920)

Eggers, Rheinhold *Colditz, the German Story* (1961)

Evans, A. J. *The Escaping Club* (1921)

Foons, Herbert C. *Prisoners of War* (1924)

Foot, M. R. D. and Langley, J. M. *M.I.9* (1979)

Forsythe, J. W. *Guerilla Warfare and Life in Libby Prison* (1967)

Fowler, Kenneth *The Age of Plantagenet and Valois* (Elek, 1967)

Hain, Sir Edward (ed) *Prisoners of War in France from 1804–1814* (1914)

Hawkins, Christopher *Adventures of Christopher Hawkins*, unprinted in 1968

Hesseltine, W. B. *Civil War Prisons* (1964)

Hewitt, H. J. *The Organisation of War under Edward III* (Manchester University Press, 1966)

Hibbert, Christopher *Agincourt* (1964)

Hinsley, F. H. *British Intelligence in the Second World War – Vol. 1* (1979)

HMSO *Treatment of British Prisoners of War in Korea* (1955)

Holmes, C. W. *The Elmira Prison Camp* (1912)

Horace Marshall & Sons Ltd, on behalf of the British Red Cross Society and the Order of St John of Jerusalem *Prisoner of War* (1941)

Hunter, Edward *Brainwashing – the story of the men who defied it* (1956)

Hunter, E. J. (and others) *Resistance Posture and the Vietnam Prisoner of War* (1976)

Jackson, Robert *A Taste of Freedom* (1964)

Johnson, W. Brench *The English Prison Hulks* (1957)

Jones, E. H. *The Road to En-Dor* (1920)

Jones, Francis S. *No Rice for Rebels* (1956)

Kellogg, R. H. *Life and Death in Rebel Prisons* (1866)

Kinkead, Eugene *Why they collaborated* (1960)

Kinne, Derek *The Wooden Boxes* (1955)

Knauss, W. H. *The Story of Campchase* (1906)

Mason, W. W. *Prisoners of War – Official history of New Zealand in the Second World War* (1958)

McCarthy, Daniel J. *The Prisoner of War in Germany* (1916)

McGrath, Lt-Cdr J. M. *Prisoner of war; six years in Hanoi* (1975)

Miller, F. T. and Lenier, R. S. (ed) *The Photographic History of the Civil War, Vol. 7* (1911)

Mitchell, Broadus *The Price of Independence* (1974)

Naughton, Cdr R. J. 'Motivational factors of American Prisoners of War held by the Democratic Republic of Vietnam', *Naval War College Review* (Jan/Feb 1975)

Oliver, Dame Beryl *The British Red Cross in Action* (1966)

Page, J. M. and Haley, M. J. *The True Story of Andersonville Prison* (1908)

Pasley, Virginia *22 Stayed* (1955)

Plusdnow, G. *My Escape from Donington Hall* (1922)

Post, Laurens van der *The Seed and the Sower* (Hogarth Press, 1963)

Rivell, Rohan D. *Behind Bamboo* (1947)

Roxburgh, Ronald F. *The Prisoners of War Information Bureau in London* (1915)

Russell, Lord, of Liverpool *The Scourge of the Swastika* (1954)

Schein, Edgar H., with Inge Schmeir and Curtis H. Barker *Coercive Persuasion* (1961)

Schemmer, B. F. *The Raid* (1970)

Scotland, Lt-Col A. P. OBE *The London Cage* (1957)

Seward, Desmond *The Hundred Years War – The English and France 1337–1453* (1978)

Stockdale, Rear-Admiral J. B. 'Experiences as a POW in Vietnam' *Naval War College Review* (Jan/Feb 1974)

Sturgis, T. *Prisoners of War, 1861–65* (1912)

Sullivan, Matthew Barry *Thresholds of Peace* (1979)

Summers, Gerald *The Lure of the Falcon* (1972)

The Chinese Committee for World Peace, Peking *Shall Brothers Be* (1952)

United States House of Representatives Committee on Foreign Affairs Sub-Committee on National Security Policy and Scientific Developments *American Prisoners of War in South-East Asia* (1970)

United States Sanitary Commission *Narratives of Privations and Sufferings of United States officers and soldiers while Prisoners of war on both sides during the War of the Rebellion, 1864*

Velter, Hal *Mutiny on Koje Island* (1965)

Walder, Thomas James *The Depot for Prisoners of War at Norman Cross Huntingdonshire 1796–1816* (1913)

War Office *A Handbook for the Information of Relatives and Friends of Prisoners of War* (1943)

Wentzel, Fritz *Single or Return* (1954)

Williams, Eric *The Wooden Horse* (Collins, 1949)

Williams, Eric *Great Escape Stories* (Barker, 1964)

INDEX

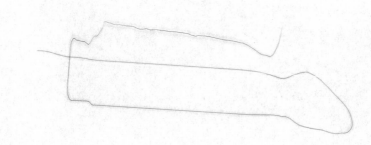